GEORGE ADAMSON

My Pride and Joy

SIMON AND SCHUSTER
NEW YORK

Copyright © 1987 by George Adamson.
All rights reserved
including the right of reproduction
in whole or in part in any form.
Published by Simon and Schuster
A Division of Simon & Schuster, Inc.
Simon & Schuster Building
Rockefeller Center
1230 Avenue of the Americas
New York, New York 10020
This edition published by arrangement with William Collins Sons & Company Ltd.,
London, England. First published by Collins Harvill, 1986.
SIMON AND SCHUSTER and colophon are registered trademarks
of Simon & Schuster, Inc.
Manufactured in the United States of America.

1 3 5 7 9 10 8 6 4 2

Library of Congress Cataloging in Publication Data

Adamson, George (date).
My pride and joy.
Bibliography: p.
Includes index.
1. Adamson, George, 1906-   . 2. Adamson, Joy.
3. Zoologists—Kenya—Biography. I. Title.
QL31.A32A3 1986   590′.92′4 [B]   86-26324
ISBN: 0-671-62497-0

By the same author
BWANA GAME

By Joy Adamson
BORN FREE
ELSA
LIVING FREE
FOREVER FREE
ELSA AND HER CUBS
THE STORY OF ELSA
THE PEOPLES OF KENYA
THE SPOTTED SPHINX
PIPPA: THE CHEETAH AND HER CUBS
PIPPA'S CHALLENGE
JOY ADAMSON'S AFRICA
THE SEARCHING SPIRIT
THE QUEEN OF SHABA
FRIENDS FROM THE FOREST

Contents

Author's Note   7

PART I   INTO AFRICA

1 A Day at Kora   9
2 Early Man   25
3 The Day of the Game   42
4 Joy   64

PART II   THE COMPANY OF LIONS

5 The First of the Free   85
6 On Playing With Lions   109
7 The Chance of Freedom   132
8 A Chapter of Accidents   150
9 By Lake Naivasha   170

PART III   A SEA OF THORNS

10 A Lion from London   187
11 The Shadow of Death   201
12 Christian's Pyramid   219
13 Daniel's Pride   237
14 The Last Walk   254
15 Seven Commandments   272

Epilogue Evening at Kora   293
Acknowledgements   300
Index   302

Colour Plates

(Following page 96)

Early Days at Kora

1. My early walks with the lions introduced them to all the sights, sounds and smells of their new world.   2. Our camp at Kora, set in a sea of thorns.   3. The hut which served us as a sitting room, bar, office and mess. 4. My brother Terence has only once left Africa in the last sixty years. 5. An evening visit to the lions with Tony Fitzjohn.

At Meru and Lake Naivasha

6. Two cheetahs from Pippa's first surviving litter at Meru. 7. After lunch at Meru we all feel a little sleepy. 8. Joy with one of the colobus monkeys at Elsamere on Lake Naivasha. 9. Girl with her cub Sam, at Meru. 10. Boy with the newly arrived Katania at Elsamere. 11, 12. After asserting his supremacy over Christian, Boy walks away and contemptuously marks territory.

At Kora and Shaba

13. Boy after the fight in which he was badly bitten on the back. 14. Only after the dominant male has satisfied his hunger can the rest of the pride share a kill.
15. Some of the sixteen lions we had round our camp when the pride finally established itself at Kora. 16. Joy with Penny, the leopard, at Shaba. Each day they walked for an hour together.

Later Days at Kora

17. Arusha, from Rotterdam, who tried to drive away some of the other lionesses.
18. Komunyu, from Paris, one of the first two leopards released at Kora. 19. Friendly but dangerous. On the right is Shade, who went for Terence.   20. Koretta (right) with her two sets of cubs. 21, 22. White henna flowers, red salvadora berries and violet Resurrection plant.   23. A gerenuk browsing.

Maps

Kenya	8
Northern Frontier	34
Meru	135
Kora	189

Family Trees

Boy's Pride at Meru	151
Christian's Pride at Kora	222
Daniel's Pride at Kora	252

Author's Note

This book is a work of collaboration between Bill Travers, Adrian House and myself. In 1963 Bill came out to Kenya to play my role in the film of *Born Free*. Since then he has made three documentary films about my work, we have corresponded continuously and he has never missed a chance of taking photographs of the lions, many of which appear in this book. Adrian House first met Joy in 1959 while working with Billy Collins and Marjorie Villiers, of the Harvill Press, on the publication of *Born Free*. When Billy died he published Joy's last two books and persuaded me to begin this one.

For reasons which I later describe, the book was easier to start than to finish. Bill therefore recorded many hours of answers that I gave to his questions about my life with Joy and the lions. Apart from these conversations I have drawn on my letters and diaries, my only previous book *Bwana Game*, Joy's own writings and unpublished letters, and the memories of some of our friends. Adrian has helped me to weave these together to tell the story of my life among lions and with Joy.

If I travel over ground which Joy and I have already covered it is partly because it would be difficult to explain what I have been doing in the last twenty years without describing some of my previous experiences. Then, at the age of eighty, some of the highlights, shadows and significant detail seem to have changed. I also feel that the passage of time enables me to say things which could not be written before.

I am much indebted to Georgina Edmonds who has helped sort out my papers at Kora, transcribed many hours of recording and typed the final draft of this script.

3 February 1986   GEORGE ADAMSON

KORA

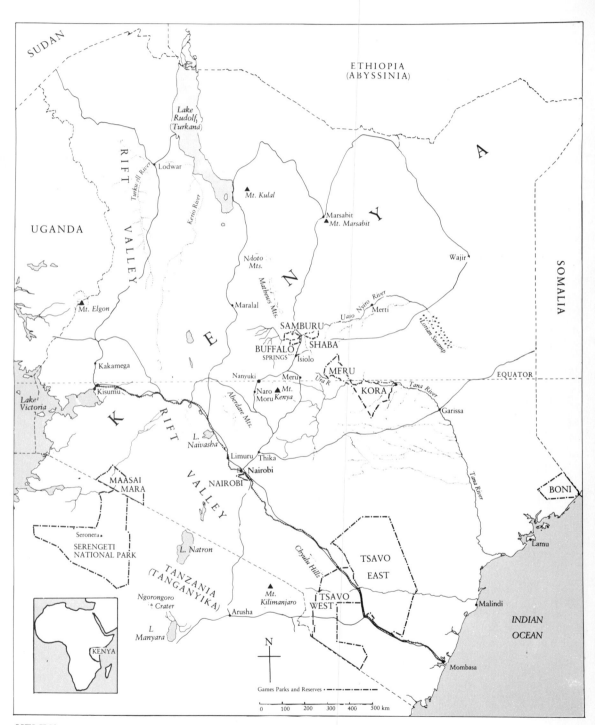

KENYA

Showing the Principal Game Parks and Reserves mentioned in this book

Chapter 1

A Day at Kora
1970–1985

Each morning I wake up to the disappointed glare of Bourne and Hollings-worth; the pair of hooded vultures stare down from the fence round our camp, no doubt hoping that one day my eyes will fail to open.

Every day as I put on my shorts, walk over to breakfast, or go about more private business, an American satellite sails overhead and photographs this remote tract of Kenya beside the Tana River. They say the pictures are so clear that experts can decide whether an egg or a golf ball has been set on the table.

The African wilderness is shrinking fast. When I first came to Kenya its grey thorn-bush country, scorched by a blazing sun in a clear blue sky, offered few promises. But those promises, of solitude, of wild animals in a profusion to delight the heart of Noah, and of the spice of danger, were always honoured. Today, of these three, you are only likely to encounter the danger.

It is not just vultures and spacecraft that invade our privacy. Fifteen years ago, to reach Kora Hill, the mounds of pink rock below which we set up our camp, we hacked our way through the resinous thorn bushes for days on end; it was weeks before we could clear a track here from the nearest road, and another to a rough little airstrip, twenty miles off. Nowadays, although the temperature is over 100° at noon and after lunch I feel sleepy, I dare not take a siesta as it is so frequently interrupted by unexpected visitors.

Subdued and disappointed because they have not been harassed by elephants or charged by infuriated rhinos on the way, they watch with delighted wonder the pride of lions that gathers round the camp at dusk. Just why the elephants and rhinos have ignored them is part of this story.

To find out which lions have come to camp I go out to greet them and toss them some meat. If I am away my companion, Tony Fitzjohn, will give them a welcome instead. In his thirties, tall, bronzed by the sun, and recently invited by a film company – admittedly Japanese – to play Tarzan, he is treated by the lions as one of their pride. Half my age, he has taken over the more demanding tasks of their care, wild as they are.

My younger brother Terence, now in his late seventies, shares our flimsy cage. An expert self-taught engineer, he built and keeps up our huts, our fence, our airstrip and our roads. A gifted amateur botanist, he knows every tree, shrub and plant within a hundred miles, by its English, Latin and Swahili names. But although he is on the side of the animals, he has one unaccountable failing – he prefers elephants to lions.

The other long-term human resident is Hamisi, a grizzled Sudanese, who provides us with three good meals a day from almost any ingredients or almost none. Like Terence he seems to regard my weakness for lions with melancholy indulgence.

The four of us do, however, have one distinction in common. Each of us has been mauled by a lion or a crocodile and bears the marks on our skin. Terence's scars, I suspect, go deeper. Some of the other habitués are two-legged but feathered; the majority have four, six or eight legs; the least desirable have a hundred, a thousand – or none. Wire link is effective for keeping out lions but it presents no obstacle to a guinea fowl bent on getting our millet or the hornbills who demand and steal our nuts. Acacia rats use the trees as a bridge into camp. Mongooses and civets climb easily over the fence, while feverish ground squirrels drive tunnels underneath it. Mosquitoes, hornets and ants, large black scorpions, carnivorous centipedes and venomous snakes – boomslangs, puff-adders and spitting cobras – slip through its mesh with the greatest of ease. As they all seem to find our company irresistible, we make friends with the pleasant and come to terms with the rest. But our lives revolve round the lions.

Ever since I shot a charging lioness in 1956, and took her three tiny cubs back to my wife Joy, I have lived in the company of lions. We kept one of the cubs, whom Joy called Elsa, and when she grew up we prepared her to go back to the wild. She became world famous when Joy told her story in a book called *Born Free*. After Elsa, each lion, and later each pride, has led to another. Over the years I have released twenty-three young lions in the wild, all of them otherwise destined to live behind bars.

Only two of the lions were born in a zoo; some were trapped for the sins of their fathers and mothers; others went astray on their own. Mating together or with lions from the bush, they have produced fifty cubs that I have seen and perhaps as many more that I have not. In the manner of lions when a pride gets too big it breaks into groups and disperses. At one time we had sixteen lions round Kora.

Living for animals means that we have to live like animals, or at least like our earliest ancestors. Our clock is the sun, our shelter is primitive, our food is simple and our water is drawn from the Tana, three miles away. Our eyes and ears have to pick up sights and sounds that most others would miss. I have not taken a morning paper for forty years: the news I need is printed on the ground.

Lions are nocturnal and most of their significant activities take place while I sleep. If I want to know what has happened, I have to go out at dawn and study the clues in the dust and the grass, on the sand, the rock or the bushes. If I get there too late the sun, wind, or rain will have destroyed them. At first as a hunter, and then for twenty-five years in the Game Department, my livelihood, if not my life, depended on interpreting footprints and getting it right.

While Elsa was growing used to her freedom I had to be able to read her spoor as easily as handwriting. By learning to do this I could help her over her difficulties and could follow her courtship and mating.

At Kora Tony and I have to memorise many sets of prints at any one time. It is essential, both to follow the lions and to keep abreast of the rest of the news in the bush. Two years ago Tony came back and told me of a typical and violent story that could be read in this way. A family of Somalis had stopped him and asked for his help, as their daughter had been mauled by a lion. They had kept her at night in their camp, wrapped in a dirty old sheet, as they were not allowed in the reserve and were at first all too frightened to ask for help.

The drought had been harsh and each evening they watered their herd at a spring a few miles from our camp. Tony was afraid that one of our lions might have gone for the girl but then he remembered seeing an unfamiliar and sickly old lion near the lugga – the sandy bed of a dried-up water course. He felt it was much the most likely culprit.

When Tony and some friends got to the waterhole he checked the spoor of the lion, to make sure it was not one of ours, and it was possible to read the whole story. As all the signs were still visible the attack must have taken place within the previous twenty-four hours. But since there had been no stampede and only a few hoof marks, leaving the lugga, crossed the tracks of the lion, it must have struck just as the last cows were slaking their thirst.

A flurry of dust and some blood showed where the girl had been seized by the lion. Tony's friends traced its progress, dragging the child between its legs, across the sand to the edge of the lugga. Finally, where the undergrowth started there was a larger patch of dried blood, surrounded by stones, and a confusion of footmarks that told their own tale. Casting around in a circle and into the bush they saw where the lion, deprived of its victim, had run into cover.

Tony and his friends cleaned up the girl's wounds and handed her over to an Anti-Poaching Unit of the Game Department and persuaded them to take her to hospital. Her family then described how they suddenly heard her screaming for help. When they saw her in the jaws of the lion they surrounded it and bombarded it with stones till it fled. Their courage and presence of mind saved her life, as she quickly recovered.

*   *   *

I cannot explain why I have devoted so much of my life to lions without trying to convey the depth and range of their personalities. They are as distinctively different from each other as people. Like people, they can look impressive, beautiful, curious, ugly or plain. As with humans you get the large and the small, the strong and the weak.

They are creatures of character and mood, who are not only sociable but may be affectionate or shy, gentle or fierce, friendly or hostile, generous or possessive, mischievous or grim, impulsive or restrained, promiscuous, wanton, steady or frigid. If some are aloof, nervous, introvert and mean, others are playful, confident, extravert and fun. Most are intelligent and inquisitive. The best are adventurous, loyal and brave. All of them have been designed and perfected by nature to kill.

I know that in using these terms I risk falling foul of some scientists, but I can find no others that are adequate. I do not know exactly where the border lies between "instinct" and "conditioned reflex" on the one hand, and "experience" and "intelligent decision" on the other. But I do know that in some circumstances lions cross the border into territory normally reserved by philosophers for man.

From my earliest days in Kenya I was fascinated by the behaviour of lions and elephants because of this extra dimension in their lives. But I did not sense how powerful their spell could become until we set Elsa free, and I realised that she not only reciprocated our love but could keep up our friendship without disturbing the bonds with her mate and her cubs.

After he had been out to Kenya, and had watched Elsa and her cubs at our camp, Sir Julian Huxley, one of the most distinguished biologists of his generation, was so impressed by her ability to bridge these two worlds that he recommended scientists to study the implications of her behaviour for the future understanding of animals. Sir Frank Fraser Darling, another outstanding naturalist, believed that in some respects we can only decipher an animal's world if we resort to a human vocabulary. What Elsa did, and the way in which it could best be explained, were both of interest to science.

"Innocent Killers" was the phrase coined by Jane Goodall, famous for her scientific studies of chimpanzees, and her husband Hugo van Lawick, the brilliant wildlife photographer. They applied it, as a title for a book, to the hyenas, jackals and wild dogs of the Serengeti. I have seen a herd of sixteen goats wantonly killed by a family of cubs so I am not sure that killing by lions always deserves the verdict of "innocent"; but it is never as guilty as man's, whose destruction in Kenya and interference with the balances of nature is relentless and irreparable.

With his own increasing numbers, and his ever growing hordes of cattle and goats, the herdsman is denuding the bush. With the lure of rich pickings the poacher works through the country to bring out his haul – the last rhino horns as handles for daggers; ivory, bloodily culled from the diminishing elephants; the silken coats of gazelles; and the lovelier skins of the cats. Destroying the wilderness, and robbing its prospects of peace and of game, man leaves only the promise of danger. He has killed ten of my lions and murdered my wife.

Few couples can have had a more rewarding life together in the bush than Joy and I. After we married, in 1944, we lived at Isiolo, on the frontier of Kenya's northern provinces. For the next twenty years we spent most of the time on safari, out on the plains, into the deserts and forest, up to the lakes and the mountains, and down to the coral reefs of the coast. Often we travelled together and sometimes apart. Mine was the life of a warden, keeping a check on man-eating lions, crop-raiding elephants, poachers. Joy's was the life of an artist, painting the pictures of the flowers and the tribes which now hang in the National Museum and the President's State House, in Nairobi.

Towards the end of these years Elsa came into our lives and not long after that I retired, just in time to help train the lions for the film of *Born Free*. When the filming was over Joy and I, with Virginia McKenna and her husband Bill Travers who played our roles in the film, were determined to save at least some of the lions from consignment to game parks in Europe, or zoos.

Joy and I therefore spent the next five years in Meru Park, where I released a small pride from the film led by a magnificent lion called Boy. A few miles away Joy successfully prepared a tame cheetah called Pippa for a life of freedom in the bush.

When this phase was over Bill Travers and I brought a lion from London, called Christian, to Kora. Once more our intention was to give a lion freedom. I hoped Joy would join me and take on some leopards but she found the climate too hot and the camp too remote for the rest of her work, writing books, and raising money for wild animals all over the world. When she did adopt a leopard she took it to Shaba, near our original home in the north – and there she was killed.

* * *

Over the years Joy paid us a number of visits at Kora. My daily routine aimed to put into practice what I had learnt from our experiences with Elsa and the pride I had released in Meru.

Day starts when the fan-tailed ravens, regular as clockwork, call us with their raucous croaking at dawn. For the next twenty minutes the rumpus rises to a crescendo as they flap around Hamisi, trying to steal his eggs. He usually fobs them off with a biscuit.

As my campbed is next to the two lion enclosures, at the end of the camp, I sometimes wake up to find a pair of cubs lying only a few inches away from my nose, on the other side of the wire. By sleeping next to me they learn that human beings do not necessarily represent a threat. I had to keep two young lions, Suleiman and Sheba, who had been sent to us by a ranching friend called Ken Clarke, penned up for several weeks before they calmed down; Suleiman had been grazed by the bullet which killed his mother. They were over a year old, and their mother had been shot for persistent cattle-raiding; I took them as I could not bear the thought of them going to a zoo. Once the young lions are settled, I wander in as soon as I am up, with a bucket of water or tit-bit of meat. If they rub their heads against my knee the first battle to win their trust has been won.

After a quick cup of tea I get ready to walk the lions down to the river. Hamisi breaks off washing the pans and gives my tracker a cold thermos and packet of biscuits. Tony arranges for our driver to hitch the trailer to the Landrover and fetch water. Terence briefs his road gang for the day. There is a fearful cackle as the guinea fowl and hornbills clear off with the last of the millet or Terence's Weetabix. Most of the lions spend the night outside camp and it is intriguing to see how newcomers react to their first taste of freedom. Usually they have got the measure of the pride after watching them carefully through the wire: once outside they approach their elders with diffident greetings, like dogs.

So far none of them has bolted. Nevertheless this initial introduction to the rest of the pride is an acid test of their nerve. The younger the cubs the sooner they are likely to be accepted. Normally they approach the dominant male and work their way down through the hierarchy. The warmer the feelings between two lions, the more affectionately they rub cheeks and run them sinuously down each other's flanks. This tactile sense is obviously of great importance. Suleiman and Sheba were treated much more suspiciously than most other newcomers, partly because they were at least a year old and partly because the pride was already over a dozen strong and beginning to break up. Nevertheless they were tolerated on occasional walks.

As soon as the pride moves off all its senses are alert to the engrossing world of the bush. Lions have superb vision for spotting movement and instinctively shift to the highest ground for the best look-out: that is why mine have always lorded it from the tops of my Landrovers. Being nocturnal their night vision is excellent too.

When I came to Kora I grew even more aware of how important scent is to lions. In this dense bush, where visibility is often down to fifty yards or less, I have seen them set off after a giraffe which has been browsing five or six hundred yards away. They also have a different and no doubt instinctive understanding of scent. When they come across a big ball of elephant dung, or one of those middens made by the families of little dik dik antelopes, they love to roll in it. I suppose it is to disguise their scent, which to the human nose is rather like honeyed tobacco, for they never roll in the droppings of lions, hyenas or jackals.

Lions have very keen ears. I have known them pick up a sound eight miles away, which was well beyond the power of human hearing. Their voice plays an important part in their social life and they seem to appreciate that a rock or a cliff can boost their full-scale territorial roaring. They have a whole repertoire of lesser noises – puffs and whuffs, miaows and purrs, moans, yowls, grunts and growls.

Although their basic diet depends on the local game they certainly have a discriminating palate. They relish zebra meat as much as they scorn baboon, unless they are starving. Like dogs they occasionally feel the urge to eat grass. Once I put out poisoned meat to get rid of some hyenas, but found to my dismay it had been taken by lions. I followed their tracks and came to a place where a lion had been sick. In the vomit were some chewed berries of *Cordia gharaf*. They have a bitter taste and I am sure they were eaten as an emetic.

While roaring is the most obvious method of proclaiming territory the pride is constantly employing another on our walks – marking. Young lions piddle, females squat, and adult males deliver backward, well-aimed squirts, scented from an anal gland. By this means the native lions and mine are constantly exchanging challenge, information and insult.

The principal aim of our walks is to provide fun and game, but sometimes we run into trouble. If they try to take on the rare buffalo we meet, the younger lions are in for a shock, but it is essential for them to be completely at home in the bush and to get the measure of the different game. I cannot teach them to hunt, any more than their mothers or their elders can. Lions are born with the instinctive ability to stalk and to kill – I have seen it proved over and over again – but only experience will perfect these skills and experience is what I can offer.

While we are walking I talk to the lions. They must know my voice so well that they automatically pick up its intonations of encouragement, approval, reassurance, caution, command and rebuke. It would be lunacy, not to say disastrous, to try to dominate them as some people train dogs.

They know very well when you are angry, will often respond to a shouted "No!", and will respect you if you stand your ground and move towards them – whereas retreating is dangerous. What matters is that they recognise a voice and authority. Even so you can never rely on them entirely. When it rains, and the temperature drops, they can become uncomfortably boisterous. I do not carry a rifle or revolver whenever I leave camp just for protection against irascible rhinos.

By the time we get down to the river I am ready for a cool glass of gin from the thermos and, as the sun will be getting warm, the lions are quite happy to flop down on the sand or mess about in the shallows. Lions are among the laziest animals on earth and like to spend most of the day dozing, although if very hungry they will spring up at the chance of a kill whatever the heat.

It is extremely beautiful down by the Tana. The stretch we make for is more than a hundred yards wide if you take in the stream, the pools, the shallows, the rocks and the sand. There is shade from the palms and acacias, which are much taller here than those in the bush round the camp. Terence has identified all the plants and the shrubs – the deadly datura or moonflower with its lovely white trumpets, the sweet scented henna and the red-berried salvadora, so attractive to birds.

The game fades away at the approach of the lions but the baboons chatter and bark on the opposite bank, while the hippos wallow and snort out in the silted red water. Close in it is hard to tell if a dark ridged shape, gliding along with the current, is a log or a crocodile. The birds seem to have no fear of the lions and if I sit quietly a succession of waders will drop down to the river – silent white egrets and honking purple-black hadada ibis, mottled Egyptian geese and the formidable carnivorous sentries, goliath herons, tall yellow-billed storks and the large marabous, with their wicked beaks pressed against the scrotum-pink sacs on their chests.

Peaceful as it is, warmed by the sun and cooled by the contents of my thermos, I am always a little uneasy when I am here with the lions. After it has rained they make a frightful fuss when they have to walk through a puddle, but if something excites their interest on the other side of the river they plunge straight into the stream and swim directly across, despite the strength of the current. My worry is that crocodiles have drowned at least one of my lions and may easily account for others.

I usually walk the younger lions back to camp for lunch; in the first few weeks they are inclined to come to a call, like a dog. I leave the older ones by the river, or on Kora Rock, which we pass on the way. They are probably still there when I go down in the evening – or will come to me quickly if I call them with a megaphone.

I have had some tricky moments up on the rocks. Early one morning, in 1977, I let Suleiman and Sheba out of their enclosure to spend the day in the bush, while I drove to the hill to look for a lioness with cubs. I climbed to the foot of some cliffs where I thought her lair might be, but could see no sign of them.

As I started down Suleiman and Sheba appeared. They were in a playful mood and while I fended off Sheba, who butted me from the front, Suleiman jumped on my back, grabbing me by the neck and bringing me down on the steep hillside. I tried to beat him off, whacking him over my shoulder with a stick. This made him angry and he started to growl, sinking his teeth in the back of my neck. It was no longer play.

Luckily I was wearing my revolver because my search for the lioness and cubs might well have brought me face to face with a cobra or leopard while I was poking about in the rocks. I drew the gun now with the notion of firing a shot over Suleiman's head to scare him off. When I pulled the trigger there was just a dull click. It happened a second time and with a fearful chill I realised I had probably forgotten to load it. My hand was no longer steady as I broke the gun open to work out my chances. At least there was a round in each of the chambers and as Suleiman still had his teeth in my neck – I could feel the blood trickling down my shoulders and the sweat coming out on my forehead – I decided to try again. This time I managed to get two shots off into the air. They had not the slightest effect.

Suleiman bit harder. In sheer desperation I pointed the revolver backwards over my shoulder, and fired straight at him. Immediately he let go and, looking startled, went and sat twenty feet off with Sheba, who had leapt back at the sound of the first two shots. I could see blood on his muzzle and more on his neck.

I was bleeding profusely myself and wondered what the hell to do next. Tony Fitzjohn was away in Nairobi. Terence was off on safari and our radio was out of action. I therefore concentrated on getting down to the car and back into camp, where at least I had disinfectant and dressings. By the time I got the Landrover into camp I was feeling exceedingly groggy.

To my surprise it was Terence who opened the gates at the sound of my engine. He had got in only a few minutes before me. He helped me clean up the bites, and then he set off on an eighty-mile journey to the nearest medical post, which was in permanent touch with Nairobi. I did not get much sleep during the night and felt very worried about Suleiman, as I had no idea how badly I had wounded him. I rather feared the worst as Sheba had appeared in the evening without him.   Next morning, much to my

The borderline between a playful embrace and a spurt of irritation is a slender one — as I later found when Suleiman sank his teeth into my neck.

"By the time we get down to the river I am ready for a cool glass of gin from the thermos, and the lions flop down on the sand."

relief, Suleiman turned up. The pistol bullet had run across the top of his shoulders and lodged under the skin. He looked little the worse for it and was as friendly as ever. My own damage might have been worse too. The Flying Doctor took me to hospital in Nairobi and as the wounds did not go septic I was out in a week.

Few of our morning walks end as eventfully as this one and the camp we return to at midday has calmed down after the bustle at breakfast. By now the temperature is 100 degrees. The lions lie flat out under the trees. All the other animals too, the reptiles, the birds and even the insects are silent and still, each in its own patch of shade. Our lunch is like a movie in slow motion with the sound turned down. It is an effort to eat, to drink, to puff my pipe. Terence and I nod in our chairs. Dry leaves crack under the scorching heat of the sun like tiny pistol shots.

I know that if I surrender to sleep, just as I get on to my bed, I shall hear the persistent and approaching drone of a small plane heading for camp. I recently counted from my visitors book that two hundred and ninety-seven people made their way to Kora last year. As always, while friends bring their news and their views, strangers ask questions. I do my best to give answers.

"Yes, after their first week or two the lions are entirely free to come and go as they please – unless they are damaged or ill, in which case I bring them into camp to look after them."

"I'm sorry, I can only take people out on foot if I know that the lions are well away from camp."

"Sadly it is true. One of the lions did kill a man here; but that's a long time ago now."

"Well, the danger is really more to Tony and me than anyone else, as we spend so much of the day with the lions."

"No. In a funny way the danger is part of the attraction – as it presumably is for racing drivers or people who sail round the world single-handed."

"As a matter of fact nobody pays us. We have to raise money to keep ourselves going as best we can."

"Why do I do it?" That is the most difficult question of all. "Well, I suppose it is to give the lions the chance of a decent life. A lion is not a lion if it is only free to eat, to sleep and to copulate. It deserves to be free to hunt and to choose its own prey; to look for and find its own mate; to fight for and hold its own territory; and to die where it was born – in the wild. It should have the same rights as we have."

"Suleiman died like a lion." After he had been killed by a slicing crunch of a hippo's massive jaws…

…Sheba had guarded his body. I could see from their prints that crocodiles had tried to claim it, but she had driven them back to the water.

They are serious questions and I cannot stay on at Kora unless people go on being interested in my work. The Tana River Council only created the Reserve here, and the Government only support it, because it is constantly drawing attention to the country's unique and beautiful wildlife. The longer I am kept from siestas, the better for all of us here.

In the afternoons we either drive visitors down to the river, to look at the lions, or Tony and I go off on our own. The late afternoon is the best time to search for a lion with cubs, as it is hot work climbing about on the rocks, and I am grateful for the cool of the day. Another job I kept for the afternoons, when I had recovered from Suleiman's attentions, was to call on him and Sheba his sister. When they came to us, two of the three adult lionesses – each with several cubs of her own – took against them and never let them become full members of the pride. I therefore moved them to a dry sand lugga about five or six miles away and drove out every few days to see how they were getting on.

One morning, as I was reaching their favourite haunt on the river, Sheba burst from the bushes. She was scratched, trembling and kept up a low moan of distress. She peered intently into the undergrowth that grew along the top of the bank, and as she edged persistently towards it I followed her for a few hundred yards till we came to a gap.

At first all I could see was a chaos of footprints in the mud and sand of the river bed. But they drew my eye to a tawny shape slumped in the scrub under a giant acacia. Suleiman lay dead, from bloody and terrible wounds round his rib cage.

Gradually, from the evidence of the tracks and the flattened saplings, I pieced the tragedy together. Suleiman and Sheba had surprised a great bull hippo coming back from a night's grazing in the bush. They had attacked it, suicidally, as a hippo weighs more than a ton and is at its most dangerous when cut off from water. In the struggle which followed the lions must have got a hold on the hippo with their teeth and claws, until it had backed Suleiman against a clump of bushes. There it had killed him with one slicing crunch of its massive jaws.

Suleiman "died like a lion" and I reckoned that for two nights, with even greater courage, Sheba had guarded his body. I could see from the prints of their feet and the scrape of their tails where crocodiles, smelling Suleiman's blood, had waddled out of the river to claim his corpse. But Sheba would not let them have it. She had circled round, darting backwards and forwards, finally driving them into the water.

I buried Suleiman close to where I found him, just above flood level, with Sheba sitting by. She refused to leave his grave even when the light began to fail. Suleiman had been given his chance of freedom and its span was brief. But Joy and I always felt, rightly or wrongly, that life in a dangerous world was better than bars or a bullet for lions, as we reckoned it was for ourselves.

Three months later I was driving down this stretch of the river, thinking of Suleiman, when I noticed a scarred and limping bull hippo making off into the shallows. The next day I saw it on the bank, looking rather sickly under a shady tree, and I got out for closer look at it through my field glasses. What happened next took me completely by surprise. The hippo let out a mighty snort and charged me. I leapt into the car but before I could start it the hippo rammed into it and heaved it up until I thought it would roll over. Next, he bit deep into the mudguard before retiring once more to the shade. My fingers tingled with shock. The hippo's back was furrowed by deep claw marks and he must have been the animal that killed Suleiman.

When we get back to camp in the evenings, Tony and I check that there is water in the trough outside the wire, and prepare some meat for the pride's regular evening appearance. I feed the lions for several reasons: so that the mothers with cubs do not have to leave them alone for too long; so that any new lions are not threatened with starvation if they cannot get a share of the kills in the bush; and to reinforce the pride's association with the territory round camp. In the wild lions may only kill and eat every few days and I am very careful not to blunt the incentive to kill for themselves. The last thing I want to induce is dependence. On the other hand the lions are the reason I am here and the more I know about them and their needs the more use I can be in emergency.

Strictly speaking there is no need to put out water either, as the river is within easy reach. During the worst droughts lions survive on liquids from their prey and I have sometimes seen them chewing succulent plants broken open by antelopes. The water trough is therefore a luxury enjoyed by a number of visitors, including a family of owls who use it to bathe in.

We are only three miles south of the equator and night falls fast every evening, at about seven o'clock. Hamisi brings out a table, our dilapidated camp chairs, bottles, glasses and ice. The lions materialise like silent and ghostly figures from the dusk and sink contentedly to the ground, just outside the wire. It is a magical hour; the stars grow brighter and brighter; the chirrup of frogs and the liquid call of the nightjars take over from the daytime hum of the crickets.

I was scribbling away at my diary one evening – I have kept one for most of my life – when a squabble broke out between two cubs. Tony and Terence were trying to see which they were, when I pricked up my ears.

"Watch out, George!" hissed Tony, with an odd note in his voice, "look quickly behind you." I turned and found myself staring straight into the eyes of a quivering lioness. I feared the worst, for a second, as none of our lions had broken the rules and managed to get into camp.

In fact it was a shy and attractive lioness called Juma, who had suddenly mastered the art of wriggling under the wire. It was a little time before Terence succeeded in outwitting her, and until then I had to entice her to one of the gates with a tit-bit of meat on the occasions when she decided to join us for a sundowner. I was rather sorry that she was preoccupied with her first litter of cubs when Joy came up for a memorable Christmas at Kora, bringing with her the novelist Hammond Innes and his wife. Innes was out in Kenya sniffing the air for the scent of a plot. I thought he might enjoy Juma's company and even put her into his book.

Joy had been brought up in Austria and wherever we were in the bush she managed to make a sparkling celebration of Christmas Eve, as she did now. There were presents, decorations, candles, a cake, champagne, and even a glittering Christmas tree. Joy loved a party, and this was the last one we ever gave together.

Supper on an ordinary evening at Kora is a humble affair, but a good deal livelier than lunch. The birds that pestered us at breakfast have all gone to roost but the acacia rats and ground squirrels drop in, almost literally, for some crumbs and the dregs of our coffee. The air and our soup are thick with squadrons of insects and bugs homing in on the lanterns. Sundowners have loosened our tongues.

"Nonsense," said Terence one evening. "George is not like a lion – hair a bit yellow – that's all – just needs to wash it."

"But Terence," protested Tony, "*everyone* starts to look like their animals. Take . . ."

"I grant you Ionides," interrupted Terence, uncharacteristically. "Caught more snakes in Africa than any man, animal or bird that ever lived. Had eyes and beak of an eagle. Claws too, I dare say."

"And what about Thesiger?" I asked. "After all those journeys in the desert I always think Wilfred looks just like one of his camels."

"Come on, face it, Terence," chipped in Tony. "Even you – you're just as sticky and prickly as one of your bloody old thorn bushes."

Terence lowered his head in disdain, and the scars on his cheek, where Juma's grandson had raked him, showed pink in the lamplight. Perhaps Tony had gone too far.

My thoughts had drifted away to the memory of what Desmond Morris, an expert on animals, and professional manwatcher, had thought about

Joy: with her pale golden hair, her prowling gait and her eager eyes – to him she resembled a lioness.

For some reason we never seem able to organise supper so that it doesn't coincide with the evening radio routine. Tony usually handles the calls. I hate the infernal machine, with everyone else on the network listening in, but Tony has no inhibitions. He uses an extremely effective code of *doubles entendres* for dating his girlfriends.

We get an odd miscellany of calls in any one week. The Director of Wildlife is seriously worried about threats from the local Shifta – Somali bandits from across the river – and is coming up to discuss our security. A television company is bringing Ali McGraw out to Kenya, please could she interview me – up in a balloon – about the great migration of wildebeest. Bill Travers and Virginia McKenna are arriving to help choose photographs for my book; they know about our desperate need for White Horse whisky, but what about butter and mangoes?

If Tony has friends in camp I usually hear the murmur of voices as I slip off to sleep. It is very dry here – the average rainfall is ten inches a year, less than a third of the temperate zones of Europe and America, and almost instantly evaporated by the equatorial sun. In a drought we get one inch – and most of the time I sling my mosquito net from a fence post and sleep under the sky. Beside me are a loaded rifle and a slit trench.

The country on the other side of the Tana is grazed by the herds of Somalis, a tough tribe, who spread from Somaliland up on the coast down through the heartland of Kenya. They are allowed on the other bank of the river but in a drought cannot resist the temptation of driving their stock into Kora. The Shifta come with them.

The Director of Wildlife has some cause to be worried about our safety. We have just learnt that Ken Clarke, who gave us Suleiman and Sheba, heard shooting on his ranch and went out to find Somali poachers hacking the horns out of three rhino carcases. When he chased them they ambushed him. A bullet which hit his belt buckle was deflected up into his heart. He died instantly.

As a result I have been ordered to evacuate Kora. I think this is too drastic and refuse to leave unless they take me in handcuffs. Instead I hand out a scratch arsenal of pistols and shotguns each night to my recently recruited Home Guard and put my faith in the funk holes we dig.

As I close my eyes the sounds of the bush drive out all thoughts of Somalis. A tremendous roar goes up from the rocks on the hill: it may be from Juma's young lions, or Christian, asserting their rights. I think of Boy and of Elsa, and remember my earliest safaris in Kenya, and the first shot I fired as a child, in India.

Chapter 2

Early Man
1906–1938

The first gun I fired was my mother's. So far as I know she herself only once killed an animal with it – a black buck. The little railway in the Indian state where we lived ran through a forest, and if he saw game in a clearing my father would pull the communication cord and stop the train. It must have been on one of these journeys that my mother claimed her buck.

She came from one of the many British families whose lives were interwoven with India. Her mother had lived through the fear and excitement of the mutiny in 1857. On the other hand, my father Harry, an Irishman, did not come to India until after a spell in the Royal Navy, with whom he sailed round the Horn. He must have infected me with his reminiscences as my favourite book has always been *Sailing Alone Around The World* by Joshua Slocum. He came out to India to plant indigo, married my mother, Katherine, and soon after 1900 joined the service of the Rajah of Dholpur.

They lived in Etawah where I was born in 1906 and my brother Terence a year later. Terence remembers our being put into the bath to eat mangoes: when we finished them we would turn the skins inside out and slide down the sides with a satisfying splash. Before the summer temperatures rose to 120 degrees in the shade we would be packed off to Simla with the other British families. My father stayed at home and stuck out the heat. He was a versatile man. He taught himself building and engineering and set up the railway system in Dholpur: they were aptitudes he passed on to Terence. Later he reorganised the Rajah's army, and it was one of his Sergeant Majors who taught us to shoot with my mother's rifle. Sometimes I was allowed out pig-sticking, but my real ambition was to kill a bear, though I never achieved it.

Whatever they may feel when they grow up, most small boys are bloodthirsty. At school in England and during our holidays in Scotland, Terence and I dreamed of big game hunting. Believing, as I now do, that the larger social animals are closer to man than is usually admitted, I believe also that they have moral rights which are similar to man's. The corollary of this is that people are much closer to animals, in their genetic impulses and social behaviour, than they care to admit. I sometimes examine my own nature in this light.

The social drive of the Romans was like that of safari ants. Their armies hurried across the land, in disciplined ranks, carrying all before them, first in one direction and then in another. Centuries later a strain among the English, Scots and Irish produced behaviour more like ants in their alate or flying form. Restless and enterprising individuals responded to an impulse and took off overseas, where they set up trading posts, and then colonies, where they were largely dependent on their own initiative and ingenuity. This was my own background and when my father retired from India he made not for Ireland but for South Africa, where I was to join him.

At the age of eighteen I duly caught a boat to Cape Town and when it docked I found a telegram from my father. His boat had put into Mombasa, in Kenya, and he had liked the country so much he had decided to stay: please would I join him. By the time I reached Kenya my parents had bought a small coffee farm at Limuru, near Nairobi. They were living in a grass hut or banda, not unlike my palm huts at Kora today.

Terence came out the next year and has only left Africa once. In the nineteen-fifties, a friend saw him digging up a debbie – a tin fuel can – at the back of his hut. It had been carefully sealed and was difficult to open. My friend asked Terence how long the debbie had been buried, what treasure it contained and why he was disinterring it now.

'Seven years. My suit. Going round the world," was his laconic reply. During the war he had been commissioned as a Garrison Engineer and on demobilisation was presented with the customary suit; it is the only one he has ever owned. After his cruise it was reputedly returned to the debbie where it rests to this day.

When Terence and I joined my father, Kenya, as an English settlement, was about twenty-five years old and offered all the conditions and opportunities most attractive to the colonial species. In the nineteenth century two outriders of empire, the explorer and the missionary, had brought to London news of East Africa's challenges. There were excellent ports in Mombasa and Zanzibar, magnificent landscapes and the largest lake on the continent – Lake Victoria – which gave rise to the Nile. But urgent action had to be taken to stop the Arabs from trading in slaves, confine the Germans from extending their bridgehead round Zanzibar and prevent the French from controlling the headwaters of the Nile. Here was excuse enough for the Prime Minister to sanction completion of a railway, in the last ten years of the century, which would run from Mombasa, right across what is now Kenya, through the new capital, Nairobi – still only a tented camp near a swamp – to Lake Victoria and Uganda in the West. All went well until two native forces fought a rearguard action at Tsavo as the railway snaked towards the interior. These were not the Maasai, or other tribes who had repulsed Europeans and Arabs, but the mosquitoes and lions.

Tens of thousands of coolies had been brought over from India to lay the line. Two and a half thousand died from accidents and malaria. It is a disease I have caught myself and I sometimes wonder whether the antidotes, which have once or twice driven me literally insane, are not as bad as the complaint. Certainly the quinine in them has damaged my hearing.

Even more frightening and obstructive than malaria were the lions. Two in particular terrorised the camps which the Indians had put up for their women and their children. Their murderous attacks were carried out with unprecedented bravado and ferocity, resulting in a mutiny and the flight of many of the labourers to the coast. Work on the line stopped as more than a hundred coolies were killed. The lions ate them, or stripped them of their skin and sucked their blood. The chief engineer, Colonel R. J. Patterson, put out marksmen at night but on more than one occasion they found themselves being stalked by the man-eaters. Patterson had the daunting experience of hearing lions crunch the bones of one of his men, purring as they did so. In the end Patterson himself sat up over bait and nailed the two culprits, whose skins were stuffed and sent for display in the Natural History Museum of Chicago. Even then other lions took over the attack. One night three Europeans sat up in a box-car to deal with them but a lion pushed open the sliding door and made off with a railway superintendent named Ryall.

It is not always easy to kill a lion and seldom that one can do it from the relative safety and ease of a platform or machan. For instance the shooting of Elsa's mother might well have led to disaster. I was out with Ken Smith, a colleague who had just joined the game department and who has remained a close friend ever since. We were after a man-eating lion and I wanted to give him first shot. Before we could find the lion, Ken was charged by a lioness and fired. She was wounded, not killed and when we followed her up she suddenly leapt at him from under a rock I was standing on and both of his next shots went wide. I could not fire myself as the lioness was in line with him. It was only after a bullet from one of our rangers had turned her that I was able to kill her myself.

Two of the most cunning man-eaters I have ever known persecuted the Boran who lived near Merti. They took a variety of men and women in many different ways. They set on a mother with her baby strapped to her back; when she tried to climb a tree they simply clawed her down, and ate her and the child. A man was pulled from his hut and screamed for help, which no one dared bring him. Two dogs gave chase, but the lions dropped the man, drove the dogs back, picked up the Boran again, and killed him in the bush. They had claimed twenty-one victims and it took me nearly a month to account for them both. When I finally did so I found they were perfectly healthy, without any of the disabilities that weaken or slow down a lion so that it has to abandon its more natural prey and take to a diet of humans.

Once the railway from Mombasa to Lake Victoria was finished, in 1901, Kenya Protectorate – as it then was – offered British settlers two options: the hard and the soft, depending on their means. Having few means but my wits and my hands when I arrived there in 1924 I took the hard route, for the next ten years of my life.

I built roads, but the work was gruelling and thankless. I went into transport; my first load of matches combusted with the friction, I very soon ran out of spare axles and wheels and my mail service was overtaken by others. I farmed, but one coffee bean looked like another and sisal, which I grew for sacking and ropes, was just as monotonous. I traded in goats, bee's wax and resins milked from wild thorn bushes. The goats languished and died from changes in altitude; my African suppliers treasured the wild honey but forgot to keep the combs for the wax; and the bazaars favoured Arab above African resins. When I became a salesman I ran out of whisky bottles for my milk rounds and my competitor in life assurance – a defrocked priest with D.T.'s – was better at the game than I was. As a civil servant, in locust control with stirrup pumps and arsenical spray, I was a danger to the Africans and lethal to the locusts. When the last remaining hoppers grew up and took wing I was out of a job.

Then I hit on something which I was convinced would make me a glittering fortune; I went gold prospecting with my great friend Nevil Baxendale. We collected equipment, staked our claim on a stream near Kakamega and were rewarded by the occasional flash in our pans: it was exhausting work. Our cook Yusef did his best to sustain us with variations on the guinea-fowl we shot and wild vegetables prepared on his traditional fireplace of three stones. He also brewed us hooch. One day a toto, six or seven years old, arrived with a strand of plaited grass round the neck of a magnificent rhinoceros horn viper which we bought from him. We christened it Cuthbert Gandhi – he frequently "fasted nigh unto death" – and set it to guard our meagre finds. But our ambitions began to falter, we returned to Nairobi no richer than when we arrived and handed Cuthbert Gandhi over to the museum. He is still there today, in a large glass jar.

These were the years of the depression which hit Kenya as badly as anywhere else. Terence prospered no better than I. He built my parents a stone house at Limuru and after my father died in 1927 ran the farm, replacing the coffee, which was unsuitable at the altitude, with wattle from whose bark a tanning extract was derived. Then he worked in a sawmill for £12 a month. He had nothing to spend on smoking, drinking or women. At the age of nearly eighty he has still not touched tobacco or alcohol and I swear it has damaged his health.

Although Terence and I never made our fortunes there were others in the twenties who took the hard option and flourished. Abraham Block arrived with only a few ponies and sacks of vegetable seeds. His interest in hotels began when he sold them mattresses, made with the sacks and stuffed with hay cut from the railway line. Eddie Ruben began his famous Express Transport company with one team of mules he bought with an army gratuity after the First World War. Both established extraordinarily successful businesses in this country and both Kenya and I owe much to them and their sons.

Some of the settlers who arrived and took up the soft options transferred immense wealth from England, America or elsewhere to acquire properties in Kenya of fifty or a hundred thousand acres, but they led very tough lives. The third Lord Delamere was so carried away by his vision of farming in Kenya that he gave up a life of hunting and pleasure, pledged his British estates and threw himself into the life of the country, becoming the unofficial spokesman of the settlers. He was as unconventional as hard-working, became a blood-brother of the Maasai, was Winston Churchill's host when he visited Kenya, wore shoulder-length hair, and potted bottles and lanterns with a revolver from the verandah of the Norfolk Hotel in Nairobi.

Another landowner on a similar scale but a totally different character was Gilbert Colvile. A miserable looking cove, he was not merely a misogynist but a misanthrope too: the only exceptions to his dislikes were the Maasai and their cattle. He hunted lions with packs of ruthlessly disciplined dogs. When he suspected a European neighbour of harbouring a pride he set fire to two island sanctuaries he owned, destroying many of the birds and their habitat, and forcing the hippos to seek their grazing elsewhere.

The life of these ranchers was extremely demanding, as was that of the rich men who devoted most of the year to killing game – driving themselves after the animals with the finest physiques. But not all the affluent worked and played so energetically: many preferred racing, fishing, polo or golf. They went down to the coast or simply on safari – a journey – to enjoy some of the loveliest scenery in the world. Two further pastimes, flying and adultery, quite often went together.

The women who lived with these pioneers, settlers, hunters or remittance men were just as colourful but much more articulate. Unlike their counterparts in England, they had plenty of servants and were free to express themselves in whatever way they chose, by travelling, writing, painting, taking photographs or making love. In fact the most vivid accounts of Kenyan life, in words and pictures, all come from women.

The most entertaining and probably best known is our friend Elspeth Huxley's autobiographical sequence, which was adapted for television, *The Flame Trees of Thika*. Perhaps the classic is Karen Blixen's *Out of Africa*. It brilliantly conjures up the atmosphere of life for a European on an African farm — its sights, sounds and smells; its struggles, mysteries and sudden shocking horrors; the loneliness, the touching loyalties and the precious moments of companionship and love. Known to her family and friends as Tanne, she wrote under the name Isak Dinesen.

Karen Blixen was a Dane. Her husband, Baron Bror Blixen, was an irrepressible, extravert Swede — an expert hunter of animals and women. Her lover, the Hon. Denys Finch Hatton, was a sensitive, introvert old Etonian. He was also a professional hunter and used his small plane to scout game, as did another of Kenya's flying pioneers in the twenties, Beryl Markham.

I did not meet the Blixens but I did know Beryl, whose book *West With the Night* has recently enjoyed a revival. It gives an enthralling account of her earliest flying in Kenya — sometimes on mail runs — and her marathon solo flight, the first to be made from England to America. I met her in Muthaiga with her step-brother Sir Alec Kirkpatrick, who was a bit of a playboy and an odd man out in the Game Department. I have sometimes blamed myself for his death as I had arranged to meet him one evening in Limuru and had to cancel at the last moment. That night Alec was shot or, I suspect, committed suicide.

Beryl has led an astonishing life. As a child she ran barefoot and hunted with the Nandi. When she grew up she not only wrote and flew planes but trained race horses until she was well into her eighties. Strikingly attractive, she has been loved by royalty, married three times and was said to have had romantic liaisons with both Bror Blixen and Denys Finch Hatton. When the Prince of Wales, later King Edward VIII, came out to Kenya in 1928 she helped entertain him. Among the social events of this tour was a patriotic gathering at Nanyuki, near Mt Kenya, to which all the settlers with good English sounding names, like Nightingale and Fletcher, Bastard and Hook, were invited. The Prince noticed three angelic looking children dressed up in sailor suits, asked who they were, and was told they were young Bastards.

"Good God!" he said. "This must be the only country in the world where they put them into uniform."

By the time the Prince was in Kenya Bror Blixen's marriage to Karen was over and he had married a sparkling lady known to her friends as Cockie.

She is still alive, although a South African newspaper reported her death, some time after she had remarried – for the second time. She regarded the obituary as a slur on her undisputed vitality. When she demanded a retraction the editor grovelled and agreed to print whatever she dictated. According to Elspeth Huxley, in *Out in the Midday Sun*, the notice appeared as "Mrs. Hoogterp wishes it to be known she has not yet been screwed in her coffin."

The Prince of Wales was determined to shoot a lion, and placed himself in the hands of Denys Finch Hatton, who asked Bror Blixen to help with the safari. Before it began Karen Blixen gave a dinner party, hosted by Finch Hatton, at which Beryl Markham was one of the only two women present. Towards the end the Prince and his party turned up in Cockie Blixen's tumbledown house, quite unexpectedly, at lunchtime and demanded food: Cockie had nothing but eggs which she scrambled herself. This cat's cradle of intimate relationships epitomises Kenya's reputation in the twenties and thirties.

When he left Mombasa the Prince said he had found Kenya a wonderful land of promise. He might have added he had found it a wonderful playground, much in line with his own private tastes. His visit, so different in tone from his niece Elizabeth's twenty-five years later, nevertheless ended exactly like hers, with a sudden summons to London. His father, George V, was thought to be dying.

*   *   *

One of the few things I had in common with the Prince of Wales was a taste for hunting. It was the only recreation Terence and I could afford. Our transport was limited to a motor-bicycle and side-car, we shared a rifle, and every bullet had to kill. It was touch and go getting up some of the hills with the three hundred pound carcase of a hartebeest in the sidecar.

We would never have got anywhere without Mosandu, our Dorobo tracker, whose tribe are probably the only aboriginals left in Kenya and have gradually been pushed into the forests as other tribes have occupied the grazing and farming land. The Dorobo are past masters of the ancient traditions of the hunt. Mosandu taught me to understand wind, scent, sound and spoor. He could interpret the age and sex of an animal from its tracks, and knew how fast it was moving, if it was lightly or badly wounded, and if it was dying. He could tell from the clarity of the trail, from rain drops or dew on the spoor, or perhaps from the trace of an insect, how old the prints were. If the spoor petered out he would pick it up again from dislodged pebbles, broken twigs, bent blades of grass, or torn cobwebs. If an animal had lain up, under a rock or bush, he would identify it by licking his palm and pressing it to the ground, so that any hairs there would cling to it.

From Mosandu I also learnt to use my ears, to catch the rustle of a leaf or twig, the sudden alarm of a bird or the abrupt silence of a chorus of frogs. On safari Mosandu only brought a scrap of blanket round his middle and a small stick. After the hunt I gave him a share of the meat. He and his friends would camp round the carcase, like lions on a kill, until it was finished.

Sometimes Terence and I would go out after game birds with one of my dogs and a shotgun. More often we would take a rifle in search of an antelope. Occasionally we would hunt for a fine specimen of one of the big five – lion, leopard, rhino, buffalo and elephant – which have always excited sportsmen in Africa. We had to buy a licence from the Game Department to shoot any of these but I could get something back on a rhino horn and the feet sold for tobacco jars. If I was really broke I would save £25 to buy an elephant licence so that I could sell the tusks – at a tiny fraction of today's values – for £50 or £100.

*   *   *

I had not entirely lost my itch to find gold, so in 1934 Nevil and I embarked on one final quest, almost as much for the adventure as the prospect of riches. We set out to discover the Queen of Sheba's Mines, which legend located on Lake Rudolf in northern Kenya, near Abyssinia (since Kenya's independence in 1963 it has been known as Lake Turkana).

The lake, with Mt Kenya and Mt Kilimanjaro, was one of three geographical features that had caught the imagination of nineteenth-century travellers. When the German missionaries, Krapf and Rebmann, had brought back to Europe stories of mountains on the equator capped with snow, they were greeted with scorn – not least by the Royal Geographical Society of London, who set themselves up as the ultimate authorities on African exploration. On the other hand the explorers Count Teleki and Lieutenant von Hohnel were listened to with respect when they described crossing a blistering desert to reach a vast inland sea, 170 miles long and 20 miles wide.

Twice my size, robust in every way, an expert boat builder and with a highly developed sense of humour, Nevil was the ideal companion for such an enterprise. We could not have done without Yusef, our cook from Kakamega days. He could perform miracles with dried meat, scrawny game birds, wild spinach or mushrooms and tiny doles of maize flour. He was equally clever at handling donkeys which, until well after the second world war, were the Landrovers of the Northern Frontier.

Left: With Terence. He always hated being photographed and his ability to anticipate the camera was uncanny. *Right:* "I was convinced I would make a glittering fortune." Panning for gold near Kakamega.

Terence and I. "If I was really broke I would save £25 to buy an elephant licence so that I could sell the tusks…"

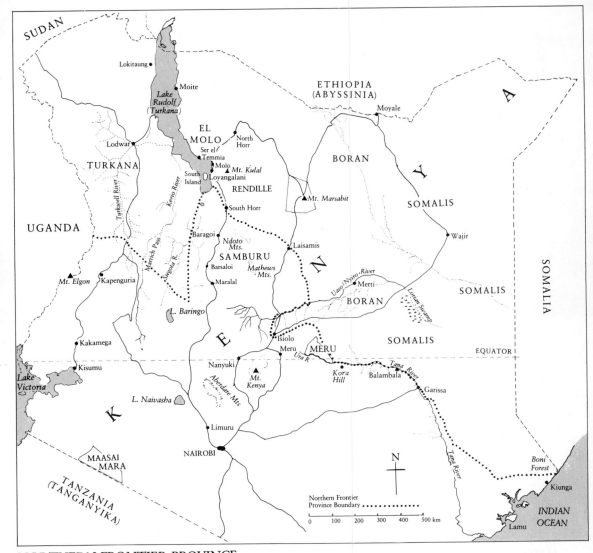

NORTHERN FRONTIER PROVINCE

Previously Northern Frontier District and Turkana
showing the principal tribes mentioned in Chapters 2 and 4

We spent the first two months of our safari following first the bed of a tributary and then the Kerrio river itself, searching systematically for traces of gold. The doum palms and acacias shaded the sand and rocks from the blazing sun and we ate the sweet, glutinous berries of *Cordia abyssinica* to keep off scurvy. Not long ago I saw a satellite photograph of northern Kenya which represented vegetation in reds. The forests were scarlet, and the desert round Rudolf was white. But the course of the Kerio shows up as a tiny pink vein curving down to the western shore of the lake. It was at this point that tradition placed the Queen of Sheba's Mines. Tradition had made a mistake.

Cheated of our gold Nevil and I were determined not to be done out of our adventure. We therefore decided to trek a hundred and fifty miles round the southern shores of the lake to Mt Kulal, which we could see thirty miles away as the pelican flies. We might even find gold in the gulleys, which we spotted through our binoculars, on the flanks of the volcanic mountain. While Yusef loaded the donkeys we engaged two Turkana who volunteered to come with us. Tobosh, the younger, was about twenty, well over six foot tall and superbly built. He wore no stitch of clothing, not even sandals, and carried nothing with him, not even the traditional Turkana spear, the *rungu* – knobbed stick – wristknife or headrest.

The donkeys were exasperating but indispensable. At various times they were scattered by hyenas, a rhino, a herd of elephants and a thunderstorm. Squeezing past a boulder above a precipitous gorge, the donkey with our bedding rolls lost its footing and I seized its ears as its hind legs slid over the abyss. Thanks to Nevil's massive strength we saved it. One morning we woke to find the donkeys had vanished in the night. Tobosh finally came on them as they were being stalked by two lions. Without hesitation, although he was unarmed, he got behind the donkeys and drove them back to camp, followed by the lions until they saw Nevil and me. It is remarkable how almost all animals sense danger at the sight of a gun.

Lake Rudolf lies in a harsh, barren, rocky cauldron. The desert round it is strewn with a hail of volcanic boulders which are hell for man and donkey to pick their way through. There is an unremitting and merciless force to the sun and also to the wind, which gusts at forty miles an hour for most of the day, and sometimes rises to eighty. It blew the food from our plates, covered it with grit and whipped up angry white horses on the lake. If this malignant wind did drop, in the late afternoon, the heat would strike like breath from a furnace. To obtain respite at night from stinging particles of sand we built ourselves low parapets of stones. Once or twice we came across screens which I am sure had been left by Teleki and von Hohnel.

As we fought our way round the lake, sometimes forced into detours by the largest outcrops of rock, one of the donkeys died of exhaustion and our food ran low. When we had virtually nothing to eat for two days I shot a cormorant that was too rank for Nevil's stomach and mine but which Tobosh and his friend accepted with relish. Just in time Nevil caught a delicious forty-pound Nile perch.

Whatever the hardship there was always something to look at, terns and waders, divers and ospreys, plenty of crocodiles and a few wallowing hippo. The colour of the water frequently seemed to change. According to the wind and the sky it could be grey, muddy, blue or the green which has given it the name of "The Jade Sea". What surprised us was that we did not see a single tribesman, Turkana or Samburu, Rendille or Boran: later we were to discover why.

At last, near the foothills of Mt Kulal, we came to the beach on which all one hundred of the tiny Molo tribe lived – in a cluster of palm leaf huts, like up-turned baskets. The party which greeted us were naked, except for their young chief Kurru, who sported a red fez, a striped pyjama jacket and red hair on his arms and chest. I speculated on the alien origins of all three. But the fish they gave us, Nile perch, came from the lake. Most of them were speared from the palm log rafts on which they braved the treacherous waters, morning or evening, when the wind dropped. Smaller fish, tilapia, were caught in nets woven from palm fibres.

Finding plenty of game on Mt Kulal – including greater kudu, for which it was famous – but no trace of gold, Nevil and I pushed on up the shore to Moite before we were forced by shortage of time and food to turn back. On our way south again camping in a dry river bed called Serr el Temmia, Nevil made one of the most idiotic suggestions I have ever heard, just as I was dropping off to sleep.

"Instead of walking a hundred and fifty god-forsaken miles back to the mouth of the Kerrio, why don't we go straight across the lake?" he said. "It's only twelve or fifteen miles just here."

I actually thought he was suffering from heatstroke or off his head and had religious delusions of crossing the water on foot. Then I remembered his reputation as a boat builder. Much later that night I realised nothing would stop Nevil from putting his skills to the test and that I would have to share his lunatic adventure.

The design of his boat was based on a wooden frame, made from the branches of the acacias growing above the river bed. None of the branches were straight, so they had to be broken and rejoined with thongs from an antelope we had skinned a few days before. My job was to sew our groundsheets together for the hull and to tailor a sail from our bedding. Donkey boxes were adapted for the rudder, a lee-board and oars. When we launched this object of mad ingenuity it was ungainly but floated.

In high spirits we sent Tobosh off with his companion, the donkeys, the remains of our food and all our possessions except for a gun, and a cooking pot we kept as a bailer. We told them that if desperate they could eat one of the donkeys but they left us on their hazardous way without hesitation or murmur of complaint. That evening we weighted the boat with stones, so it would not be blown away, and retired to sleep in the riverbed. When we woke in the morning the boat was in pieces. Jackals had come in the night and devoured all the thongs. Our predicament would have seemed catastrophic were it not also ridiculous.

As there was no game anywhere near us to replace the thongs, I had to strip the inner bark off a species of acacia growing some way inland. At first our only food was salvadora berries which look and taste a little like blackcurrants, with a tinge of nasturtium. When I found a goose, nesting up in an acacia, I had to climb another tree so I could blast off its head without damaging the eggs. Yusef, who had rashly elected to sail with us, as the lesser of two evils, made an excellent job of preparing this windfall.

Needless to say, when the boat was once more ready to sail the wind had risen; we therefore decided to wait for the evening calm and take our chance with the oars, even though there was no moon and darkness would fall long before we made land. At three p.m., ten days after Tobosh and the donkeys had left us, we pushed out onto the lake. While Yusef bailed, and the little boat concertinaed with the waves, Nevil and I rowed until well after dark and our hands were raw. As we paused to check our position against the silhouette of the Loriu hills, which had appeared dimly ahead of us, I heard a sound in the distance, like rising waves under a gathering wind.

Nevil and I strained our ears; we suddenly realised it was the croaking of a thousand frogs and we must be close to shore. Half an hour after we landed the wind really did get up and a gale blustered over the lake until well into the following day. For the next twenty-four hours we had to survive on a half bottle of brandy given me by my dear mother against just such a moment of joy or despair. Then Yusef succeeded in begging a single cupful of milk from a ravenous family of Turkana. Finally Nevil bagged four ducks and a goose. Unable to see a sign of our donkeys, impatient to get to our rendezvous with Tobosh, we threw caution literally to the winds and clinging to the shore let the gale carry us up to the mouth of the Kerio.

Within twenty-four hours Tobosh arrived with all the donkeys. They had fought through the heat, the wind, and the terrible rocks; they had risked death from starvation, exposure and lions. From that day on my admiration for the fierce courage and pride of the Turkana has never wavered. Before parting from the two men and leaving them the donkeys as part of their wage, we called at the District headquarters at Lodwar, on the Turkwell River.

The Nairobi – Arusha Mail Service. "I went into transport but matches in bulk burst into flames and my mail service was overtaken by others."

Jackals ate the thongs of our home-made boat in the night and it took ten days to rebuild: our food had gone on ahead!

There we were greeted by the District Commissioner, and his assistant William Hale. First Willie filled us with mounds of bread and butter, which seemed the most desirable food in the world, and a goat stew of such size that it had to be cooked in his safari bath. Next he and the D.C. gave us a gentle lecture on the facts of life.

They told us that we should never have gone round to the other side of the lake without a permit – which we knew. What we had not known, however, was that the eastern shore was deserted except by the primitive Molo because raiders from Ethiopia had swept over the border, massacred any Turkana and Rendille they had encountered and made off with their women and camels. The D.C. also looked askance at our boating expedition. A few months before, Vivian Fuchs had led a geological expedition to Lake Rudolf and had left two scientists on South Island. They had never been seen again, although an oar had been found from their boat – a seven-foot canoe made of canvas.

As we made our way back to civilisation we once more kept our eyes open for gold – in vain. Had we gone a bit further, on both sides of the lake, or had we looked instead for oddly chipped stones and fragments of bone, we might have made a discovery of quite a different kind. Forty or fifty years later expeditions led by Richard Leakey, in both East Turkana and West Turkana, have disclosed settlements of *Homo erectus*, the immediate forerunner of *Homo sapiens*.

Between half a million and a million and a half years ago when the lake was much higher – in fact at one time water flowed from it into the Nile – *Homo erectus* occupied huts of palm or simple brushwood near the shore. They had fires for warmth and cooking. They gathered roots, leaves, fruits, berries and shellfish. They made bows and arrows, and stone tools for butchering their prey. They wore skins, hunted in groups and shared their food. Their life style enabled them to travel and explore not only Africa, but Europe and Asia as well.

It was an odd coincidence that I had spent the whole of my early manhood, until this safari, looking for a livelihood among the choices offered by twentieth-century colonial society; but from now on I abandoned the search and adopted the life of man's ancestors. Allow me a rifle instead of a bow and arrow and there is a remarkably close parallel – with obvious exceptions – between the life I have lived ever since, and that of early man. Nevil Baxendale's existence became rather more urbane as he decided to marry and settle: his son Jonny is my godson and we, too, have had our adventures together.

*   *   *

Early in 1935 a firm called Gethin and Hewlett employed me, presumably for qualifications in survival and hunting, to conduct some professional safaris. By good fortune the first people I took out were a charming Austrian brother and sister – Ernest and Angela Ofenheim. Apart from the smaller game, I enabled them to shoot a buffalo, a rhino and a lion. Angela became a surgeon and the safari was the beginning of a curious association with Austrian medicine. Angela and I have kept in touch ever since and fifty years later, not long after she came to visit me at Kora, an Austrian surgeon arranged for me to fly to Vienna for a cataract operation, while my brother Terence was in the care of a third Austrian doctor living in Kenya.

Unlike my motor-bike days, these professional safaris entailed hiring a Bedford truck, a pick-up and a driver; a tracker and two gun bearers, a skinner, two cooks, a waiter and a turney-boy – the assistant driver, originally engaged to turn the starting handle. This was modest. When Theodore Roosevelt came out to Kenya on safari in 1909, just after he ceased to be President of the United States, he had a retinue of five hundred porters, excluding the gun bearers and other hunting specialists.

The safari which remains most clearly in my mind from these days was a photographic expedition to the Serengeti plains, which lay in Maasai land, just over the Tanganyikan border. We saw more migrating wildebeest and zebra than we could conceivably count, innumerable gazelles, and large numbers of giraffe and buffalo. We stopped to photograph rhinos and elephant, and even came across that rare creature, which looks like an armadillo, called a pangolin. We were allowed to shoot antelope to lure lions in front of the camera: in three days we photographed thirty-six.

The glorious sight of these animals, living in a natural paradise, sparked off a reaction in me that early man would have found incomprehensible, but which was so powerful that I wrote it down.

> One evening we came to a magnificent lioness on a rock, gazing out across the plains. She was sculpted by the setting sun, as though she was part of the granite on which she lay. I wondered how many lions had sat on the self-same rock during countless centuries while the human race was still in its cradle.
>
> Civilised man has spent untold treasure preserving ancient buildings and works of art fashioned by his own hand, yet he destroys these creatures of ageless beauty. And he does so for no better reason than to boast of his prowess, achieved by means of a weapon designed by man to destroy man, and to use the skin of his victim to grace some graceless body or abode.

Emotions of this kind continued to work away inside me until one day an eccentric game warden called Tom Oulton, an incomparable raconteur who refused to eat unfertilised eggs, insisted on carpeting his camps with green leaves, used to sleep every night with his head towards north and believed implicitly in the "pyramid prophecies", persuaded me to apply to the Game Department.

In July 1938 I was enrolled as Temporary Assistant Game Warden, at a salary of £8 per week.

Chapter 3

The Day of the Game
1938–1942

There was a large clock in the Chief Game Warden's office. As Captain Archie Ritchie sat at his desk he could watch it over his visitors' shoulders during the morning's business. When the hands reached eleven he would stretch out for a leather bag that hung by his chair.

"Would you care for a gin?" he would ask as he pulled the bottle from the bongo skin bag. A bongo is a rare, beautiful and secretive antelope found in only a few of Kenya's mountain forests. The bag was not the only exotic touch in his life. Tall and upright, by the time I knew him his hair and moustache were white. Impatient to fight in the First World War, he had quickly joined the French Foreign Legion. Then he had transferred to the Grenadier Guards with whom he had been wounded beside his friend Harold Macmillan, later the Prime Minister. Ritchie was decorated for gallantry by both the French and the English.

He was perfectly cast in his present role for he was a man of action with a brilliant brain, had a degree in zoology and was a passionate naturalist – he also became an excellent photographer and amateur film maker. He inspired total devotion in the Game Department and managed to penetrate the most inaccessible parts of the country in his motor car: a Rolls Royce with a box body and a hippo tooth mounted on the bonnet. Wherever he went the gin bag went too, and was produced at precisely eleven o'clock. I found the habit catching.

Archie's natural authority was put to the test in some unusual ways during the Prince of Wales' visit in 1928. He was reputedly involved in a scuffle at a dinner party in Muthaiga and seen hustling another man out of the room. When asked what was going on Archie is said to have replied that he thought that there were limits even in Kenya and that when someone offered the heir to the throne cocaine in the middle of dinner, something had to be done about it!

Archie found himself watching a second undesirable approach to the prince when he came back to Kenya two years later. His safari was once more in the hands of Denys Finch Hatton, and this time he insisted on photographing a charging rhinoceros, head on and not from a car. Archie helped to manoeuvre the rhino into position, while Finch Hatton waited as long as he dared before dropping the rhino with a perfect shot between the eyes, six yards or so from the camera. Even then it was still too early for the prince who had wanted the rhino to fill his frame; he was highly respected by Finch Hatton for his courage and endurance when they were out on safari together.

There were less than a dozen wardens in the department when I joined it. Apart from Alec Kirkpatrick, who helped run the office in Nairobi, it included two experts on lions: Jack Hunter, who once found a large male in the back of his truck when he was carrying a carcase, and Lyn Temple-Boreham down on the Mara. Temple-Boreham kept two large males of his own, Brutus and Caesar, whom he had brought up from cubs.

The department had been set up by the government for several reasons. It administered the sale of licences without which game was not permitted to be hunted; it attempted to keep poaching under control; it was responsible for safeguarding life, stock and crops from lions, elephants, buffalo and any other four-legged miscreants; and it otherwise tried to protect all creatures with backbones – furred, feathered, plated or scaled – from persecution by man.

I was posted to Isiolo, on the southern boundary of the Northern Frontier Province, and was lucky to be lent a thatched house twelve miles outside the town by a family called Brown. I had little time or money to call my own and would have found it hard to make ends meet had I not been able to live off game.

I was expected to cover an area at least as large as Great Britain. There was not a single tarmac road in the country, and my only truck was a small private pick-up. It was, of course, quite incapable of carrying me, my six rangers and a cook, with all our kit, on patrols that would last several months. I clearly had to sort out some priorities.

One of the first was to recruit dependable rangers from the tribes in my area which surrounded the lower half of Lake Rudolf. To the west were the Turkana and south of them the Samburu. To the east were Somalis and Boran, and north of them the Rendille. They were all pastoral and semi-nomadic; in the north they favoured camels, in the south cattle. They largely subsisted on milk, often mixed with cow or camel blood drawn from the jugular veins which were afterwards sealed with dung. If there was enough water nearby they planted maize, millet or sweet potatoes. The forests on Mt Marsabit and the Ndoto and Mathews ranges were inhabited by the Dorobo.

One of my staunchest rangers was Lembirdan, a Samburu with plenty of goats and cattle, who joined me for the fun and excitement. He had a cool head and once killed a charging elephant at such short range that he was smothered in its blood; it was a classic shot to the centre of its head, just below the line of the eyes. Later, he saved my life. I missed an elephant and turned to run, but then I tripped and fell. I expected to be trampled or tossed in the air but Lembirdan stood firm as a rock and turned the elephant with a shot of his own. For all Lembirdan's qualities, and there were others like him, I often found that the very best rangers were reformed poachers. Adukan made a marvellous tracker. A notorious Turkana poacher, he eluded me for years but finally gave himself up when his omens, a tossed pair of sandals, fell in such a way as to predestine his capture.

I depended for transport on camels and donkeys; they carried our kit. If I wanted to ride I bought a mule; I had a sweet-natured one called Artemis with whom one of the donkeys fell in love so noisily that I had to get rid of him. The camel, in spite of its air of invincible discontent, is with its convenient hydraulic system and soft splayed feet ideal for the desert. They were a way of life for the Rendille and northern Somalis – wealth, transport, meat and their source of milk. There were said to be a quarter of a million camels up in north-eastern Kenya and on the borders of Abyssinia.

On the other hand, donkeys, obstinate as they can be, are tough, nimble-footed and perfectly suited to hard going and heights which would finish off camels. The Samburu have a way of putting forked sticks through the noses of recalcitrant donkeys, which bleed whenever they graze. I therefore made a point of asking for these animals when I had to buy new ones and found that, once the sticks were removed, like the reformed poachers they were often exceptional assets. One can grow very attached to a donkey. I had a lead male called Korofi who had an iron will but was so game and dependable that I could give him his head and let him run on to graze till the others caught up. He had an uncanny way of alerting me to the presence of lions but after we had been together for sixteen years he rushed on one day, when I was not there to protect him, and fell prey to a pride.

Having chosen my rangers and transport I tried to understand the country and its people. The tribesmen had been learning for centuries how to make the most of the land, the seasons and the wildlife. They knew by heart the rhythms and reasons of this world in which I was really a trespasser. I wondered why we talked about "poaching" when they had been subsisting on game and living in balance with it until Europeans arrived and started to draw lines on the map. National frontiers cut the routes of the annual migrations; new boundaries circled white settlements; on one side of an invisible line hunting was banned or needed an expensive government licence. By what right did I stop a Turkana from eating a crocodile (which

A patrol of my rangers in the Northern Frontier District. Some of the best recruits were reformed poachers.

"I think I was the first European to see Mohamed. His tusks are preserved in the Nairobi Museum. The longer was over 11 feet."

tasted rather like chicken)? An elephant might feed a Dorobo manyatta or communal dwelling for a week and its tusks fetch some sacks of desperately needed maize flour. Why shouldn't a Wakamba shoot a kudu in the bush with his bow and arrow? These feelings partly prompted me to recruit the more responsible and resourceful poachers we caught. Nevertheless there were times when I came across killing so cruel or so wanton that I had not the slightest compunction in applying the full force of the law to capture and punish offenders.

This was still, just, the day of the game. It was only later, after the 1939–45 war, that Africa ceased to live off the dividends nature provided and to dig, disastrously, into her capital. As a game warden I had above all to become familiar with the ways of the animals I was paid to protect. In 1938 I could read plenty of books which told me how to approach an elephant or a lion with the least danger and to kill it with the least mess, so that it kept its maximum value as a trophy; but I could find hardly one which told me how an animal behaved for the greatest part of its life, when it was not being threatened with a gun. Still less could anyone except the canniest African and European hunters tell me *why* it behaved as it did. To be any good I would have to find out these things for myself.

It was not just because of its size that the elephant intrigued me so much. Its strength and dignity, its silent movement and sudden trumpeting fury, its sociable life in the herd, the humour of its young, the threatening beauty of its tusks, the delicate twist and touch of its trunk and the intelligent look in its wise old eye if I managed to get close to it, all these enthralled me.

The more I saw of them, particularly the groups of mothers and young, the more they seemed human. The care they took to bring up their offspring, the way families continuously kept in touch and even the length of their lives were so like us. Chimpanzees later became famous as tool-users when Jane Goodall observed them sticking grass into ant-hills and sucking the ants off the stalks. But I have seen elephants holding sticks in their trunks to get at an inaccessible itch. In the South Horr valley I camped under a large acacia, smoothed and polished by the rubbing of elephants. The Samburu told me it was the favourite scratching place of one old elephant that would carry a branch to clear away the goats and sheep that gathered in its shade.

Of course Indian elephants trained for forestry learn to use "tools" but Colonel Williams in *Elephant Bill* gives an amazing example of their intelligence. He saw one elephant, lifting heavy timbers to build a bridge, which was obviously worried that they might roll back over its forehead and crush the mahout, who was riding on its shoulders. It therefore picked up a long wooden mallet, wedged it upright between its trunk and a tusk as a safety device, and continued the work. No elephant had ever been taught how to do this.

My brother Terence has always believed in the brotherhood of elephants and man, and when we were once discussing their virtues he told me about one he had found trapped in a well. His road building gang begged him to shoot it for meat but Terence told them to bring him barrows of stones which he dropped, one by one, into the pit. The elephant understood exactly what was happening and carefully lifted its feet as the stones raised the floor of its prison. The labourers fled as it reared up and finally heaved itself out but Terence had kept murmuring reassurance to the elephant throughout its ordeal and occasionally patted its anxious and questioning trunk. Once free, the elephant moved slowly towards him as if in thanks; it was some time before Terence could persuade it to return to its herd.

I was reminded of this when I read a book by Iain and Oria Douglas-Hamilton, who lived among the elephants at Manyara for a number of years and studied them closely. Although a few were undoubtedly killers, others were marvellously trusting. Iain describes how, when they took their baby into the forest for the first time, a young female they called Virgo came to take fruit from their hands and then returned . . . to present her own tiny calf to them.

A large herd of elephants is one of the most thrilling spectacles in Africa. I once camped above a pool at Barsoloi and soon after sundown a party of elephants began to appear, until the riverbed was seething with animals pressing towards the water. The noise was deafening and continued through most of the night. Early in the morning I followed them up river and watched about three hundred elephants feeding. Among the many bulls, four were carrying tusks of a hundred pounds and over. The tusks, incidentally, are specialised teeth. I saw two pairs of elephants mating, a very rare sight I had not witnessed before. The penis of an elephant can extend to four feet long and must curve like an "S" to penetrate the female. The act was performed in a manner common to most animals but on this occasion a number of cows and calves gathered in a circle and appeared to be greatly excited.

I always feel it ought to have been possible to find an effective way of keeping elephants off farmland without killing the greediest or the ring leaders. I had a district on the Tana in which, during the dry season, the elephants could only make their way to the river by walking through crops that they raided or trampled as they went. The sad but inescapable side of my job was to shoot the leading or most persistent offenders and to supervise the hunting, under licence, of some of the grandest tuskers in Kenya if not Africa. Many had taken refuge in the dense bush on the Tana, round Kora.

Usually the bulls lived apart from the females and young of a herd, though they tended to form groups of their own. One morning, in the Ndoto mountains, I came on two huge old bull elephants. The larger carried tusks of at least a hundred and thirty pounds each. The local Samburu told me these two had been in the valley for many years without molesting a soul. Today, once their presence was known, they would not last a month before some well-organised poacher moved in.

I wondered about the age of these big tuskers: were they eighty or even ninety years old? To grow very large tusks an elephant must live to a great age, although a cow will never produce one of more than fifty or sixty pounds however long she lives. Before the war a well known Dutch hunter called Van Rensburg was with a party camped on Balambala Island not far below Kora on the Tana. One morning he felt too ill to go out – possibly he had a prize hangover – when an elephant with the largest tusks he had ever seen burst out of the trees. He shot it and found that both tusks weighed over one hundred and seventy pounds each.

The greatest thrill I ever had was to see a four-tusked elephant near Isiolo. The ivory was not large but I know of no similar sighting in Kenya – although the skull and ivory of a four-tusked elephant shot in the Ituri forest of Zaire ended up in the Explorers Club in New York.

Tusks have always excited curiosity – and admiration for the beauty of the ivory when it is carved by an outstanding craftsman or artist. I find them more beautiful on the animal. I rather think I was the first European to see Mohamed, one of the two great tuskers of Mt Marsabit. Like the other one, Ahmed, his tusks – the longer is ll feet – are preserved in the National Museum in Nairobi. Both these old bulls were usually accompanied by one or two younger ones. I suppose that elephants sense safety in numbers and some young bulls, after they have been evicted from the herds – as all of them eventually are – remember the leadership of the matriarchs and find security in the company of a venerable bull. They also seem to feel a need to protect him.

In moments of sickness, danger or death elephants show a loyalty to each other which moves me very much. I was once summoned to Marsabit where four marauding bulls had been robbing maize-storage cribs. It was not only costly but dangerous as the cribs were in the heart of the police lines. On the night I arrived I sat for two chilly hours, down wind of the maize, waiting for the elephants to appear in the moonlight. When they emerged into view I aimed at the shoulder of the leader and fired. He fell immediately. But then his comrades gathered round him and, supporting him, made off with him into the forest. It would have been futile, not to say suicidal, to have pursued them that night so I waited until dawn.

Lembirdan and I followed the spoor and splashes of blood till we came on the elephant lying dead in the forest. It must have taken enormous strength and determination to get him so far.

I was even more impressed to discover that elephants seem to attach special significance to death. An old Boran told me that he was familiar with a small group of bulls who always stayed together on the Tana. When the oldest died his companions kept watch over his body for more than a week. They then drew out the tusks and carried them off into the bush. Many years later I read Iain Douglas-Hamilton's description of an elephant family taking away the bones of a relative in much the same way.

I found it more difficult to explain the sense an elephant has of human death. At Barsoloi a Samburu had been killed as he returned to his hut from the river. Halfway along the path he came across a fallen tree and as he picked his way over it he realised, too late, that it had been knocked over by an elephant which was hidden in the foliage. When the elephant went for him he tried to escape by burrowing under the branches but the elephant pulled him out with its trunk. Then it literally pounded him into the ground with its tusks and feet. The headman showed me where the elephant had repeatedly gored its victim and an area of about thirty square feet that looked as if it had been dug with a spade. He said that every afternoon since the tragedy the elephant had returned to the spot, and stood there until evening.

We waited until the late afternoon when we heard three bulls approaching. As I could not tell which was the culprit I decided to approach to within about forty yards of them and shout. I would assume that the elephant which charged was the guilty one. In the event all three dashed off as soon as I raised my voice. Nevertheless I could tell from the spoor superimposed on the furrowed earth that the headman had told the truth. Although I waited several days the rogue elephant didn't return.

I was sceptical of other stories I had heard about elephants covering people they had killed with brushwood or leaves, until something like it happened near my headquarters at Isiolo. Gobus, an ex-poacher who was one of my rangers, was coming home with his blind and elderly mother in the late afternoon. He stopped to relieve himself and said he would follow her; but when he got home his mother was not there; by now it was dark. Early in the morning a goatherd followed some cries from the forest and found Gobus's mother unable to move.

She had lost her way and curled up under a tree for the night. A few hours later she awoke to find an elephant standing over her, feeling the length of her body with its trunk. Paralysed with fear she lay absolutely still. Then more elephants appeared and with loud trumpeting broke off branches which they piled on top of her. Perhaps they thought she was dead.

Despite all the efforts that have been made to protect them, there are perhaps only 20 per cent as many elephants in Kenya today as there were before the war. The black rhinos have suffered even worse. No one knows how many there were in 1938; by 1970 there were about 20,000; today it is reckoned there are less than 500 and they have been placed under the personal protection of the President. Over and over again in the past we had to take evasive action from charging rhino; today it is never necessary.

In a sense rhinos are to elephants rather as leopards are to lions. Rhinos, like elephants, are thick-skinned, browsing heavyweights, hunted for their horns rather than their teeth: but they are solitary. Leopards, like lions, are sleek-coated, carnivorous cats, hunted for their skins rather than their manes: but they too are solitary. This parallel is not exact as the elephant's nearest relation is said to be the hyrax which looks like a large guinea pig and lives in colonies on rocks or near trees – and not the rhino.

Archie Ritchie, who made a study of rhino, argued that for all their prehistoric appearance individuals varied in their tempers, temperaments and courage. Once fully grown they settle down for most of their lifetime on separate ranges, observing an unadventurous routine. The rhino is a selective feeder, curling its pointed upper lip round the branch or leaves of its choice and cutting them off with its teeth. It is said sometimes to eat antelope dung but I have not seen this. I am, of course, referring to the so-called black rhino which is a browser. The white rhino is largely confined to South Africa where it owes its name to its wide (*weit*) mouth, specially adapted like a mower for grazing.

In 1939, during two days marching along the Uaso Nyiro River, I once came across the spoor of more than sixty black rhinos. On another safari I saw thirteen rhinos in one morning. I found that they prefer to spend the day in the bush, perhaps sunning themselves for a couple of hours in a dust patch before retiring to the shelter of a thicket. In the evening they may travel several miles to a river. Although they are normally silent and solitary at the water they are stimulated by the company of offspring and neighbours. I watched bathing parties at which a mother arrived with her youngest calf and an older one, before they were joined by the father or another male. There were flirtations and fights, weird high-pitched screams and long drawn out groans. Male would challenge male or violently importune a female; sometimes a female would reject these attempted mountings just as rudely. After drinking and wallowing in puddles or muddy shallows the rhinos would return to the bush. In the driest weather they would have to forego these mudbaths and find enough moisture in succulent plants.

If rhinos met, when they strayed from their ranges or their ranges overlapped, they would treat each other with suspicion or hostility but it soon turned to indifference. Apart from watering places their only regular meetings were likely to be at communal dung heaps in which they deliberately scuffed their feet. Possibly the scent helped to demarcate their ranges.

Along paths to a spring called Laisamis, near Lake Rudolf, I noticed several boulders covered with thick, chalky deposits which I could not identify. Then I remembered seeing the same sort of thing, near water, in rhino country and realised that they were the result of rhinos urinating against the rocks over decades if not centuries. The Laisamis rocks were no longer used as the rhinos there had been exterminated some years before.

It is tragic that the rhino, which is harmless unless disturbed in the privacy of its home, should have been almost wiped out for its so-called horn, which is in reality a fusion of hairs, much prized and fatally overpriced in Aden for dagger handles and in the East for its supposed medicinal properties. There appears to be no scientific evidence at all for the other cause of the slaughter, the apocryphal power of powdered horn as an aphrodisiac. Presumably this erotic reputation is due to the animals' mating habits. A female in season may precipitate a quarrel between rivals for her favours or even between herself and her suitor; but once she accepts him her mate may mount her many times in a few days and coition lasts for thirty or forty minutes on each occasion, far longer than any of the other large animals I came across.

A calf stays with its mother for up to two years and is extremely vulnerable, for, unlike white rhino calves, which always walk in front of the mothers, black rhino calves tag along behind. If a mother charges or bolts, her youngster is often left to the mercy of a lion or hyena, unless it is old enough to keep up. Nevertheless Ugas, one of the big lions I was returning to the wild after the filming of *Born Free*, pounced on a young rhino and caught it – but when the calf squealed the mother turned in a fury and Ugas instantly let go of the youngster and fled.

There was a rhinoceros in the Mathews Range which often chased the Samburu and finally killed an old woman gathering firewood. I wondered what could have induced these unprovoked attacks and set out to find the rhino, accompanied by a missionary who came to see the fun: I don't think St Francis would have approved of him. When I eventually shot the poor animal I found it had a festering spear wound in its shoulder.

Solitary, myopic, dyspeptic and prehistoric-looking rhinos may be, but they are capable of forming relationships with human beings and other species too if they are introduced to them when young and are properly treated. I admired Daphne Sheldrick for raising them with her other orphaned animals at Tsavo where her husband David was the warden. They became great favourites of hers and the rest of her quaintly assorted family which ranged from ostrich chicks to elephants.

When buffaloes graze you will often see egrets poised round their feet to harvest the insects disturbed in the grass. Occasionally sandpipers take the liberty of scavenging scraps from the jaws of a crocodile: or spurwing plovers will hob-nob with a whole family of crocs and alert them with shrill cries if a figure approaches. Similarly oxpeckers or tick-birds have achieved an association with rhinos which is beneficial to both. A rhino harbours a number of ticks and other parasites and as it grows older its skin tends to crack and suffer from lesions. Archie Ritchie thought the animals sometimes took unusual interest in each other's sores. Oxpeckers certainly take advantage of lesions and parasites, deriving sustenance from them. In return a rhino can concentrate on browsing or doze in a thicket with confidence that the bird will alert it to danger. For that matter oxpeckers have several times saved me from the thundering charge of a startled rhinoceros.

On one of my most eventful safaris, to exterminate a pride of man-eating lions in Samburu country, I spent a month in search of the killers. By the end I had to shoot six, one of which I hunted for three days. Each time Lembirdan and I got close to him we found he was lying in a bush close to a rhino. If it had happened once I would have said that it was a coincidence but when it happened three times I was convinced that the lion had deliberately sought the rhino's company. It probably felt it would give him a warning if someone approached, though of course it was the oxpeckers which provided the tip-off, with the loud hissing noise they make on such occasions. It is strange that these birds, when perched on domestic cattle, ignore the presence of people.

Unlike the other big cats, leopards and cheetahs, lions have always given game wardens acute problems and left them torn between admiration for their qualities and condemnation of their savagery. Leopards and cheetahs are equally beautiful — some would claim more so — but in my experience virtually always kept themselves to themselves. My cook once slept under a tree on safari and woke to find the hind legs of a leopard dangling over his head. It had discovered some chestnut-bellied sand grouse I had shot that day and hung in the branches. The next night it came inquisitively into my tent but when I flashed my torch in its face it fled. Although they have a taste for dogs and sometimes kill goats I was never asked to deal with a man-eating leopard. They are highly intelligent and survive by keeping out of harm's way, whatever its source. In more than twenty years I had to tackle only three stock-raiding leopards.

Cheetahs are gloriously graceful and swift but never attack man nor do they threaten his stock as seriously as lions do.

The ironical misfortune of the lion was that its magnificence, strength and ferocity, combined with the royal and religious mystique which has always surrounded it, made it an irresistible challenge to the hunter. It was natural for the Maasai and Turkana to avenge themselves on the species that so often ravaged their herds – and for the Maasai to elevate this to a cult. It was inevitable that game wardens would take punitive action against individuals that killed cows or goats and sometimes their herdsmen. But it was unnatural and unnecessary that the hunting of lions should become quite such a fetish with white men.

The Prince of Wales was so keen to shoot his ritual lion and Bror Blixen so keen to provide it that Blixen risked his life by driving a stand of tall grass to make sure it was flushed. Karen Blixen was delighted to be given the title "Lioness" by an African admirer. She once watched her lover shoot two lions: when the scene appeared in her masterpiece, *Out of Africa*, one of the creatures had become a lioness and she had pulled the trigger on the lion. On my first professional safari the Ofenheims were extremely humane and discriminating but above all they wanted a lion. Angela still has its head in her house today.

To kill one lion was understandable but game wardens – and fine professional hunters like Finch Hatton too – were sickened when clients disregarded or juggled their licences to slaughter as many as possible. Keeping on friendly terms with the professional hunters was both wise and rewarding. They were as devoted to preserving the game as the wardens: their living depended on it. They had eyes like hawks for poaching, disease or rogue animals and were in effect sixty or seventy conservationists who knew the finest strongholds of game like the backs of their hands and who were utterly committed to their protection. Denys Finch Hatton, one of the most expert early professionals, collaborated closely with Archie Ritchie in his efforts to ban shooting from cars, modify killing, encourage photography and monitor the populations and migrations of game. An article and two letters he wrote for *The Times* in the thirties about abuse in the Serengeti were devastatingly scathing and uncannily prophetic.

Lions were not only vulnerable to romantic blood lust but were too often labelled "vermin". Personally I could not see how anyone lucky enough to watch a pride of lions – and who had any understanding of nature, respect for family affection or sense of the beautiful – could seriously brand them as vermin to be eliminated like rabbits or rats. I was always entranced by their noble appearance and in time learnt to appreciate how different each one of them looked, their expression and posture often reflecting character or mood.

All cubs are born with spots, perhaps to camouflage them in their most vulnerable early months — fewer than one in four survive the hazards of hunger, thirst, disease and the attentions of other carnivores. By about a year old a male begins to grow his mane; at two and a half the females first come into season; the males mature six months later. A fully grown lioness like Elsa weighs about three hundred pounds; large males such as Boy and Christian weigh half as much again.

A lion's colour can vary from pale dust or sand to rich chestnut. I have never come across an albino or white lion although I know of the white lions from Timbavati in South Africa. I have also heard of a melanistic lion in Tanzania, which was almost entirely black: he must have been an awesome sight. Manes vary too. In the very hot country to the north of Africa, perhaps because of the heat, lions' manes are very sparse or non-existent. At higher altitudes, where it is cooler, they grow luxuriant. Christian's father, from the zoo in Rotterdam, had a grand black mane which continued down the length of his belly. We named two of the most familiar wild lions at Kora according to their manes — Scruffy and Blackantan.

Apart from these characteristics each lion will have its own idiosyncratic refinement or peculiarity by which you can recognise it, just as a skilled tracker can identify it from its spoor. But it was the behaviour of lions, even more than their appearance, which I loved — the good nature of the lionesses, suckling and nurturing each other's cubs, the vivacity and mischief of the young, tugging and teasing the tails of their elders, and the warmth and dignity with which they all usually rubbed cheeks when they returned to the pride.

Their courtship and mating was both amusing and moving. When a lioness came into season and grew restless a lion became immediately aware of her condition. Instantly alert to his interest the lioness's first response might well be to withdraw. As he started to follow her she might even stretch out a pad and give him a cuff. At this point the lion would have to move in and assert himself — strutting beside her at full height, growling, pawing and finally mounting her. Sometimes he would give a yowl and nip her on the neck as he did so; she too might give voice. Between the acts, which lasted only briefly but were repeated many times over several days, the lion would rest couchant and quiet, while she would sprawl on her back. It was the only time when I myself heard a lioness purring.

There were a great many people in Kenya during those years before the war whose admiration for lions was just as devoted as mine. Mervyn Cowie, an accountant who lived outside Nairobi, had so many close encounters with lions and found them so engrossing that he decided to enlist their support in achieving his greatest ambition: the creation of national sanctuaries or Game Parks in which animals could be certain of safety from hunting. He was convinced that anyone in authority, who had the opportunity of seeing a pride of lions at close quarters, would be won over to his scheme.

His difficulty was that despite his familiarity with the local pride even he could not be certain of finding them when he wanted to. He therefore devised a foolproof plan by feeding them near a lone tree, in what is now the Nairobi Game Park. After a time "the Lone Tree pride" adopted the area as the centre of their territory. The Governor of Kenya was duly introduced to them and the establishment of the first National Park was assured — although war broke out before it was actually gazetted.

There was no danger of enthusiasts like Cowie and myself being blinded to the darker side of a lion's nature and behaviour. Its family life is nothing like so cosy as it looks on a sunny afternoon on the Mara or the Serengeti. Whenever there was an outbreak of stock raiding or man-eating I had to deal with it.

Man-eating lions have always given rise to fallacies and legends. Captain Charles Pitman, the eminent Game Warden of Uganda, had to investigate a sensational rumour in 1925 — that a pair of lions had started to attack human settlements near Entebbe, escorted by a herd of elephants. He finally established the truth. In fact, elephants had taken to raiding a number of African plantations. Whenever this happened the local chief sent out his men with drums and tins to make such a din they were frightened away. The two lions had learnt to accompany the elephants, anticipating the chance of an easy kill in the dark and confusion.

Some fallacies about man-eaters never die and can be dangerous — for instance that only sick, wounded or elderly lions will without provocation attack people, and that it is safe to sleep out among lions. Many good men, including professional hunters, have been taken in the night, all over Africa.

Up at Lalalei the Samburu once reported that nine of their men had been eaten by lions in the previous twelve months. The day before I could get there to help them a youth was killed while herding his cattle. I went to the scene and found that three lions had gone through the herd and chased the boy round a bush before killing and eating him. It was extraordinary that they should choose him in the middle of so many cattle. That night we made a particularly strong thorn boma round the cattle, the donkeys and ourselves, but a lioness tried to break in and I shot her. Two hours later I was woken by the donkeys and going to investigate with a torch and

Courtship: "When a lioness comes into season a lion is immediately aware of her condition. Her first response may well be to withdraw..."

"...As he starts to follow her she may even give him a cuff..."

"…At this point the lion will have to move in and assert himself…"

"…Between the acts she would sprawl on her back. It was the only time I heard a lioness purring."

revolver saw another lioness trying to break through. I emptied my revolver at her but she vanished.

In the morning when a ranger brought me tea, he pointed to the sand round my sleeping bag. About eighteen inches from my head was the spoor of yet another of these man-eating lions – which I found extremely unnerving. For three hours we followed their tracks until we came to some scrub, which we drove in line with a couple of rangers on either side of me. Just as we emerged from it there were loud yells and then a growl from the left of the line. I saw the end ranger go down under a lioness; seconds later the man next to him ran up and fired his rifle into her ear. We expected the first man to be badly mauled but he was unscathed and was mercilessly ribbed by his colleagues for having cried out. This second lioness, like the one in the night, appeared to have no physical cause for her man-eating though I found a fresh graze across her chest from one of my revolver shots.

We had a ten-hour chase after the third lion, a male, which finally lost patience and turned on us with a furious charge. He too showed no physical defects to account for his grisly behaviour. This experience combined with a number of others convinced me that following up a lioness, especially if she is wounded, is much more dangerous than going after a male. He will growl and give away his position: she will stay hidden in silence and is launched on her final, lightning charge before she lets out her snarl.

Such a snarl might well have been the last sound I ever heard. I was up in the Ndoto Mountains and had caught two Dorobo poachers when the Samburu asked for help with some man-eaters. I spent a morning sitting in the village while they went out to locate them and was treated to the spectacle of a local elephant first chasing one of my donkeys and then giving a herdsman the fright of his life.

A little later I went for a stroll, as no news had come in, and suddenly noticed a lioness not far from the track. I was almost certain that this was one of the killers so I fired. The lioness was knocked over but recovered herself and lay up in a patch of long grass. I could not see her when I climbed a tree and she made no response when I threw in some stones; I therefore decided to fetch help. I had just turned my back on the grass when I heard a low growl and, spinning round, let off a shot. Still the lioness came on. Not too worried, I worked the bolt of my magazine rifle – only to find that it jammed.

As the lioness flew at me I jabbed the muzzle down her throat but she simply flung it aside as if it were a walking stick. Instinctively I put up my forearm to cover my throat and she seized it, throwing me to the ground with her momentum. She then stood back for a second and watched me rise to my feet, trying to draw my hunting knife with an arm that would not work. I was utterly defenceless when she sprang at me again, grabbed me by the thigh and bowled me over once more.

At that point I must have passed out for the next thing I remember is coming to and hazily catching sight of my rifle some yards away. There was not a sign of the lioness. Assuming she was somewhere behind me I lay absolutely still, not daring even to turn my head in case the movement precipitated another attack. I remember thinking: "So perhaps this is what it is like for an animal to be killed by a lion; no pain but a fearful sense of impotence and a dread of the end." As I waited and waited for the lioness to show herself my head began to throb and I felt the sun burning my skin.

When I could not stand the suspense any longer I began to crawl very slowly towards the rifle, expecting the final charge at any second. It seemed to take an age before I got my fingers to it yet I found I had just enough strength to drag it and myself to the shade of a tree. Propped against the trunk I managed to unjam the spent case and work a new bullet into the breach.

The lioness must have been so badly hurt by my first shot that she had slunk off in her own distress. I therefore fired two or three rounds in the air, hoping they would bring help. The face that appeared in response belonged to one of my Dorobo prisoners who could not speak Swahili. As I was quite incapable of walking, even with his help and using my rifle as a crutch, I made signs to him to fetch more men to carry me back to the village.

This time several Samburu arrived, bringing my camp-bed as a stretcher. By now I was beginning to suffer from the symptoms of malaria, as so often happens after a shock, and they can be so severe that I felt I was quite likely to die from a combination of these and septicaemia. However, I luckily had with me a bottle of sulfanilamide pills I was taking for a poisoned finger; a lion wound may look clean on the outside, and can be treated with disinfectant on the surface, but the bacteria or the teeth and claws will quickly cause gangrene under the skin. While I was still conscious I scribbled an s.o.s. to the District Commissioner at Marsabit.

In the middle of the long night which followed there was consternation among the donkeys and in a daze I heard my riding mule Artemis, who was chained to a tree by my tent, snort in alarm. Simultaneously her chain snapped, an elephant screamed and a dark shape loomed in front of my tent. My cook lying beside me thrust a light rifle into my hands and propped me upright against the tentpole. Oblivious to the searing pain I raised the gun and fired.

The elephant swerved and next morning was found dead, about eighty yards away. But it was another five mornings before help arrived in response to my message. I hovered on the edges of consciousness in excruciating pain and cried aloud when my dressings were changed. In the meantime the Samburu elders shook their heads and prescribed doses of mutton fat, which I knew to be their version of extreme unction. When he finally reached me the D.C. did me proud. With war against Italy imminent the R.A.F. had brought a small force of bombers to Kenya for use against Italian Somaliland. Now they sent two, complete with a medical team, to pick me up from the airstrip at Maralal. They loaded me in like a bomb and flew me to hospital at Nairobi: it was my first experience of flying.

*   *   *

The approach of war coincided with the first serious love of my life. Now that I was over thirty and had a regular salary however small, my thoughts turned to marriage in general and to Juliette, a delightful French girl, in particular. She was secretary to what is now called the Mt Kenya Safari Club. When we were in Nairobi we would meet at the Norfolk Hotel for lunch or dinner which was much used by people from up country: the social set used Torr's Hotel, where there was dancing, or belonged to the Muthaiga Club. The café under the thorn tree outside the New Stanley Hotel (the original Stanley Hotel had been burnt down) also became a famous meeting point but at six o'clock in the evening the tarts homed in on it like sand grouse to water.

By now Abraham Block had traded his seeds and mattresses so successfully that he had been able to buy the Norfolk – reputedly for £500 and an empty field. I was with Juliette there when I met his son Jack for the first time. My friends and I were to have a great deal to thank Jack for in the years to come. Eddie Ruben, a good friend of the Blocks, had also established himself by this time. He had exchanged his mules and his wagons for trucks and had built up the biggest transport and warehousing company in Kenya.

Sadly my romance with Juliette came to nothing in the end and I was close to heartbreak when we parted. On my safaris I seldom met anyone of my own kind to talk to and there were times when I was assailed by temptations of the flesh. There was one little river on which I used to camp where the women would come down to wash and bathe. Two girls made a habit of progressively revealing their charms with the object of securing my attentions. In other places the girls seemed to have a collection of skirts which grew shorter and shorter as our acquaintance grew closer. Sometimes I left it a little late but rather than succumb to such overtures I would seize my rifle and stay out on the hills until I or the girls had grown weary. My men could not understand and asked if I suffered from some physical impediment.

In the end I allowed nature to take its course in the company of a beautiful girl from the Nandi tribe. Our relationship did not last long as war broke out in Europe, with inevitable repercussions in Africa once Italy joined in. It seemed to me the ultimate arrogance of the colonial powers to drag Africa into their European squabbles for the second time in twenty-five years.

During the 1914–18 war a German colonial army in Tanganyika, under the command of General von Lettow-Vorbeck, had fought a brilliant and unbeaten campaign against the British forces based on their colonies of Kenya and Uganda. At the outbreak of the Second World War the British prepared to eliminate the Italian armies in Italian Somaliland and Eritrea – and in Ethiopia, which they had invaded and occupied in 1935.

My first wartime task was extremely unpleasant: it was to destroy at least a thousand head of zebra and oryx which farmers complained were competing with their cattle for grazing. Only eighty miles to the north the Turkana were under-nourished or starving and yet no attempt was made to send them the meat. Two years later, after the Italians in East Africa were defeated, tens of thousands of animals were again shot, quite unnecessarily, on the pretext of feeding the prisoners of war. This time the massacre was carried out by private contract and the farmers did not weep, for the destruction of the game enabled them to put down thousands of extra square miles to wheat. The loss of this habitat and of so many breeding animals dealt some of the species a blow from which they have never recovered. Furthermore the proliferation of guns and ammunition had devastating consequences for the wildlife of Africa.

I noticed a frightful side-effect in myself at the killing of animals on this scale. However much I disliked and disapproved of what I was doing there was a part of me which, while I was actually shooting, developed a bloodlust. It gave me an inkling of how massacres can sometimes occur with so little cause.

The first military engagement I heard about was when I arrived in the remote Provincial Headquarters at Marsabit. It had just been bombed by Italians from Ethiopia and casualties, a few sprained ankles, had been sustained during the rush to take shelter in the forest.

I was anxious to play a part in the coming campaign and at last I was enrolled in Military Intelligence and sent to Wajir which was a base for operations against the Italians in Somaliland. I was to recruit secret agents among the Somalis and arrange for them to report on enemy movements. They proved to be meticulously accurate about the disposition of soldiers but having no experience of military machines were apt to confuse the identification of tractors, armoured cars, trucks, tanks and lorries, which led to some bizarre false alarms.

I only fired a few shots in anger during a number of inconclusive patrols but I witnessed a brisk air battle as the British advanced. Five Caproni bombers, escorted by four Fiat fighters, flew over and dropped their loads. Just then a lone Hurricane fighter came skimming over the bush and flew straight for the Italian formation. In a few minutes it had brought down three bombers and a fighter.

I had come to Somalia to fight a war but the campaign was so quickly over that I found myself keeping the peace. I had to prevent looting and even killing as the Italian farmers were driven from their homes and property. My first headquarters was a villa belonging to Marshal Graziani, the Commander-in-Chief of the Italian armies in North Africa. My next was a fine new house in a banana plantation that had been looted and larded with excrement. My third was a modern but isolated outpost in the desert among the Somalis.

I have a rag-bag of memories: searches for concealed arms and Italian deserters on camel and by canoe; a cavalcade of tractors returning noisily from the bush after I had decreed a series of executions should their mysterious disappearance remain unsolved; the importunities of a tame but crippled ostrich that begged for food through my window each morning; the affections of a very pretty Somali girl who shared my lonely outpost; and a succession of nights punctuated by shots, explosions and a reverberating crash. I did not discover until the following morning that the last of these, which occurred after an evening of heavy drinking, was caused by the descent of a massive and ornate chandelier onto the bedside table, a few inches from my head. Bored by my role as an unofficial policeman I returned to Nairobi on leave and applied for immediate release, which was mercifully granted.

*   *   *

At that time Nairobi held two more women who were to have a powerful influence on the image of Kenya: both were notable for their looks, character and determination. One, Friederike Bally, I was soon to know well. The other, Diana, Lady Broughton, I knew by sight: she was as beautiful and hard as a diamond.

In 1942 Kenya was still agog with a murder trial that had taken place the year before. Diana Broughton had been having an incandescent affair with the Earl of Erroll, one of the original members of the "Happy Valley" set on the edge of the Aberdares. Erroll was a handsome fascist of great charm who was also a notorious philanderer. On a night in January 1941 he was shot dead in his car, at a lonely crossroads outside Nairobi. Diana's husband, Sir Delves Broughton, was accused of his murder.

The subsequent events as recounted in a recent book, *White Mischief*, were very strange. While he was awaiting trial Broughton rented for his wife and himself a house which had belonged to her lover Lord Erroll. It was an exotic Moorish villa with a dome and crenellations which stood by Lake Naivasha and was known as the Djinn Palace. By the time I got back to Nairobi in 1942 Broughton had been acquitted of the murder by a court in Nairobi and had returned alone to England. In December he committed suicide at a hotel in Liverpool.

His wife Diana had been increasingly cold-shouldered by her friends and acquaintances in Kenya, and now to everyone's surprise the famous misogynist – and great land-owning rancher – Gilbert Colvile decided to marry her. He immediately bought her the Djinn Palace. Twelve years later there was an amicable divorce: Diana married the fourth Lord Delamere, son of the pioneer, who was a close friend of Colvile's and whose ranches were just as extensive. Colvile promised to leave Diana the Djinn Palace.

As the years went by Diana Delamere gradually became the epitome of Kenya society, famous for her beauty, chic, parties, racing and big-game fishing, at which she excelled. When Gilbert Colvile died, during 1966, she inherited the Djinn Palace. In the same year my wife Joy bought the house next to it on the shore of the lake.

It is now widely believed that Sir Delves Broughton did in fact murder Lord Erroll which was one of the reasons why he killed himself in 1942. On that same December night I was mustering a camel patrol and preparing to leave for Garissa where the new District Commissioner was Willie Hale, who had filled us with goat stew after crossing Lake Rudolf. He and his wife Morna had invited me for Christmas. A wild-flower enthusiast, Morna had asked one other couple to stay: the Swiss botanist from the Museum in Nairobi, Peter Bally, and his wife Friederike. It was to be the most fateful Christmas of my life.

Chapter 4
Joy
1942–1956

The light was fading, and I could hear the chatter and chanting of Somali and Orma tribesmen, as I moved through Garissa on Christmas Eve. The men carried spears, and the women, aflame in their brightest cottons, shimmered with beads, bangles and cowrie shells. They were making their cheerful way towards a white, Arab-style house, that stood above the river, and were obviously gathering for an *ngoma* or celebration dance.

Willie Hale left the group of people up on the flat roof and ran down the outside staircase to direct my rangers and their camels towards the picket lines. As I washed in his guest hut Willie told me that apart from his wife Morna, the others up above were the District Police Inspector, the Veterinary Officer, George Low, and George's wife. Peter Bally, the Swiss botanist and his wife, had already arrived and pitched their tent several hundred yards off, surrounding it with a few strands of wire to keep out the hippos and elephants. They were clearly intrepid or foolish.

When I joined the Hales on the roof – their four-poster bed, draped in a mosquito net, stood at one end – I felt we were typical of thousands of other little colonial parties, celebrating with cold drinks in the tropics a festival most of us remembered as children with hot turkey and snow. Willie was justifiably proud of his bar; the recent conquest of Somaliland had opened up a flow of excellent Italian white wine and a variety of powerful, though dubious, spirits.

The policeman had little to say at the start of the evening, unlike George Low, who was never averse to a party. The Ballys, too, were obviously out to enjoy themselves. Peter, with his monocle, retained a certain formality; on the other hand his wife, whom he introduced as Joy, and who turned out to be Austrian, was quite uninhibited. Fair-haired and slim, she wore a slinky, silver dress, and seemed entirely unaware that her growing animation accentuated the distortions of her curious English.

Willie was an amusing and relentless host: his wine and mysterious spirits did their work. As the *ngoma* got under way below, the singing and dance began to infect us. Some of the others went down to dance in the moonlight, while Joy and I started to sing on the parapet. From the moment we began to compete with the rising cries of the tribesmen my memories grow dim and the final events of the night had to be pieced together in the morning.

Joy was honest enough to admit that on the way to her tent she had ripped her exotic dress on their barbed wire entanglement. I then had to confess I had woken up fully dressed, with my feet on my pillow. Finally Peter Bally announced that he and Joy would be delighted to accept my kind invitation to join the camel safari. I had not the slightest recollection of asking either of them to do anything of the sort and was quite appalled. I was off to the Boni forest which was reputedly very tough going and the last thing I wanted was company – especially that of a frivolous young woman from Vienna. Nevertheless the Ballys were so keen that, as Willie's guests, I felt I could not refuse them.

The moment we set off with the camels Joy started to talk, very fast, in her Austrian accent. I gathered that Peter was collecting plant specimens for the herbarium in Nairobi and drug companies in Switzerland. Joy had started to paint them, but insisted she was only amateur. Nevertheless Peter said she was becoming first class and Lady Muriel Jex-Blake, the expert on gardening in Kenya, was so enthusiastic that she had asked Joy to illustrate her next book.

When I asked Joy how she came by her English christian name, she replied that Peter had found her original ones – Friederike Victoria – such a mouthful and her nickname – Fifi – so frivolous that he had insisted on calling her Joy.

My misgivings about her stamina were quickly dispelled. Her mental and physical energy were astonishing, and her clothes, from her khaki sun helmet to her canvas boots, were impeccable. Although she had never ridden a camel before, and her back was soon chafed and bleeding, she never complained. But I began to suffer new and more serious misgivings. Within a few days I sensed a growing attraction between us, which Joy seemed to encourage. For me to respond was out of the question: Peter was my guest and I liked him. I therefore arranged to strike off on my own, and let the Ballys join Willie Hale, who would shortly pass by on his own safari.

My life in the north was so solitary, and my meeting with the Ballys so fortuitous, that I put them entirely out of my mind, and concentrated on capturing poachers in the Boni Forest. As no warden had ever visited the place before and it was a hotbed of leopard poaching, I was extremely successful and took a number of prisoners to Lamu for trial.

Lamu is an ancient port, more Arab than African, its houses whitewashed, its people Muslim, its women black-veiled. Indian influences mingled with the English and Arab, in the faces of its people and the wording of its notices. Outside one coffee-shop there was a sign that read: "This hygene house, no spitum or other dirty business."

The District Commissioner had a reputation for the swift dispatch of business and for redirecting unwelcome petitions with one of four rubber stamps – The Business of the Police, The Business of Customs, The Will of God or Your Own Affair. Having sentenced my prisoners in the morning, he invited me to lunch in his house. I remarked with some envy a pair of elephant tusks, perfectly matched and each weighing over a hundred and twenty pounds. He also displayed on his wall a huge, seven-hundred-year-old horn, carved from a single tusk and known as the Siwa.

It was another six months before Archie Ritchie summoned me to Nairobi and when he did I managed to book in at the Norfolk Hotel, where I could park my pick-up outside my room. I was amazed, when I came out, to be seized by Joy Bally: I never discovered how she knew I was there. She immediately asked me to tea the next day. I played for time, saying I would if I could; but that evening I bumped into Peter, who repeated the invitation. I felt it was all right to go.

The next afternoon I was greeted warmly, even affectionately, by Joy and her grey cairn terrier, Pippin. I looked round for Peter, but there was no sign of him. Even stranger, for Nairobi, there was not a servant on the place. It was soon clear why. Joy said that for all her high spirits at Christmas, she was very unhappy. She and Peter had agreed their marriage could no longer work and had decided to divorce. Joy added that before my arrival at Garissa they had all talked about my narrow escape from the lioness and the elephant, and she had decided I was just the kind of man for her. Our few days on safari together had confirmed it. She fixed me with her blue eyes and smiled an unspoken question.

It took me several days to absorb this extraordinary situation, but when I spoke to Peter, he corroborated it all. Even then it was only after the divorce had been planned in some detail that I surrendered to the attraction Joy held for me and fell madly in love.

There followed the most anxious and difficult year of my life. Whatever the morals and habits of Happy Valley they were not acceptable to the Game Department, nor to some of our friends. Furthermore I had no money to pay for the divorce and Joy had none of her own. Even when Peter, heir to a shoe manufacturing business, agreed to take care of all the legal expenses, I still had professional worries. Luckily Archie Ritchie, who had a special interest in botany, knew both Peter Bally and Muriel Jex-Blake and they assured him that I had not barged in to break up the marriage. He saw the Chief Secretary and obtained his agreement that I would not be sacked if a quick and quiet divorce were followed by a wedding that was equally discreet.

Two couples were particularly helpful to Joy in riding out the disapproval of many acquaintances. For a time she and Peter had rented a bungalow in Louis and Mary Leakey's garden. They understood Joy's predicament as Louis had been ostracised in Cambridge when he had divorced his first wife, to marry Mary. Nevertheless their personalities and work carried considerable influence in Kenya. Louis' father had been a missionary among the Kikuyu. Louis spoke their language fluently, was adopted as a full member of the tribe, and had written a monograph on them. His excavations were widely known, and Joy was actually helping to piece together fragments of bone on the floor of the bungalow when their radio announced the outbreak of War. Louis immediately joined the Intelligence Service and produced a variety of unusual information through his African contacts. He also became Honorary Curator of the Nairobi Museum.

Dr Jex-Blake and his wife Muriel were also staunch friends. Her warmth and wisdom reminded Joy of her grandmother, who had brought her up through her most vulnerable age. Soon after War had been declared, neighbours had heard German being spoken in the Ballys' house, and Joy was reported to the police. As an Austrian she was arrested and interned – with Pippin – in the Aberdares. As soon as the Jex-Blakes heard what had happened Lady Muriel swept into the Governor's office and obtained her immediate release.

During the year it would take for her divorce to come through Joy wanted to camp near my house at Isiolo, collecting and painting the wild flowers. But although the Officer in Charge of the Northern Frontier and his wife were friends of both of us, they thought this would be highly improper, so I took Joy up onto Mt Kenya where she wanted to make a systematic record of the flora.

She camped at 14,000 feet in a beautiful little forest glade, close to the edge of the moorland which rose up to the glaciers and towering, snow-clad peaks of the summit. For company Joy had only a cook, her gun-bearer – and Pippin. Her tent stood next to a convenient tree, with a sloping trunk, which offered easy refuge when elephant and buffalo wandered through the camp, which they frequently did.

I joined Joy whenever I could get away from my patrols. We went for long walks across the moorland in search of plants or sat talking over the fire long into the night.

* * *

Joy, in the summer of 1931.

"She camped close to the edge of the moorland which rose up to the glaciers and towering snow-clad peaks." Joy on Mt Kenya, 1943, just before we were married.

She had been born in 1910. Her father, Victor Gessner, was a civil servant and her mother's family had owned a paper manufacturing business for two hundred years, and had large feudal estates in what is now Czechoslovakia. Joy's happiest childhood memories were of the big family parties there, playing in the forests with her cousins.

Her mother left her father to marry another man, and not long afterwards her father remarried too. Joy was twelve and I don't think she ever really got over the shock or unhappiness, although she went to live with her maternal grandmother, Oma, who came to mean more to her than anyone else. There must have been something cruel, or at least unusually cold, about Joy's mother.

When food was short during the First World War, Joy and her two sisters finished a rare and delicious stew only to be told by their mother, with a smile, that they had just eaten Joy's pet rabbit.

All through her life Joy's mind seemed to zig-zag from one subject to another. After she left school she studied the piano – at which she might have been brilliant – dress-making, sculpture and metal work. She had moved on to photography, when her mother rang her up to tell her with icy detachment that her father, who had been living in Czechoslovakia, was dead. Her mother added that the doctors had diagnosed a rare condition of his spleen, which was now on display in the Medical School in Prague.

The shock was profound. Joy had always feared death and soon after getting this news she was faced with its reality: a drunk ran under the wheels of a car in which she was a passenger and was killed. The sight, when she got out, froze into her mind. She had a breakdown and later wrote that she narrowly escaped death herself – by suicide. This experience led her on to study psychology, anatomy and medicine.

Joy's family and early friends have told me that she was unusually sparkling and attractive during these years in Vienna, while underneath she must have been so unhappy. In 1935, when she and another musical student, Susi Hock, were both twenty-five, Susi decided to marry the brilliant English scientist, Sir James Jeans, author of *The Mysterious Universe*, and left immediately for England.

Another of Joy's Austrian friends, Herbert Tichy, the well-known author, photographer and mountaineer remembers that in the same year a man came up to him at a party, pointed to Joy, and said "Please introduce me to that marvellous girl; I have never seen anyone like her; I am going to have to marry her." Victor von Klarvill was successful: he and Joy married before the year was out. Von Klarvill was well off – he and Joy travelled, entertained, and spent exhilarating weeks ski-ing in the Alps. But he was also Jewish, and the Nazis were threatening to take over Austria. He and

Joy therefore thought it would be sensible to find somewhere else to live.
When Joy had a miscarriage it was agreed that she should convalesce on
the boat to Mombasa and go to have a look at Kenya as a possible place
to settle.

Before she sailed she sent two questions to a fashionable fortune-teller:

"First, will I continue to live where I do at present? Secondly will I have
children?" She neither gave her name, nor her address, but would pick up
the reply on her return.

As fate would have it Peter Bally was on the boat to Mombasa. His
marriage had recently ended in divorce and he was planning a series of
botanical expeditions in Kenya. Joy found him so sympathetic and stimulat-
ing that their shipboard romance spelt the end of her marriage to Von
Klarvill. When Joy returned to Austria to tell him the truth she opened the
sooth-sayer's answer. It told her that she would live in the tropics and that
she would have to brush up her English. It also said that she would never
have children.

Joy, by now Peter Bally's wife, was sailing for Africa on the day that
Hitler invaded Austria, in March 1938. Undaunted by the fortune-teller,
her dresses had all been made with tucks to let out. With Peter she quickly
got into the swing of a safari life very different from mine. A hundred and
fifty porters carried their elaborate requirements up into the Chyulu Hills.
But the work itself meant long and arduous walking, great concentration
and exhausting hours. Joy had a second miscarriage. There were, however,
two consolations. With Peter's encouragement she discovered her gift for
painting the flowers they collected and she began to excel at it. Secondly
Peter gave her Pippin, the little grey Cairn. When they had finished in the
Chyulu Hills Joy went up onto Kilimanjaro with Peter, and then to the
Congo with a woman friend. By then it was dawning on Joy that the affinity
between her and Peter was not as great as they had first thought. However
much their minds were at one, their characters and energies were simply
not compatible. It was soon after this truth had dawned on them both that
we met at Garissa.

*   *   *

It was exceedingly painful having to leave Joy to her lonely vigil on Mt
Kenya, and I would sometimes write her long letters in which I expressed
my love for her. It was the best I could do.

She was entirely dependent, for most of the time, on supplies and help
from one of Kenya's great eccentrics and naturalists, Raymond Hook, who
had settled on the slopes of the mountain. A classical scholar, his unorthodox

activities included crossbreeding horses with zebras, to produce pack animals suited to the altitude, and lassoing cheetahs so they could be trained
to race against greyhounds. On Joy's last night he invited her to stay. She
found herself hermetically sealed inside his hut beside an asphyxiating
brazier which she dared not extinguish, for fear of killing the tropical fish
in the tank his servant placed over it just as she was going to bed.

On her return to Nairobi Joy was at first relieved that her divorce had
come through. But then she was suddenly smitten with doubts. Perhaps her
self-confidence had deserted her during those cold, misty months on the
desolate moorland; and possibly she was frightened of making a third
mistake. Whatever her reasons my reaction was a combination of anguish
and anger: my personal suffering was acute and my livelihood was at stake.
There was an ironical parallel with the courtship of lions. The message had
gone out from the female and had produced a response from the male,
which was being treated in return by rebuff. There was only one thing to
do: to put down my foot and mobilise the full support of our friends.

One year after we had first met Joy and I married. In accord with the
double standards of Kenya society, we did it with the greatest discretion,
at the office of the District Commissioner in Nairobi; only two witnesses
were present. It was a simple wedding, on African soil, of an Irishman born
in India to an Austrian who was leaving a Swiss. Both of us were penniless.

* * *

At last I could take Joy to Isiolo, the little town on the frontier of the
Northern Province which had been my home for five years. The wide dirt
road ran straight through it, north to Lake Rudolf and Abyssinia. On either
side stood wooden shacks with mud walls and roofs of corrugated iron, a
concrete bank, a small mosque, and a bar. Somali and Samburu tribesmen
with sticks, spears and cloths knotted at the shoulder strode about their
business. The old, the young and the crippled loitered in the sun; they sold
maize, bananas, eggs, rabbits and goatskins – or perhaps wooden combs,
copper bracelets and leather sandals. Sheep, goats, chickens and dogs
scavenged in the ordure and dust.

I still lived in my thatched house, just outside the town. Its walls were
covered in bougainvillea and I had also planted aloes and other bright
flowers. The tidy-minded government wanted to move me into Isiolo, but
I managed to coax £1,500 out of them to build a new house and George
Low, who was on the town Council, helped me get permission to use some
land three miles from the town. To make the cash go further I asked Terence
to design and put up the building. He did an excellent job and included a

large sitting room, to take Joy's piano and easels, and a workshop and gun room for me. The plumbing was simple: we brought water in drums from the river, and filtered and cooled it in bags made of canvas which hung from the eaves. Our staff consisted of a cook, two house boys, and a syce to look after the donkeys. As I had become responsible for more than 100,000 square miles, an area as large as Great Britain or New England, my rangers now numbered just over thirty. At last I was given a three-ton lorry, big enough to carry a patrol and its kit on a safari lasting a couple of months.

Soon after we had settled in, Joy and I had to go back to Nairobi. Rather than stay at a hotel, where we could not afford to entertain, we camped at Lone Tree in what is now the Game Park. Friends came out for a drink or meal, and could watch the animals grazing a few yards away. Sometimes even the lions would turn up – the pride that Mervyn Cowie had so successfully stage-managed to win the Governor's support for a park. In fact the Lone Tree lions had created a crisis. Families would come out at weekends and treat them as pets. A tragedy was bound to occur, for at the outbreak of war the army had put up a depot on the plain, three soldiers had absconded, and a search had produced only two boots and their contents. An urgent meeting was now held at the Game Department during which another warden and I were ordered to kill every member of the pride.

It was a sickening assignment, and I wished Joy had not been there to witness it. To avoid a crowd we waited till nightfall and then shot the lions as fast as we could. Limping, and pouring with blood, one lioness staggered off in the dark and I had to chase after her. Knowing how I felt later, when three of my lions were under sentence of death, I can imagine what Mervyn must have gone through when he got news of the execution.

To wash the bitter taste from our mouths I took Joy on a patrol to the coast. We drove through the Boni Forest, and in places it was so dense we could only make one mile an hour. On my previous safari we had lost one of our prisoners here; now I was told that his body had been found, wrapped in the coils of a python. In killing the snake he had stabbed his own guts. When I expressed surprise that the snake had intended to get down to a meal as large as a man, one of my rangers described how he had once seen a python trying to swallow a camel. I'm afraid I didn't believe him, but when I next saw Terence he gave me a withering look.

"I'm sure he was telling the truth," my brother said. "I have seen a python entwined round the neck of a giraffe. The giraffe had been strangled, and in its collapse had smothered the python." One friend, the great professional hunter Syd Downey, later told me he had once seen a lioness crushed by the weight of a large giraffe that her pride had killed and then left uneaten.

From the forest we emerged onto the shores of the Indian Ocean. It was a paradise of white sand and blue sea, of palm trees, dhows and whispering surf. Joy exulted in the myriads of fish, scintillating like fragments of rainbows and clustering round weirdly shaped coral, alive and breathtaking in its colours. She had brought her paints and memorised some of the fish; others she caught and sketched on the dhow, in the shade of the sail, before their glistening pigments could fade.

Louis Leakey had circulated reports that Japanese agents were blasting channels through the coral reefs, so their submarines could sneak into the harbours. When I heard this I thought it was another example of his quirky humour, for as soon as Joy had set off to the Congo he had telephoned the police at the frontier and advised them to search her, in view of her Austrian connections. She had been stripped and held there for hours. Joy was livid and only forgave him when he later apologised and told her he had done it as a misguided joke. But fishermen down the coast confirmed Louis' warning. It was sometimes unwise not to listen to his reports, however bizarre.

Joy so much wanted to show me the Congo – Zaire as it now is – that we took my first leave there. She photographed the King of Watusi and collected and painted a ruby-red orchid, one of the rarest in Africa. We straddled the rim of a roaring, crimson volcano and fought through a forest to glimpse the gorillas. We then went to look at the breeding of captive okapis – first cousins of giraffes – and the training of African elephants, in the only two places where either had been achieved.

Back at Isiolo Joy was not always easy to live with – she was restless in her body, her mind and her spirit. Too often, it seemed, I wanted to relax with my pipe and a drink at the end of a sweltering day or exhausting three weeks' safari: she would have liked to go walking with Pippin or in search of some inaccessible flower. Terence and she never really got on but she respected his botanical knowledge and he once saved my bacon while he was building our house. We were both in her bad books one day until he led her to some very rare swamp orchids she had been hunting for years: peace was restored.

She was disappointed that I had seldom listened to classical music and it was not till much later, when we went to Europe together on leave, that I fully understood the depth of her feeling for paintings. Sometimes her frustration that I was unable to share this side of her life would erupt in a torrent of reproach and I feared a return of her mood just before we were married.

Joy was an incomparable companion on any safari. Her quick eye always spotted something strange or beautiful, and her sharp mind was constantly teasing at its significance. In Buffalo Springs she noticed three-inch tilapia

Joy painted the fishes in the shade of the sail before the colours faded.

Joy, on our first safari to the coast. When I dug this old photograph out the other day the mould looked like a swarm of midges.

swimming in a pool which was fed from below, and had no other access. Near Surima she found and traced some early, unknown rock engravings of giraffe, oryx and flamingoes, much to the excitement of Louis Leakey. Two colourful species of fish in Lake Natron which she caught, painted and salted for the experts had only been discovered before in West Africa. On Lake Rudolf she saw that the Molo were using as plates the shells of a turtle much wanted by the British Museum. She obtained and sent off to them a very nice specimen.

Pippin came everywhere with us; often he rode on the front of Joy's saddle while Maeterlinck, a mongoose, peered out of her pocket. For a time Shocker, a serval cat, rode on one of the donkeys. The adoption of Egitoki, a very young buffalo orphan, caused quite a diversion. He began to thrive in Joy's care, and we could think of only one man in Africa to whom we dared entrust him – Raymond Hook. As it meant marching for more than a hundred miles to Mt Kenya, Lembirdan made him a cradle of grass and set it on one of the camels. We were a curious caravan – a travelling household of pets, orphans, camels, mules, donkeys and our milk cow, followed by her calf. On foot came the rangers and a handful of poachers we had captured.

"When Egitoki grows up," said Raymond Hook as we left, "I will cross him with one of my cows!"

I cannot remember Joy ever flagging or complaining of discomfort. When we were caught for the night on a cold and forbidding mountain top, she sacrificed her rubber sandals, to be burnt in strips as firelighters and flares, knowing full well the cost to her feet in the morning. When her temperature shot up, as it did several times on safari, she clung to a donkey while I wrapped her in soaking blankets and hurried her back to the camp. She neither flinched nor reproached me when a rhino charged her mule and she was thrown to the ground. I taught her to fire a rifle in self defence; her head was cool and her hand was steady when once she was obliged to drop an elephant in very poor light.

Most of the tensions which Joy experienced at Isiolo relaxed when we were out in the bush. But whereas my nature, a chip off the family block, was entirely content in the wilderness, Joy's was one of those outside chances that turn up in genetic roulette – a chance that produced great brilliance but much unhappiness too. While half of her craved for the freedom and peace of the wild, the other half needed the lights, the glamour and the talk of a city. While some of the time she was haunted by doubts, for the rest she was unnaturally assertive.

When thwarted, she would sometimes stamp off into forest or bush, alone and unarmed, and would walk there for hours. She had a relentless dislike for my pipe and my whisky; both habits were "extravagant", and my drinking "excessive". In the interests of peace, I stationed my whisky over my work bench, between bottles of meths, turpentine and linseed oil. One day, when I was particularly in need of a thirstquencher, I took a quick swig from a bottle, and yelled out in pain. Even a small slug of rust-remover takes the skin off your tongue.

"Just what the doctor ordered," Willie Hale, or one of his friends, remarked, "after all the water Joy's made you drink."

*   *   *

The war in Europe had been over for a year when Joy got a letter to tell her that her beloved Grandmother, Oma, had died. It lit a fuse which exploded a personal crisis. Once more Joy questioned every phase of her life, including our marriage. She claimed that each of her loves, and she included the first, a masked apache with whom she had eloped for two weeks from an Arts Ball in Vienna, had let her down one after the other. She was deeply distressed and after much talk we agreed, in a spirit of hope rather than despair, that she should go to Europe. She would have treatment for depression in London and would stay with her friend Susi, the wife of the scientist and author Sir James Jeans whom she was longing to meet. Then she would go on to her family in Vienna before returning to Kenya.

During the treatment in London Joy had decided to carve a set of ivory chessmen, representing the tribespeople of Kenya. She showed her sketches for the work to the editor of the *Geographical Magazine*, and to a painter who arranged for her to go to life classes at the Slade School of Art. Muriel Jex-Blake had also persuaded her to show her flower paintings to the Royal Horticultural Society.

Staying with Susi Jeans, she was charmed and exhilarated by the impromptu concerts given round the organ which her husband had built for her. At the end of an especially enjoyable musical evening Joy was alone with Sir James. Without any warning he turned grey and collapsed. A few minutes later he died. For the second time in her life Joy came face to face with sudden death, just after the death of her fondest relation.

Seeing her mother and sister again might have restored her morale but Joy had never forgiven her mother for leaving her father; the Nazis, and then the Russians, had stripped the family of all its possessions; and the visit to Vienna sent a shiver through Joy's heart. When she came back to Kenya her depression was verging on trauma.

Once more she needed the comfort, advice and medical care of Dr Jex-Blake and his wife. Again I turned to Archie Ritchie for moral support.

It was the last of his many great kindnesses before he retired, and Willie Hale took over as Chief Game Warden. Gradually I mastered my sorrows and remembered the vow I made to myself on the day we had agreed to get married: whatever my feelings for Joy might become, I would do my utmost to make her happy and be a good husband to her.

Although the visit to Europe had been a disaster, one after the other, seeds which Joy had sown there miraculously began to push up. In 1947 the Royal Horticultural Society exhibited some of her seven hundred flower paintings in London, and awarded her the Grenfell Gold Medal. In 1948, the year my mother died, Michael Huxley, editor of the *Geographical Magazine*, published some of the sketches for her ivory chess set with photographs of the carvings. This recognition gave Joy's confidence a great lift and rekindled a longing to paint the people of Kenya and their fantastic tribal regalia. Her work at the Slade and a quick sketch of me – to show she could catch the likeness of a face as well as of an ostrich plume headdress – led to a government contract. In 1949 Joy was commissioned to paint twenty of Kenya's tribes.

*   *   *

The six years which followed, from 1950 to 1956, were a watershed, not just for me, but for Kenya and Great Britain too. From now on Joy and I would often set off on separate safaris. It might be lonely, but there was relief from some of the stresses of the past. Joy calculated that there was one period in which neither of us saw a European for eight months. Today it would be impossible: the tidal waves of tourism and foreign aid have flung their spray of white faces into the furthest reaches of the Northern Frontier, to which we constantly travelled.

When Joy had the third miscarriage of her life, she finally accepted the verdict of the fortune-teller many years before. I had always suspected I was not cut out for parenthood, so the sense of loss was not as great as it might have been for other couples. As Pippin had died, Joy now adopted a rock hyrax called Pati, who became her inseparable travelling companion. Although Joy would venture off on many of her painting trips with only Pati and a policeman to look after her, she would come with me if I had jobs to do among tribes like the Turkana, Somalis or Boran.

During the next two years the Turkana were at the mutinous centre of an unfolding saga. They are a nomadic people, whose lives had always depended on following the rain, which sustained their grazing and watered their herds. Their seasonal wanderings took them from the shores of Lake Rudolf, westward into Uganda, and back to the lake. When the colonial frontiers were drawn the Government of Kenya both deprived them of guns and closed their route to the west. As a result the Turkana became defenceless against murderous raids from Sudan in the north, and in desperate need of alternative grazing. They adopted the only logical solution and moved south.

Alarmed that the prolific herds of these unfortunate nomads might devastate the pastures allotted to others, including the European settlers, the government in Nairobi decreed their eviction and forcible return to the wastes round Lake Rudolf. I was asked to help plan the great trek, as I had been over all the possible routes and had spent so much time with the people. The Turkana, proud as they are tough, were characteristically furious and sullen: their most respected witch doctors predicted the migration would never occur. I hoped they were right.

Nevertheless detailed preparations were made. After two years of planning the great day arrived and I waited all morning for George Low, the government vet, to give us the signal to move. But the moment I saw him I could tell from his face that something was wrong. He had found foot and mouth: the trek was aborted. Inside the hour the witch doctors proclaimed George a hero and mounted an immediate ngoma in his honour. The migration never took place.

Later in 1951 the elation of the Turkana was counter-balanced by the suffering of the Somalis. There was a devastating drought in the Lorian Swamp and Abdi Ogli, a Somali chief, sent for me in despair. Where the Uaso Nyiro River had flowed through the swamp, eight miles of dependable watering had vanished. Forty thousand head of stock were dying or dead; the vultures were so bloated that they could not lift themselves from the ground; and elephants, crazed for water that lay twenty feet down in the wells, were making daily attacks on his people and their dwindling flocks.

Joy described what we found when we got to the swamp and, in the dark, approached one of the elephants that had grown particularly aggressive to the Somalis, many of whom were starving like their cattle.

We came to the head of a camel, the rest of its body buried under mud; to all appearances it was dead, it had been exposed to the sun for thirty-six days. George touched its head, and slowly it opened its eyes, asking for the *coup de grâce* – which he delivered.

We got so close to the elephant that there was only a well between us. While he sniffed the air for the scent of water, I switched on the torch. Then George shot, a crash followed, and the bull fell over. When we examined the carcase we found a sheep buried under it, which had been too weak to move.

"The camel had been exposed to the sun for thirty-six days." When I touched its head it slowly opened its eyes.

Elephant skulls at a trial of Boran poachers. They once killed sixteen cows from one herd – and later thirty-six mothers and young from another.

For all the dedication of the British administration – and the great majority of its members did care deeply for the people they looked after – the paradoxes of colonialism were often cruel, and it was difficult or impossible to reconcile the logic of the governors with that of the governed. The thirsty Somalis were tortured by drought because they had not used their initiative to help themselves to an ample supply of water, only sixty miles away. When the hungry tribes helped themselves to meat, I often had to put an end to their killing. The Dorobo used pits, drop-spears and short bows; the Boni used long bows; the Turkana made devilish nooses, hunted with dogs and killed their quarry with spears; illegal as this was I found it difficult to condemn when they were genuinely short of food. But the Boran were incorrigible poachers. No Boran could call himself a man till he had blooded his spear. Before the British arrived the blood of a woman scored one mark, of a man two marks. Now they hunted giraffe from horseback, working the skins into sandals and water buckets; after an excited ngoma they courageously pursued the fiercest game, like lion and buffalo, on foot; and they went after elephants for the enjoyment of it. Sadly they killed regardless of age or condition. I had to take drastic and immediate action when they killed sixteen calves from one herd of elephants, and thirty mothers and young from another, which was lethargic and weakened by drought.

The Turkana, Somalis and Boran threw up just three of the problems that still haunt Africa today: resentment of the intrusion by white men, inability to cope with the forces of nature and, rapidly approaching, the end of the game. Day by day, wherever she went, aware that discontent with the past and changes in the name of progress would soon sweep the tribal and traditional chess board of Kenya, Joy recorded its figures, regalia and customs.

In February 1952 Princess Elizabeth and Prince Philip came out to Kenya. During a night they spent at Treetops, a game-watching lodge built in the trees above a waterhole in the Aberdares, her father died and she became Queen of England. It is unlikely she was fully aware of the simmering troubles, but even while she sat up that night, and looked down at the elephants, buffaloes, rhinos and two waterbuck fighting, Mau Mau rebels were at work to throw off her government. As soon as he arrived in October her new Governor, Sir Evelyn Baring, had to declare a State of Emergency and order the arrest of the rebellion's putative leaders, including the formidable Jomo Kenyatta.

Kenyatta, like the majority of the Mau Mau, was a Kikuyu, but his complicity in their obscene, sadistic and murderous activities was denied and has never been proved. Louis Leakey, whose warnings of an impending revolt had been ignored by a previous governor, was the official interpreter of the trial. It has been said that the fairness of the proceedings was open to doubt: but whether that is so or not when the verdict was given Kenyatta was banished to the desert at Lokitaung in the North of Kenya.

In the following year, at the time of the Queen's coronation, Joy and I drove across the Sahara to the Mediterranean, and thence through Spain, France, Italy, Austria – where we saw Joy's family – and to England. In Paris Joy lost her temper and made one of her sensational exits, this time from the car in the middle of traffic. Speaking no word of French, and not having the slightest idea what our hotel was called, I was reduced to casting round in circles, disregarding the solicitous offers of help from several young ladies, until I fastened on a landmark at dawn.

In England Joy seemed to have enthralled various audiences with talks on her tribal experiences: age sets, mutilation, scarification, circumcision, clitoridectomy and witchcraft seemed to go down especially well with Women's Institutes. But she looked for a publisher, for her tribal photographs and paintings, in vain.

When we returned to Kenya the Mau Mau Emergency had reached new heights of tension and violence. I volunteered my services and my most serious work was to train patrols in the Aberdare Highlands: I tried to get across the rudiments of tracking, and how to move silently in the forests. The only prisoner I ever saw taken was a wounded gang leader brought in by my trackers. At one point I was sent to investigate a rumour of Mau Mau activity on the Tana: it proved to be quite unfounded, but I came on some previously unrecorded falls.

In 1954 we got news of one of Mau Mau's grimmest atrocities. A gang walked into the house of Louis' cousin, Gray Leakey, and strangled his wife. They then took Gray, who was nearly seventy, diabetic and deaf, dug a hole and buried him head first, probably alive.

It was another two years before the rebellion was quelled. Twenty-six Asians, ninety Europeans, and eighteen hundred "loyal" Africans died. About 11,500 African "terrorists" were killed by the security forces. But the violence was so closely confined to the Kikuyu areas that Joy was able to go on painting the tribesmen throughout the emergency. She did in fact paint one Mau Mau prisoner, clad typically in an old army great coat and a shabby felt hat. He chatted and smoked as she painted, but to her horror he was executed as soon as she had finished his portrait.

The Kikuyu lost the fighting, but they were about to win the battle for freedom and to dominate the first independent government of their country. Ironically although they had resorted to the most arcane rituals, oaths, curses and clothing to mobilise the revolt, they now set their minds on

Largely on the strength of this portrait of me, the government commissioned Joy to paint the principal tribes of Kenya and their regalia.

M.IKWINGA
URINGU
GANIA

CHAPKWE KIB
KAPSABET
NANDI

eradicating the symbolism and tribal traditions recorded by Joy in her paintings. She felt it was touch and go whether the pictures would be allowed to survive once the new men came into power.

The Mau Mau rebellion took a great toll on the strength of the Governor, Sir Evelyn Baring, who had always found inspiration in the open – climbing, sailing, fishing and watching Africa's wildlife. In 1955 he asked me to take him and his family fishing on Lake Rudolf. Joy painted him a map of the Northern Frontier, complete with vignettes of its tribesmen, game, birds and the fishes he was hoping to catch.

As soon as he had gone she and I secretly embarked on a forbidden crossing to South Island in a fourteen-foot dinghy with an outboard engine. We spent several fascinating but exceedingly uncomfortable days and nights there exploring its mysteries. We discovered relics of Dyson and Martin, the scientists who had been drowned just before my crossing in 1934; a herd of two hundred goats, creeks swarming with crocodiles of exceptional length and shoals of Nile perch in such numbers as I have never seen elsewhere – many of them were forced above the surface by crowding as they fought to get at a pink substance encrusting the rocks. Although our return to the mainland was delayed by bad weather, and its timing was uncertain even to us, a party waded out to the boat. A Rendille girl, gifted with second sight, had told them when and where to meet us.

The Provincial Commissioner in Isiolo could have done with her services. Alarmed by our disappearance, he had not only alerted the police and an aerial patrol, but, according to a rumour picked up by Joy, had reserved two graves in the Nyeri cemetery. Had we needed them, Joy's paintings of its flowers and its people would have remained, as a legacy, in her country of adoption. As it was she arose from the waves of Lake Rudolf to embark on another adventure, which left Kenya an even more remarkable legacy.

Chapter 5

The First of the Free
1956–1963

No one knows more about violence and sudden death in Kenya than the surgeon Michael Wood. One weekend he answered an s.o.s. to fly in his small private plane to help a Turkana wounded in a fight near Lake Rudolf. From this single flight grew his Flying Doctor Service, which saves thousands of lives every year all over East Africa. Without it I and several others living with me at Kora would probably be dead.

Michael is familiar with the deserts round the lake and has operated there to save the life of Turkana damaged by lions. He says that sometimes half the beds in the little hospitals of the north are filled with the victims of maulings. In a country so short of game there are running battles between herdsmen and the lions. I am sure that is why the Turkana regarded Joy and me with such surprise when we next went back to the lake together, for we were accompanied by a large lioness who frequently shared Joy's camp bed in the heat of the day. The lioness was later to become famous as Elsa.

It was eighteen months before, in February 1956, that I had shot Elsa's mother. Soon after she was dead we heard some weak cries from a crevice in the rocks, which she had obviously been defending. With a hooked stick we pulled three tiny cubs out into the sunlight.

Knowing Joy's devotion to the various orphans she had adopted I took the cubs back to our camp. Joy left her painting unfinished and immediately took over the little lions, feeding them through a teat I improvised from a sparking plug. At Isiolo we built them a wire annexe to the house. To our surprise Joy's hyrax Pati Pati, who had been with her for six years and been bitterly jealous of previous rivals – mongooses, squirrels and bush babies – immediately adopted the baby lions and joined in their fun.

They loved romping, especially with children, and were forever testing their strength. At an early age many instincts asserted themselves. They began to drag blankets, gripped in their mouths, as they would later drag a kill. They would always be silently stalking some new victim from behind. Out of doors they grew increasingly boisterous, and learnt how to trip us with a deft twist of their paws.

Opposite: Joy with Elsa and her sisters. It was a mistake, I realize looking back, not to have kept all three cubs.

Just as Pati was quite undismayed when her charges grew far larger than her, the cubs were far from intimidated by the donkeys. They charged them, in line abreast, and put them to flight, before changing their tactics and dropping into a stalk. Sociable and inquisitive, they resented being kept off the verandah at the end of the day, and would press their noses to stare and to eavesdrop as we sat with our sundowners. When they held back one evening I felt something was wrong, and went to investigate. Once again their instincts were at work: a red spitting cobra was slithering along the foot of their wire.

The timing of the cubs' arrival was ideal from Joy's point of view. Until now her energy had been almost continuously absorbed by her paintings. As soon as she had handed over her pictures of the tribes to the government — in the end there were more than five hundred — she had started to concentrate on writing and photography. On our return from the clandestine crossing to South Island she wrote up five versions of the adventure and sent them, with five different sets of photographs, to five magazines. They all published them, including the journal of the Royal Geographical Society in London. Having a methodical approach to all her work Joy meticulously numbered her negatives and contact prints for future reference. She also began to keep an album of photographs devoted to the lions. It was bound in lion skin, an irony that escaped her at first.

As Chief Game Warden, Willie Hale kept a weather eye on the cubs. He had been quite happy for Lyn Temple-Boreham to raise his two young lions, Caesar and Brutus, down on the Mara; even though they had grown enormous, they were no more dangerous than spaniels. But unfortunately, like dogs, they were playful, and when they knocked Willie down, and proceeded to sit on him, they were banished to a zoo. I knew about this incident and, not wishing to lose all of our cubs, Joy and I quickly agreed when Willie said we must send away two.

We decided to keep the smallest, whom Joy had christened Elsa — after Bally's mother — and made plans for her sisters to go to Blydorp Zoo in Rotterdam. Joy took them to an aeroplane at Nairobi and during the days she was away Elsa joined me in my work and my walks in the bush. I had no idea when to expect Joy back, but Elsa did. One afternoon she refused to budge from the gate by our house. An hour or two later Joy drove up. It was my first experience of a lion's power of "telepathy".

Elsa almost smothered Joy in her relief to see her back, for although the cubs had been faithfully looked after by our gardener called Nuru, it was to Joy that Elsa now looked for affection and snacks. She would suck Joy's thumbs, and knead her thighs as if pressing her mother's flank for milk, when she was anxious or tired. It was pathetic to see her searching for her sisters, and while she got over the loss of them we let her sleep on our bed. In the meantime we began to plan her education for life in the wild, for Joy and I were as one that she should not end up in a zoo. Despite all my years as a warden, and my particular interest in lions, I had no real knowledge about how to set about our self-appointed task. So far as I could discover, literally no one had attempted such a thing before. It would have to be a programme of trial and, no doubt, errors; and we would have to start soon, in the bush.

As Elsa's first safari we took her camping on the banks of the Uaso Nyiro river. At home she had bumped into a rhino, and had got on friendly terms with a herd of giraffe, but now she was loose in a garden of Eden. She chased mongooses round their fortress in an old termite mound, sneaked up on a family of bat-eared foxes, teased and was teased by the baboons, and found herself chased by a flock of vulturine guinea fowl. When she took on fifty giraffes she worked round them, to give them a whiff of her scent, so that they instinctively turned off towards us: presumably she thought we were bright enough to spring an ambush. As soon as she came across fresh elephant droppings she rolled in them, and then followed the herd into the forest; single-handed she started a colossal stampede. I was surprised that the unmistakable grunt of a lion left her completely unmoved.

When I shot sand grouse or guinea fowl she knew that the report meant a dead bird. She would retrieve them and claim the first as her own. Later, when I took her fishing, she would watch my line and, as soon as it twitched, plunge in to recover the catch. She was inclined to deposit the fish, in distaste, on my bed. Twice she saved us from snakes. Quite often her company meant mischief, but a swift smack with a small stick, and increasingly the sharp command "No", restored her to order.

Elsa's second safari was to the Indian Ocean. Joy wanted to show her friend Herbert Tichy the glorious beaches and coral gardens at Kiunga, but what was to have been a holiday became work for me, when local fishermen claimed that their goats were being taken by a young lion. It was more seriously spoiled for Joy when Pati, her hyrax, died of old age. Elsa did not let any of this upset her fun. She chased coconuts bobbing in the surf, played with the seaweed, and stalked a goat all too successfully. For the first time she discovered opponents, other than guinea fowl, who refused to be routed: the crabs stood their ground and nipped her on the nose.

Elsa slept in my tent. Joy, who was a few yards off, woke us one night and said that a lion had come up to her bed and was now near our truck, in the process of stealing a buck I had shot. I did not believe her, but when I got up with my rifle I was greeted by a growl that certainly came from a lion. I therefore positioned the buck where I could get a clear shot, and

Hunting with Elsa. The first real understanding I had of lions came with bringing her up.

The sight which so surprised the Africans we met on our safari to Lake Rudolf.

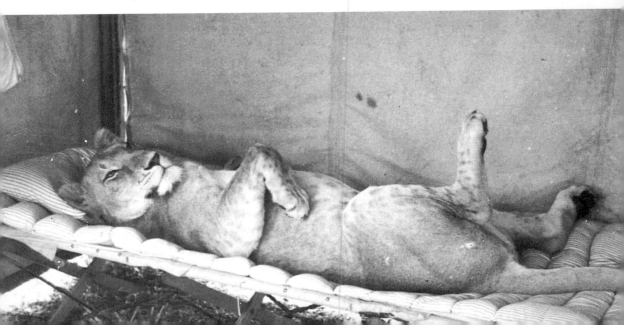

waited. Half an hour later I saw the lion and fired – or tried to. I had forgotten to load my gun! Sometime towards morning he came back: this time his luck had run out. Elsa had been a spectator of the whole performance, but never uttered a sound.

Our third safari was the one to Lake Rudolf, when the Turkana had been so amazed to see Elsa and Joy on a camp bed together. I had decided to go up the east shore of the lake and beyond it, right to the frontiers of Ethiopia, from which raiders were said to poach game. We would return by way of Mt Kulal, to find out if it was true that the mountain was being so heavily grazed by the Samburu that the greater kudu had deserted its forest. Although we would follow much of the route Nevil and I had taken, twenty-five years before, it was rather a different expedition.

To carry all the tents, stores and equipment for a large patrol of my rangers we had two three-ton lorries. We also took Joy's large truck and two Landrovers. Apart from our drivers and personal servants we were accompanied by thirty-five donkeys. We were also joined by my assistant, Julian McKeand and Herbert Tichy.

Elsa still kept her close attachment to Joy, but at eighteen months, although not yet fully grown, she was a very good size and must have weighed at least 150 lb. She began to mark territory with urine heavily scented from her anal glands – and always pulled a grimace when she had finished squatting. (Males perform the same function with a ten-foot squirt, often tickling their faces on the target first.) We dared not trust her with the donkeys, and kept her in an advance party, or rearguard, when we were all on the move. At night, or when we encountered the Rendille, watering thousands of camels in their wells or the pools of a gorge, Elsa was firmly held back on her chain.

When we reached the Ethiopian frontier there was no game of any kind to be seen – the poachers had been over in force. Equally, on the slopes of Kulal, where Nevil and I had searched in vain for our gold but had seen plenty of game, there were no greater kudu in sight. Once or twice we came across their spoor, but the mountain was trammelled with the footprints of cattle and goats.

At one point Elsa looked down a sheer 2,000 foot rockface into the gorge below, without the slightest sign of concern. She gazed wistfully up at the eagles, perhaps mistaking them for vultures circling over a kill, and was infuriated by a pair of fan-tail ravens which started to mob her. When the time came to leave the mountain and cross the scorching lava to the lake, Elsa tried to bolt back into the cool of the forest. It was a long march and after it got dark the advance guard had to fire tracer bullets in the air to guide us. Both Elsa and Joy were too exhausted to eat. Elsa's extraordinary good nature on this testing safari was, I think, due partly to her character and partly to the use of persuasion, rather than force, if we had a difference of opinion.

Elsa seemed to grow in both size and confidence after our return from Lake Rudolf. It was interesting to see how our friends reacted to her: she was always a little more impish with those in whom she detected a trace of apprehension. Most of them were aware of this, and treated her calmly but firmly. Ken Smith, of course, took Elsa completely in his stride.

Willie Hale also remained on good terms with Elsa, but was less fortunate with Joy. Anxious that Elsa should not divert me from my work, he most reasonably asked me not to use my rangers to look after her. Joy took umbrage at this and ceased to regard him as a friend. But both we and Elsa benefited from Willie's intervention, as I appointed a faithful Turkana, Makedde, to help Nuru, and he has remained in and out of our lives ever since.

Joy and I always enjoyed it when Elspeth Huxley and her mother, Nellie Grant, came to stay. They were amusing company and had a gift for eliciting mild indiscretions from inspectors of police and provincial commissioners. But Joy realised there was a limit to their admiration for the adolescent Elsa, and would withdraw to sketch her inside her enclosure. Joy once asked Elspeth if she would write a book about Elsa, but she said she thought Joy should tell the story herself.

When she was two years old Elsa's voice developed a deeper growl, and she showed signs of coming into season for the first time. She grew restless, insisted on taking the lead on our walks, was clearly seeking the company of other lions, and spent the night in the bush. The peace was disturbed by grunting and snarling – unmistakably lions in a fight – and, when Elsa failed to show up after several days, we both feared the worst. But she did come back, and the tell-tale scratches, with a scent far stronger than usual, were signs of a typical mating encounter. In soliciting the attentions of a lion, she had obviously incurred the wrath of a rival.

It was time to find her a home in the wild, away from us, away from Isiolo, and as far away as possible from human habitation of any kind at all. Had it not been for my colleague, and fellow devotee of lions, Lyn Temple-Boreham, it might have taken a long time to find one.

*   *   *

Lyn Temple-Boreham was in charge of an area known as the Mara Triangle: it had been designated as a national reserve, but as yet had not been fully taken over. Today it is known as the Maasai Mara Reserve.

The Mara offered the most spectacular concentration of wildlife in the whole of Kenya. It is a continuation of the Serengeti Plain and together they form an apparently endless ocean of grass, growing from a bed of volcanic ash. Dotted by kopjes, or islands of rock, the plain is a paradise for game, watered by streams – and pools when it rains – shaded by patches of woodland and bush, and offering seclusion in the valleys and combes of the hills which surround it. Animals and birds, amphibians, reptiles and butterflies abound here, in breathtaking variety, beauty and numbers.

There was only one blot on this otherwise idyllic landscape. Thanks to the colonial rulers – of both kinds – the Mara lay in Kenya, while the Serengeti was in Tanganyika, yet both were the home of the Maasai. For generations the Maasai had fought all comers to defend the heartland of Kenya. It was an unhappy coincidence that the British arrived just as the Maasai and their precious herds were afflicted with small-pox and rinder-pest, and that shortly afterwards they were persuaded, some would say misled, into leaving their pastures in central Kenya to trek south. Decimated by disease, traduced by a treaty, they were now not only bisected by a frontier but deprived of part of their grazing. When the government later proposed to reserve it for game, from the worthiest of motives, these once magnificent warriors, who gloried in fighting on foot with the lions and had defended their freedom so bravely, felt as if they were being treated as trespassers.

It says a great deal for Lyn Temple-Boreham that in a situation like this he was able to retain the respect of the Maasai. Perhaps his passion for lions had something to do with it. Although he had lost Caesar and Brutus he cultivated a wild lioness he called Sally and the rest of her pride; they appreciated his reliable provision of water and meat in hard times, and came to recognise his voice and respond to it. Like Mervyn Cowie in Nairobi, Lyn knew that the pride could just tip the scales in his favour: waverers on the issue of the Maasai's rights in the Mara might well be won over by the sight of his lions.

Having familiarised lions to a human acquaintance I think he was intrigued to see if we could do the reverse – familiarise our humanised lion with the wild of her kind. He gave us three months to try. The journey to the Mara was 350 miles, and it took us over seventeen hours of continuous driving to get there. We had given Elsa a tranquilliser, and she swiftly recovered from the effects of the drug and the drive.

As the first step in her introduction to the Mara we decided to give her a view of the country – the landscape, the game and the resident lions. For a start we took off her collar, as a symbol of freedom. Luckily she loved to travel about on the roof of the Landrover, which caught all the breezes and provided an admirable look-out. Nothing would induce her to approach any of the prides, though she made tentative overtures to a blond young lion who was living on his own.

So far we had always cut up her meat so she would not associate food with the animals she saw on the hoof. But now, as the second phase, we gave her whole carcasses, and let her sleep out for the night. One by one additional instincts began to assert themselves. She opened her first waterbuck correctly — starting with the softest skin between the hindlegs — and then went on to bury the stomach to conceal these remains from the vultures. Very soon she took to dragging her "kill" into the shade, and defending it from the hyenas, jackals and vultures. Next, she gave up the random stalking of prey, and only leapt down from the car if her quarry's attention was distracted in courtship or fighting. Even so she never succeeded in making a kill, and since I could not shoot inside the reserve there was no way to help her. Nevertheless she did begin to lose her shyness or fear of other lions, and to seek out their company.

We had noticed that Elsa came into season about every ten weeks, so when this was due to occur we began the third stage of her initiation. We started to leave her alone for days on end. But although once or twice we could tell she had briefly joined up with a pride, she got little to eat and was losing condition. At the end of two months Elsa suddenly became very ill; her coat became mothy and dull; the hairs on her face grew ash grey. It was obviously more serious than the effects of hunger, or the changes of climate and altitude.

We sent blood slides for diagnosis, and while we waited for the results Elsa slept in my tent, looking very lethargic. As it happened the infection she had caught was quite easily treated, but by the time she recovered Temple-Boreham's three months had expired. She went off in search of one last honeymoon, but still had not killed for herself. How I wished her sisters were here in the Mara, instead of thousands of miles away in the Rotterdam Zoo. I was sure that the three of them together would have brought down a kill, and captured the heart of a lion.

I feared Willie Hale might take a poor view of our failure, but he remained sympathetic and suggested we take Elsa back to the north, and release her on a tributary of the Tana — in country then known as the Meru County Council Reserve.

*   *   *

Elsa's new and, we hoped final, home was on the banks of the Ura, a small river close to the place where she was born and which we could easily visit from Isiolo. It was uninhabited, and likely to remain so as it was suitable for neither farming nor grazing. The Meru County Council had recently appointed a Tsetse fly officer, Larry Wateridge, to be its first Game Control Officer.

This was truly a corner of Africa where, as Joy put it, "even the foxes say goodnight to each other". The river banks were lined with luxuriant green undergrowth above which rose doum palms, acacias and tall fig trees. A little way back from the water the bush quickly thinned out, and apart from the thorns, only the big, bulbous baobabs had been left standing by the elephants. Looming over this picturesque African landscape was a long ridge of reddish rock, which provided ideal lairs and look-outs for lions.

Instantly Elsa responded to her native climate; her muscles rippled again, and her coat grew glossy and shone. Here I could help her on the next, vital, stage of her education: I could give her practice in killing. She caught a warthog but could not finish it off. I therefore gave it a merciful bullet. But very soon afterwards, when I shot at a waterbuck, Elsa was on to it before it even fell, and went straight for its throat. From now on she realised that a stranglehold on the throat, or a suffocating grip on the muzzle, was the quickest way to kill.

Joy and I were later much criticised for killing to support Elsa but we never shot more than a lioness would have killed in the wild on her own. It has been calculated that a lion can eat up to 75 lb of meat in one night, and this may be true, though it will often take half an hour's break in the middle of feeding. On average a fully grown lion might eat the equivalent of twenty large antelopes in a year, at uneven intervals, and sharing the larger kills with the rest of the pride. Lions are never too proud, when hungry, to resort to scavenging, and I have seen them eat meat that has been crawling with maggots.

Like all lions Elsa was perfectly evolved for her hunting: her eyes were set at the front of her head to give her judgement of distance; her jaws and teeth were thrust forward, and pointed, so she could strike straight to the most vulnerable spots on her prey; her claws were sharp for clinging and slashing, yet retractable when handling her cubs. Her muscles had immense strength – although she cannot have weighed more than 300 lb herself, she once lifted a 400 lb waterbuck up the very steep slope of the river bank, at least ten feet high.

Probably Elsa's most remarkable step forward at this time was in exercising extraordinary self-control; she somehow learned to reconcile the reactions of the new, wild lioness who was emerging, with those of the young lion who had imprinted, almost at birth, on her human foster parents. One day, we decided to move closer to camp a fresh kill she had made. But her blood was still up and she suddenly put back her ears, her eyes went to slits, and her tail began to flicker in an ominous threat. Joy saw what was happening, spoke to her softly but firmly, and showed her how she could help. In a few moments Elsa got the point, and then began to drag the kill into the back of the Landrover. At the other end she helped to unload it.

Knowing that Elsa was now able to kill for herself, Joy and I began to leave her on her own for a week at a time. She was often waiting for us near our camp, or up on a ledge which we called "Elsa's Rock". If she did not appear very soon we would fire three shots in the air, to which she responded. Although she was sometimes hungry it was clear she had always found food.

Joy had often made sketches and paintings of Elsa; now she began a book about her. There was a particularly handsome fig tree down by the river. Its leafy branches rose to form a cool and shady dome above the sandbank, on which Joy built a bench and a table of driftwood. Baboons would sneak down a branch to tease Elsa or Joy, and little ones sometimes got over-excited and fell into the water. Through the hanging leaves Joy could watch lesser kudu or bush buck coming down to drink, and wading birds stalk through the shallows after fishes and frogs. Joy's dedication to the animals she adopted was gradually spreading to others. Never one to hide her feelings, she was so outraged to find some monkey traps, set by Larry Wateridge near the Ura for a zoo collection, that she immediately let out his prisoners.

My work as a warden was as demanding as ever but on our visits to Elsa Joy would get on with the book while I went fishing. She would sometimes reproach me for this, but she seemed so sure of the blend of anecdote, atmosphere and personal feeling which would convey the story to her readers that I thought it wiser to leave it to her, although she leafed through my diaries and reports when she wanted to fill in the dates or check some of the facts.

We had taken great care to photograph every stage of Elsa's upbringing and the lion skin book had grown almost to bursting. There is no doubt that our shared devotion to Elsa had brought Joy and me as close to each other as we had ever been, just as a child might have done – and Elsa took the place of a child in our family album.

Apart from the photographs we had started to make a record of Elsa on 8mm cine film. The light was often poor, in the shade by the river and so we only captured Elsa's most astonishing feat in stills. She dashed into a thicket by a stream one morning and suddenly we heard a thunderous

Opposite: Elsa's most astonishing feat. She brings down a buffalo, allows Nuru to cut its throat and helps to drag it from the water.

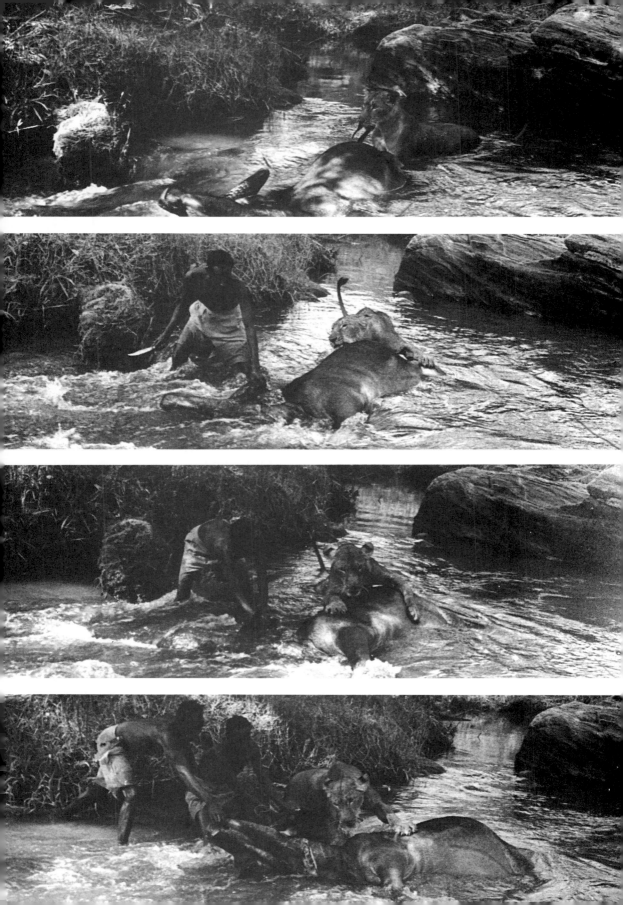

bellowing. I struggled after Elsa and found her on top of an enormous buffalo bull, which had obviously slipped in the rapids.

Elsa had left its throat and gone to the soft flesh round the tail when Nuru, a Muslim, came up. If he was to enjoy some of the meat he would have to cut the buffalo's throat and his knife was already out. Elsa's ears went back dangerously as she realised his plan but we talked to her soothingly, and she understood we would help her get the buffalo out of the water and into the shade of a tree – it must have weighed over a ton. It was an impressive achievement to bring the beast down on her own – even when it was unsure of its footing – and much more amazing when her blood was up to allow us to take a share of her kill.

We were equally impressed that after Elsa had been in season for a few days, and had enjoyed the company of other lions – even if she had not consummated a courtship – she could come back to us and doze beside Joy in her studio, as she called it, on the sandbank.

                              *   *   *

Early in 1959, when Elsa had proved she could survive on her own, and seemed on the verge of finding a mate, Joy went to London to find a publisher. She had failed with her tribal pictures: it would not happen again. Normally an author approaches a publisher direct or appoints a literary agent to do this for her. Joy collected lists of both agents and publishers, and wrote to several at once. What is more she secured promises from *two* distinguished men to introduce her book!

In response to the first expressions of interest, she decided to send off two copies of the script, and her photograph albums – there were now two. But for all her elaborate preparations she was still a novice in the world of books: her prose (like her speech) was idiosyncratic, her typing apparently dyslexic; and her paper not only slippery and thin, but discoloured by the light and the insects of her riverside studio. For reasons of bulk, and in the hope of speeding her search, the scripts were airmailed separately, from each other and from the albums. The albums too were separated, and since neither was captioned, and each showed only half of the story, the crux of our experiment was manifest in neither.

Thus it was that when Joy arrived in London she was greeted with both bewilderment and a number of outright rejections. Luckily she remembered that one publisher, Marjorie Villiers of the Harvill Press, had shown genuine concern over her tribal paintings, so she bundled up her lion skin albums and walked round to their offices without an appointment. The Harvill Press was run by two partners. Marjorie Villiers was sensitive and kind,

6

7

9

10

13

14

17

18

20

23

21   22

concealing this, and also great cleverness, behind a camouflage of poodles and tweeded reserve. Her partner, Manya Harari, possessed exactly the same virtues but was ceaselessly curious and animated. She was as Russian as Marjorie was English, and had recently discovered, and translated into English, Boris Pasternak's *Doctor Zhivago*.

Marjorie Villiers remembered Joy's persistence from her previous visit to London and was reluctant to see her without warning. But Joy refused to leave the landing of the shabby little office which served as its waiting room. When the poodles could contain themselves no longer both women were rewarded – Joy for her determination and Marjorie for her earlier interest in the tribes. At first from politeness, and then with rising excitement, she listened as Joy told the story of Elsa, and turned the pages of photographs – which proved the truth of all she was claiming. It was the first time that anyone in London had the opportunity, or the patience, to appreciate both together. Marjorie felt in her bones that here was a book whose sales might almost match those of *Doctor Zhivago*.

As soon as Joy had left, with the promise of an offer for her book, Marjorie rang up Billy Collins, chairman of the big publishing house which owned an interest in Harvill. He urged her to acquire the world rights in Joy's book. She did so at once.

*   *   *

During Joy's absence in London I continued to make visits to Elsa. She always seemed pleased to see me, but if in season she would make her usual disappearance. I wrote Joy details of her daily activities, and warned her to be ready for a tremendous greeting when she returned. I had seldom seen Elsa so affectionate since the day she welcomed Joy back from the airport after sending her sisters to Europe. She bounded up to her, embraced her with her paws and licked her face and her arms.

In August Elsa took up with a young lion, who was so besotted by her that once he nearly knocked me over without seeing me, and another time sat tight under a bush a few yards away, with his eyes fixed on his bride. They shared kills together, and he frequented the bush round our camp, roaring loudly and long through the nights. Six weeks later it was clear, from the softness and sheen of her skin, and from the size of her teats, that Elsa was pregnant. Although she still spent much of her time with the lion, she was affectionate with Joy, who laid in a feeding bottle and tinned milk, in case she chose to have her litter in camp and lacked the support of another lioness in suckling them.

On 20 December we heard Elsa giving weak cries from her rock, and she slowly walked towards us, in pain, with blood trickling from beneath her tail. She rubbed her head against our legs and when she made for a crevice in the rocks we left her, as many animal mothers kill their young if disturbed during birth. That night her mate put up a magnificent performance of roaring and the next day bolted out of a bush only six feet away from us.

We began to get very worried when Elsa had still not appeared by Christmas Eve. But the next day at lunch she burst into camp, swept the table clean with her tail, and smothered all of us – Joy, me, Makedde and Nuru – with energetic embraces. Her figure had gone back to normal, and we assumed she had felt it safe to leave her cubs hidden, during the heat of the day, when there was the least chance that danger would be stalking abroad.

*   *   *

We cabled news of the birth to Marjorie Villiers and Billy Collins in London. The telegram was included in Joy's book which, after endless debate, carried her original title, *Born Free* – from St Paul's boast in *The Acts of the Apostles*: "But I was free born." Marjorie performed the unusual task of translating Joy's "English" into English – the content of her story was untouched. As soon as each edited chapter arrived for approval, Joy went through it with an English–German dictionary, to check that no nuance had been added or lost.

In Billy Collins Joy found a publisher whose drive was equal to her own. Tall and an excellent athlete, he played tennis not only for Oxford University but also in the men's doubles at Wimbledon. An enthusiastic naturalist, his publishing adviser was the famous biologist Sir Julian Huxley. Billy was dissatisfied with his list of best-selling war books until he captured Field Marshal Montgomery. It was not enough to publish the Archbishop of Canterbury, he wanted a Pope – and he finally acquired two.

All his skill went into making *Born Free* a success. He filled it with photographs; kept the price as low as he dared; bombarded the booksellers with promotion displays; persuaded the *Sunday Times* – quite against their own judgement – to carry a pictorial serial; and printed a very large run. The impact was instant and phenomenal. The *Sunday Times* begged for more pictures and copies of the book were gone in a week. All over the Commonwealth the orders came in and the edition sold out. We were told that people were unwrapping their books on the pavements to gaze at the pictures. Very soon the success in Britain and Europe was repeated in America, Japan and even in Russia.

I was flabbergasted by all these reports: Joy was not. She, Marjorie and

Billy had known what they were doing, but I don't think any of them knew what they had started. From now on Joy would have to live with unending invasions of her privacy. She would also have to handle vast sums of money. In the next ten years she must have earned half a million pounds. From the start she made it quite clear that as I had written only a few pages of the book she did not propose to give me a share of the royalties. Instead she made practical arrangements with accountants, in London and Nairobi, to accumulate money for the benefit of wildlife.

We often speculated on the reasons why *Born Free* appealed to such a phenomenal number and mixture of people. Partly, of course, it was a love story. Then partly it owed its impact to the fact that we had stayed on terms with an animal in the wild which up till now had symbolised majestic strength and ferocity: only one other man I know of, Norman Carr, has ever done this. The response also owed something to the popular impact of a few exceptional films. In America Walt Disney's *Living Desert* was widely regarded as a classic, while in Britain a Belgian called Armand Denis – a friend of Julian Huxley's – was showing a television series called *On Safari*, shot by brilliant cameramen like Alan Root, Simon Trevor and Hugo van Lawick who were soon to become aces on their own.

In the meantime Joy caught this new wave and established her Elsa Wild Animal Appeal, with the status of a charitable trust, in England and later in America.

*   *   *

At first Elsa moved her cubs from lair to lair every few days. Her mate hovered nearby but as he did not kill for her we had to play the role of a fellow lioness and bring her meat, which her mate would sometimes purloin.

Nevertheless for six weeks Elsa made sure we kept well away from her offspring. Then, one afternoon in February, she called from the river, in an unfamiliar way, and stood near the bank with three cubs at her side. It was a moment we never forgot.

From the first day the different characters of the cubs were perfectly distinct. The first male, who was the boldest and kept up with Elsa whenever he could, we called Jespah – "God sets free". The second grew larger and stronger than Jespah, but never equalled his spirit; he was called Gopa, that is "Timid". The third cub, a female, we christened Little Elsa; she was the replica of her mother at the same age.

It was not long before a series of distinguished visitors came to see Elsa's young family. One of the first was Julian Huxley and his wife Juliette. Larry Wateridge was so excited by the appearance of the Chairman of UNESCO

that he erected a special "choo" or latrine. Unfortunately he embellished it with creepers and the whole thing collapsed. The Huxleys were infinitely more concerned with the lions, and Julian described the powerful impact they made on him, both personally and as a scientist, in his foreword to Joy's next book.

Another early visitor, David Attenborough, made a television film about Elsa and her cubs for the BBC. He was a delightful companion and utterly unruffled by Jespah's persistent attacks on his shins, which Elsa, who had just been nastily hurt in a fight with a lioness, was ineffectual in discouraging. Far more serious, however well-meant, were Elsa's own assaults on another of our guests, Billy Collins.

We put him in a tent between Joy's and mine, and thought he would be safe when we surrounded it by a thick barricade of thorn branches and tightly secured its wicker gate. But just after dawn I heard a call from Billy's tent. I found that Elsa had brushed aside the thorns, was sitting on her publisher, who was entangled in his mosquito net, and was nibbling his arm. When we remonstrated with Elsa, and apologised to Billy, he told us not to worry.

"I realised Elsa was determined to come and see me, and as I had once owned bees, I knew I must try to keep my head, and not make too much noise or fuss," he calmly explained. "I was sure she was friendly and that you would come and get her off me."

But the next night Billy nearly did lose his head. Elsa tried the same trick again; I quickly evicted her, doubled the thorns, and went back to sleep. However, I was suddenly aroused by yet another summons from Billy — this one more urgent. I cursed as I fought my way through the vicious but useless thorn-spikes and arrived almost too late. Billy was using all his weight, strength and balance to keep his footing on the tottering camp bed. Elsa, on her hind legs, was clasping his shoulders, wrapped in mosquito net, with her paws, and holding his cheek bones between her teeth. I could see threads of blood on his face and his neck.

"We had often watched her doing this to her cubs," wrote Joy afterwards. "It was a sign of affection, but the effect on Billy must have been very different." I am sure that it was, but he still came back six months later, to plan the publication of the new book Joy was writing about Elsa and the cubs – *Living Free*.

Just before Christmas 1960, and the cubs' first birthday, we received a nasty shock. The local Council, who held authority in the area, gave us notice to leave, taking Elsa and the cubs, whom they regarded as a threat to their livestock. After the episode with the monkey traps, I doubted if we would get much support from Larry Wateridge; and as Willie Hale had

Opposite above: Elsa bringing her cubs across the river for the first time. It was one of the great sights of our lives. *Opposite below:* Joy and Elsa. "The best and perhaps the only method of eliciting hidden potential . . . is by way of understanding love" wrote Sir Julian Huxley about them.

retired as Chief Game Warden I started to make enquiries about yet another new home for Elsa and her cubs. Without much success, for we had never handled them like Elsa, we tried to get Jespah, Gopa and Little Elsa used to the trucks in which they would have to travel there. What should have been a doubly happy Christmas became rather a muted affair.

And then Elsa fell ill. I was not too worried at first, and Joy went off to Nairobi. But Elsa suddenly grew worse, and I sent an s.o.s. to Ken Smith, at Isiolo, to find a vet and contact Joy, asking her to bring antibiotics as fast as she could. Later that night Elsa collapsed in the bush, and I lay down on a camp bed beside her. Twice she got up to rub her head against me; Jespah made off with my blanket; and we all got a fright when a buffalo nearly stumbled over my bed.

The next day Elsa scarcely could move, except to stagger into the river. Pathetically she tried to lap water, but was unable to swallow. She dragged herself to a little island, and then with a tremendous effort, and some help from me, she made it back to the studio. As she lay on the sand Jespah pressed up against her. It was beginning to get dark when a messenger came from Isiolo with a drug sent out by Ken Smith. But by now Elsa was incapable of swallowing it. I wrote down for Joy what happened that night.

> At about a quarter to two in the morning, Elsa left my tent and went back to the studio . . . she reached the sandbank under the trees where she had so often played with the cubs. Here she lay on the sodden mudbank, evidently in great distress, alternately sitting up and lying down, her breathing more laboured than ever.
>
> I tried to move her back to the dry sand of the studio, but she seemed beyond making any effort. It was a terrible and harrowing sight. It even crossed my mind that I ought to put her out of her misery, but I believed that there was still a chance that you might arrive with a vet in time to help her.
>
> At about 4.30 a.m. I called all the men in the camp. Together we put Elsa on my camp bed and with much difficulty carried her back to my tent. As dawn was breaking, she suddenly got up, walked to the front of the tent and collapsed. I held her head in my lap. A few minutes later she sat up, gave a most heartrending and terrible cry and fell over.
>
> Elsa was dead.

Jespah came up to his mother and licked her face. He seemed frightened, and went to hide under a bush with the others. All three were in a state of distress.

At tea time that day Joy arrived in the camp. Ken Smith had driven two hundred miles to fetch her, and had brought her back in a plane. The extent of her shock may be imagined. We were wholly united in our grief, and also in our gratitude to Ken for his unstinting efforts to help us. He alone, who had been with me on the day I brought Elsa to Joy, four years ago, could realise the depth of our sorrow.

The senior government vet from Isiolo had reached me just after Elsa had died. He performed an autopsy and we buried Elsa together, not far from the Ura. She had been killed by a tick fever which, with anthrax and sleeping sickness, is one of the three diseases that are fatal to lions. We later discovered she might have responded to a treatment of Veronil.

*   *   *

We were now faced with a frightful predicament. We were under notice to take away the cubs. It had been difficult enough to prepare them for the journey before Elsa had died: now it would be next to impossible to get them into a crate or a lorry. Anyway, we still had to find them an alternative home and would have to look after them in the meantime. If Elsa had belonged to a pride another lioness would almost certainly have adopted them, but there was no question of their father taking on the job.

Quite recently I had helped a clever young vet, Toni Harthoorn, experiment in capturing game with tranquillisers shot by bow and arrow. He might have helped solve our problem, but we would never get hold of him in time; and the drugs were still in their infancy, and might not be suitable for lions. We put out food for the cubs, in the hope it would keep them close to the camp, but they were driven away by wild lions and disappeared without trace. We hunted them all day and were so exhausted by night that once we were nearly drowned in our sleep when a flash flood swept down the lugga where we were camping.

Joy thought the cubs might have joined up with a pride after all until we got a message which made my heart sink. Herdsmen over the river had found three young lions attacking their goats and sheep, and driven them off with arrows and spears. One of the lions had been hit. I hurried to the village, and sat up over the carcase of a goat. It was not long before the cubs, who looked starving, succumbed to temptation – when they turned up, Jespah was carrying an arrowhead in his rump. He had been cornered, but had successfully dodged a volley of poisoned arrows. The only one to find its mark had been fired by a child, too young to be entrusted with poison.

We now had a desperate race against time to save the cubs' lives. The unlucky herdsmen obviously wanted revenge and the papers carried a rumour that the new Chief Game Warden had ordered them all to be shot. I built three traps, with drop doors, controlled by ropes which led to my Landrover. For several nights on end I baited the cages, sitting up without sleep and praying the cubs would fall for the lure, each going in to a separate trap. We put small blocks below the gates so that no damage would be done to a tail. Joy was asleep when I finally slashed the ropes and the doors came down. She was woken by the crash and lay still in the deathly silence which followed. Then all hell broke loose as the cubs fought to get out of their prisons and we attempted to calm them.

*　　*　　*

One of the authorities with whom I had been in touch before Christmas was John Owen, Director of National Parks in Tanganyika. His responsibilities included the Serengeti Reserve on the far side of the Mara. As soon as he had heard of our plight he came to our rescue and invited us to bring down the cubs.

The six hundred mile journey was a nightmare. We dared not risk it in the heat of the day, and the cold at night was excruciating, the road was appalling and rain fell in torrents. The lorries skidded and lurched over the ruts; the cubs were rubbed raw, and wretched. A sympathetic vet examined Jespah's arrowhead on the way but he was too restless to take an anaesthetic, and we dared not hold up the journey for long. Assured that the wound was not septic, and that the arrow would soon be rejected, we pressed on.

John received us at Seronera and gave us a heart-warming welcome. He led us to a valley which was ideal, with its shelter of bushes and trees – and even a stream – for the cubs. Thomson's gazelles and an impala ram were quietly grazing nearby. For the first few days we might shoot game for the cubs, and sleep in our trucks near the valley. Their reunion, when we put them in one large cage together, was enormously touching. Their bodies were battered and bruised, but their spirit unbroken.

The Serengeti was probably the greatest of all the game reserves in Africa. It had recovered from the decimation of the lions by hunters in the thirties, and from the unnecessary slaughter of game during the war, and owed its renaissance to three men.

The first was Monty Moore, who held the Victoria Cross, and the second John Owen, who had thrown himself into its protection by making the world aware of the unparalleled richness of game to be found there. He had also established a scientific research centre, in its heart, which was soon to be responsible for some of the most important work on animal behaviour in the next twenty years – including George Schaller's masterly study of lions.

The third great guardian of the Serengeti was Bernhardt Grzimek, Director of the Frankfurt Zoo. He had realised that failure to resolve the conflict between the Maasai's herds and the game was pushing the greatest congregation and migration of animals on earth towards the brink of destruction. To prove his case, and discover a solution, he had to have facts. At the age of forty-eight he and his son Michael taught themselves to fly. Together, from the air, they counted every single wildebeest, zebra, antelope, elephant, lion, rhinoceros and ostrich that was visible. On the ground they listed the plants, sampled the soil and studied the pastoral needs of the Maasai. Everything they saw was photographed and filmed. On the last day of this unique study Michael's small plane collided with a vulture and he was killed in the crash. He was buried just outside the Park on the lip of the Ngorongoro crater.

When we finally opened the door of the big cage on to these great hunting grounds, Gopa was the first to move off into the valley. Jespah stayed for a moment beside Little Elsa, and then he too made for the river, looking over his shoulder as if inviting his sister to join them. Quite soon the three young lions were lost in the reeds.

For several days we kept in touch with the cubs as they explored this immense new world. They would come to our trucks for meat, and for the milk and cod liver oil – they had developed a taste for it – we always put out in an old tin helmet. But one night they did not turn up.

Our searches each day were a failure and our allowance of time began to run short. In the evenings we sat and talked over the extraordinary twists in the saga of Elsa which had finally led us to the glorious world of the Serengeti. Joy knew how much its survival depended on the work of Grzimek, who raised vast sums through his appeals in Germany, by his best-selling book *Serengeti Shall Not Die* and from his own films, which had appealed to enormous audiences and also won an Oscar. I think all this planted a seed in her mind, but when we discussed what Joy would say if someone offered to make a film of *Born Free* she said she would refuse: she did not believe it could be done without falsifying the story. Almost anything else she would do for the sake of her Appeal to help conservation in Kenya.

We searched for the cubs day after day without a glimpse of them. Unless we could discover their new home, we would not be able to bring out a vet to extract the arrowhead from Jespah's rump. As a special concession John Owen allowed us to remain till the end of July and to sleep out in our cars for yet another week. We were finally rewarded. A few hours before leaving we did find the cubs, and saw Little Elsa, Jespah and Gopa for the last time together. Jespah stood while Joy patted him, and even worked at the arrowhead, but it was still too firmly embedded to come out.

Once more we asked to stay on, but this time our request was refused.

The cubs were eighteen months old, they had survived for two months, and now they would be taking their chance on their own.

*   *   *

Most conveniently, just at this moment in September 1961, I retired after twenty-three years in the Game Department. Ken Smith took over from me in the Northern Frontier, and I was free to go down to the Serengeti, camp there and search for the cubs, with the rights of an ordinary visitor. I had managed to accumulate 928 days overdue leave to my credit!

A year later, in 1962, I found Little Elsa and saw her seven times in a fortnight, before she disappeared again: she would jump in and out of a tree to have a look at me and came right up to the car. Just then Joy was in England on a lecture tour and promoting her third book, about Elsa's death and the cubs, which she called *Forever Free*. She talked to packed houses, and showed them our own little film about Elsa and the cubs. Elspeth Huxley said this tour was Joy's bravest achievement. Her accent was only marginally improved by an elocutionist, who sat in the front row and waved a red flat when she got carried away. On the first night she was literally sick.

The next year, in July 1963, when he would have been three and a half years old, Joy and I saw a lion with a scar on his haunch that could well have been Jespah. It was getting dark, and he was gone the next day, so we could never be certain.

In September Joy and I said goodbye before a long separation. She was off on a lecture tour to South Africa, India, Singapore and Australia. She was so exhausted by the time she got to New Zealand that she had to be carried into the country on a stretcher. She was to spend a few days at Christmas in Fiji and Honolulu, and then lecture for another six months in America. Apparently she was so stressed, and distressed, by talking continuously about Elsa, who was as close to her heart as a daughter, that psychiatrists, seeing her physical tension when she lectured, could not understand how she was surviving the strain: while talking she stood as if she were locked rigid.

The hazards of lecturing were worlds away from the hazards of the Serengeti where we had crashed into unseen holes, frequently broken down and been bogged in the worst of the floods. Twice we had witnessed the stupendous migrations that Bernhardt and Michael Grzimek had done so much to protect. We had moved among the hundreds of thousands of zebra and wildebeests, barking, grunting, and bellowing for mile after mile, as they started their annual trek towards Lake Victoria.

We had seen more than five hundred lions, of all ages, in prides and alone, by day and at night. We had observed their mating in our presence or with lions lying near, when we had thought they required seclusion and privacy. One pair coupled close to my camp, every twenty minutes for five days on end – and were continuing when I left them. For a week I was kept awake by lions and a hyena attacking our stores. When the hyena persisted in stealing our tins, puncturing them with its teeth, and sucking out the condensed milk, I baited a rat-trap with bacon. The nip on its nose taught it a lesson it evidently didn't forget. Joy had once woken to find a lion, with a splendid mane, standing in her tent. On another night she realised that the strange noise which had disturbed her was a lioness drinking from the bowl by her bed.

Some Kenyan farmers came and slept near Joy for a few nights, without tents, and laughed at her when she said she thought it was unwise. A week or two later we were aroused by the sound of a car before dawn; it was the warden who had come to ask us if we could lend him some morphia. A newly arrived party of three men had gone to sleep with their heads in the mouth of their tent a quarter of a mile away. One of them had just been taken by a lion, and although his friends, and two courageous African servants, had quickly driven it away, it was unlikely the man would live. I went to check the spoor, and found the tracks of two males who were hunted, and shot, by the warden. Their victim did not recover.

When Joy set off on long journeys alone, I would sometimes accompany her on the first leg to Nairobi over the worst part of the road to the Ngorongoro Crater. Driving back one night, past the rim of the crater where Michael Grzimek lay buried, I saw a magnificent lion sitting beside his grave. I was moved by this unconscious tribute to the young man who had lost his life in preserving the treasures of the Serengeti.

Late one afternoon in December 1963, I had to drive back to my camp through such heavy rain that I could see only a few yards ahead. Suddenly a lioness got up almost in front of the car. I stared, and stopped, and stared again, for I was sure it was Little Elsa, now four years old. There was an older lioness, and a young lion, behind. I knew for certain it was her when I saw her several times during the next three days. Then there was a radical improvement in the weather and I never saw her, or her brothers, again. However much we would have liked to see Elsa's grandchildren, I knew that in a place like the Serengeti it would have been almost impossible.

Over the border in Kenya the political climate, too, had radically altered. Harold Macmillan, the British Prime Minister, had blessed the winds of change on the African continent. To Kenya he had sent, as its last Governor, a man ideal for the moment, Malcolm MacDonald, the son of a socialist

Prime Minister. A lover and photographer of birds and wild animals, he later lent us his invaluable support. Now he had a more important task. He stood beside Prince Philip, twelve years after his wife became Queen during their visit to Kenya, when the prince formally handed over the country to its first President, Jomo Kenyatta.

Henceforth this lovely place – my home for forty years – its mountains, forests and rivers, its animals and birds, would once more be in the hands of the people who had lived here for centuries. I was happy to think that Elsa's earnings would help to support them, but it was unlikely they would require the services of a retired outsider like me. If I wanted employment I would have to look to neighbouring African countries or conceivably India, where I could perhaps start all over again with some tigers. I was just wondering where I should go when a letter arrived from Joy.

She said she had changed her mind about a film of *Born Free*. She had received an offer she felt she shouldn't turn down and, if I would agree to advise the film company on how to handle its lions, she proposed to accept on the condition it was shot in Kenya. It did not take me long to make up my mind.

Chapter 6

On Playing With Lions
1964–1965

When the filming of *Born Free* was finished, but before it was shown to the public, the producer, Carl Foreman, invited Joy to visit his office in London. "Joy, darling," he said, "two of the greatest mistakes of my life have been to get involved with this film, and to allow you on to the location."

She came back to Kenya a few days later still spitting with rage. Her fury was not caused by Carl's use of "darling" to embellish the twin blades of his dagger – in fact it amused her. She was only mildly irritated by the suggestion that she had abused her right to appear on location as she knew she had behaved impeccably: I had never seen her show such perfect restraint in the face of provocation. What made her really angry was the implication that after all the money, effort, skill, imagination and courage that had gone into the film it might prove a failure.

Such a lack of confidence came oddly from Carl Foreman. Without him there would not have been a penny to make such an impossible movie. But he had fallen for the story and saw, in the phenomenal sales of the book, good omens for the success of a film. His stock in the film world was high, with box office hits like *High Noon, Bridge on the River Kwai* and *The Guns of Navarone* to his credit. He persuaded Columbia to put up most of the million dollars he needed, carried the project into production and in moments of crisis held the wavering ship to its course. He was clear headed, decisive and ruthless.

Joy was a woman of equal resolve, but she was also a romantic – a dreamer of dreams. If her more ambitious ones frequently came true she usually deserved it, as reward for the willpower and energy she committed to them. After the success of the book she was determined the film, too, would break records. By comparison I have lived with my feet on the earth. The only time in my life I have entered a world of make-believe was when I agreed to help with the film. In a way I could not have foreseen it altered the course of my life.

In April 1964 I drove my old Landrover up through dripping coffee plantations to the farm at Naro Moru where the film was to be shot. It was on the plains below the peaks of Mt Kenya, a country far greener and softer than the dry bush where Elsa had lived, but was chosen with care for its purpose. The farmhouse, on its 750 acres, stood at the heart of the fantasy world we were to live in for the best part of a year.

Already the house was being extended, and surrounded by a village of huts. There would be forty Europeans and a hundred and twenty Africans making the film. They needed a laboratory, a cutting room, stores and a number of garages. There were cages for two lions and a hyrax, and opening on to the compounds a preposterous version of our house at Isiolo (which was quickly replaced). One look was enough to decide that the safest place for Joy and me would be in tents, near the lions.

The director, Tom McGowan, was proud of his lions, as he must have been proud of his ingenuity in initiating the enterprise in the first place. If Carl Foreman was the wizard who had produced the money, Tom was the magician who had conjured up everything else. To begin with, and much to my surprise, he had persuaded Joy to part with her film rights. He had worked with Walt Disney, not on his embarrassing cartoons about wild deer with long eyelashes, but on some excellent wildlife documentaries. He promised the film would be true to the book and he would show Joy the script in advance so she could check it. He paid a fair price for the rights and guaranteed a generous share of the profits. While I was to help with the lions, Joy was to be allowed on the set to make certain the animals were properly treated.

Having sailed over the hurdle of Joy's stringent conditions in selling the rights, Tom next turned to the question of lions. He travelled round the zoos and circuses of Europe and returned with an address book bulging with candidates. When he persuaded two stars, Virginia McKenna and her husband Bill Travers, to take on our parts – over tea at the Mayfair Hotel in London – he told them he had found lions "all over the place, as friendly as dogs". They must have believed him for they agreed to appear in the film although Virginia had read only half the book in the hairdresser, earlier that afternoon.

The first thing I did, when my tent had gone up, was to have a good look at the two lionesses brought over from Germany to impersonate Elsa. These middle-aged ladies called Astra and Djuba were scarred and massively heavy and I thought had a malevolent look in their eyes. They came from a circus and were under the care of two trainers, one of them called Monika, an attractive and intelligent girl with a shock of dark hair. As she never went in to the lions without pointed sticks in her hands and a man with a loaded rifle standing by, and as she never once turned her back to them, I wondered what Miss McKenna would make of some of the tenderer scenes between

Elsa and Joy. The scriptwriter had been liberal in his use of "affectionate embraces". When I asked McGowan how he himself got along with these companionable creatures the look which he gave me said a great deal more than his mumbled "just great".

I shall always remember the day I first set eyes on Virginia and Bill. I had just finished giving Monika one of her lessons in driving the Landrover. On this particular day we were standing on the grass outside Astra's cage and Monika was describing her technique for guiding and warning the lions with her sticks, and for rewarding their efforts.

As Bill and Virginia walked up my concentration was divided. I was naturally curious to size up this enormous young man who was to take over my life, as it were. At the same time I could not take my eyes off Virginia; I was enchanted by her beauty and wonderful smile. Many thoughts rushed through my head as we exchanged the cards of politeness. How on earth would this very tall man get inside my modest figure, and what would he do with me? Even more disconcerting: what havoc would the rigours of Africa, and Djuba, play with this lovely, fair-skinned and delicate girl? I knew that Joy would be thrilled by her appearance but worried to death by her fragility. I wished Joy were here to help her, but she was on the other side of the world at the time promoting her books and her Appeal.

"I really don't know anything at all about lions," said Bill apologetically, when we got on to the subject. "I've ridden a horse and we have got a couple of dogs in England. In Malaya and Burma I had to sleep out in the war, but we didn't get very close to the elephants and I'm glad the tigers kept out of the way. Ginny, you had a lot of animals at home, didn't you?" Ginny smiled. "They were my father's, really. We had four dogs, two cats, four budgerigars, two bush babies, a parrot – and a snake called, er, George. Forgive me." She went on to relate McGowan's belief in the friendliness of lions and we looked at Astra and Djuba in silence.

Some time after this she told me how her heart was thumping and her mouth had gone dry at this moment. She was thankful that she was playing this dangerous game with a husband, and that at the end of each day they would be going back to a house with their three young children. It was wise to keep the children at a distance, for whatever the respect for grown-ups a lion may develop it will always treat a child as legitimate prey or a plaything.

The film company had chosen Naro Moru as their base for a number of reasons. The least significant was its spectacular view of Mt Kenya; the most important was its reputation for a reliable climate. In a country which has two rainy seasons each year, and with a film that is costing ten thousand pounds a day, you don't want to waste time in the dry seasons sitting indoors, waiting for the rain to stop or the clouds to blow away. Another reason was the supposedly excellent communication with Nairobi, 120 miles to the south, from which would have to come all our food, drink, photographic supplies, reinforcements of lions, sealing wax, string and, of course, visitors from America and England.

Finally the farm was chosen for its amenities and proximity to Nanyuki and places like the Mt Kenya Safari Club. This club represented the apex of luxury with its lake, swimming pool, tennis courts, restaurants and boutiques. On its acres of emerald lawn strutted sacred ibis, crowned cranes, egrets, flamingoes and peacocks. Joy and I preferred the nearby Nanyuki Sports Club. It looked like a shabby and overgrown cricket pavilion whose decoration inside had not been touched since the thirties. There the menu included delicacies like lamb chops and trifle. Its acres of grass were brown, and were occasionally graced by a lonely polo pony or a homesick Scotsman swinging his mashie.

As filming approached Tom McGowan thumbed through his Almanac de Gotha of the lions of the world to find some suitable cubs and one or two males. The Marchese and Marchesa Bisletti, who lived on Lake Naivasha, bred lions on their ranch and said they could provide the baby Elsa and her sisters. Failing them the Emperor Haile Selassie, the Lion of Judah himself, was prepared to hire Tom cubs from the royal menagerie. Tom was worried that these aristocratic animals would be snapped up by the Marquis of Bath, who was about to stock his park at Longleat in England with lions, and hired most of them immediately.

The first new recruits to arrive were lent to us by the Scots Guards, who had been stationed in Kenya and were now returning to England. Their mascots were two nine-month old lions, Boy and Girl, who were brother and sister; they were destined for Whipsnade when the film was finished. Their guardian and mentor was a tough-looking sergeant, called Ronald Ryves, whose military manner relaxed whenever he handled the lions. From the moment I saw them together I felt a glimmer of hope that the film might get finished, and finished without a disaster – for we had reached an impasse with Astra and Djuba.

Bill was the first actor to go in with them. He followed Monika, with a stick and leather guards on his wrists, for a lion can extend or withdraw its claws at will and none of us cared to take a chance on these lionesses' intentions. Astra, then Djuba, allowed Bill to pat them on the rump, and half an hour later he strolled out apparently as relaxed as when he had gone in, even though it was his first encounter. But I did notice that he lit up a cigarette as soon as he sat down on the grass.

After lunch it was Ginny's turn. I stood outside the compound, as I was paid to, with my loaded rifle, and watched every expression crossing her face. I saw concentration, willpower, surprise and relief, but not a flicker of fear. As there was nothing affectionate about the two lions, and they each weighed well over 300 lb, I thought she must be exceptionally brave or a very good actress. Later, when she came out of the pen, she asked for a cup of tea to help her stop trembling, and I knew she was both.

For a month all seemed to go well. Bill and Ginny both had the courage and natural approach to the lions which were the only two qualities that would obtain a convincing performance. An experienced lion handler, who saw them in training, could scarcely believe they had not been working with lions all their lives.

One morning Bill went into the compound with Monika, and Ginny and I watched Astra suddenly lay back her ears, drop to a crouch and then advance, her yellow eyes narrowed to slits, glinting hard and bright. Time and again she circled, trying to get at Bill. Monika fended her off with her sticks. Both she and Bill had gone deathly white. I was almost as thankful as Ginny when, at last, Bill got out of the gate.

Two days later Tom came down to the compound to see how training was going and Astra behaved in the same way. This time Monika had both Bill and Ginny inside, and Astra became so menacing that I had to join them before everyone got out of the enclosure. I hoped then that Tom would put an immediate end to Astra's career as an actress.

For no reason we could understand she seemed to grow increasingly hostile. Fundamentally it was the fault of her training. Unless a lion has a steady flow of affection, preferably from a single trainer or owner, it can turn ugly. Once it has been dominated, perhaps controlled by the fear of a whip, and handed from trainer to trainer, it is bound to become unreliable. In fact, as I have learned at great cost through the years, it might be truer to say that no lion is entirely reliable. But are many human beings either?

Djuba, too, grew surlier. After a couple of months she produced four tiny cubs, but the conditions were far from ideal and within two days they all died. Her temperament never recovered. But Tom and the film company who had invested a lot of money in Djuba and Astra persisted in trying to use them.

Personally, I pinned my faith on the Scots Guards mascots and the Travers. It is a golden rule that the best hope of transferring a lion's affection from one person to another is by way of a careful introduction. Sergeant Ryves was an exceptional man and I let him and Bill work out, together with Ginny, how the handover should go.

As two old soldiers the sergeant and Bill struck up a rapport at once. Bill had served in the Gurkhas – having fudged his age to see action quicker –

and had led one of Wingate's recce groups, pushing ahead of the main column through the forests of Burma. After a couple of weeks, during which Ryves had slept in a tent with the lions, to settle them in, the transference was successfully completed. Ronald Ryves was too moved to say a proper goodbye.

"It's all over to you now, Bill; I won't be coming on any more walks," he said over his shoulder one evening. "And you buggers had better behave yourselves" – to the lions, disregarding Girl's gender and feelings.

By now Bill and Ginny had read all of Joy's books about Elsa and her cubs, and had been specially struck by Julian Huxley's introduction to *Living Free* in which he stressed the importance of love in bringing out an animal's finest potential. The Travers had made it a condition of their contract that no one should double for them in any of the scenes, for they realised that unless they could develop the same kind of relationship with the lions in the film that we had with Elsa, the movie could never succeed.

With the daylight so short, and the schedule so tight, they had to get up in the dark to train with the lions before breakfast. Their breaks and even some of their meals they took with the lions: and at the end of the day would sit in the compounds until they went home to the children.

The three of us would talk about the characters of new lions whenever they arrived, for the film covered Elsa at various ages and also her cubs, her sisters, her rivals, her suitors, and her mate. By the end we had to use twenty-four lions. It was an amazing opportunity to see how varied their characters were, and how differently some would need handling.

Among the smallest to arrive was the one we called Little Elsa, after her namesake. She was probably the most affectionate lion on the set and Ginny's favourite. Her growing up coincided with the growing up of "Elsa", as we filmed, and she was used for many of the linking shots.

Henrietta, from Uganda, was beautiful and a clown. She arrived like a skeleton and was jumpy with nerves. Tom McGowan tried to dismiss her at once. But after a few weeks' careful feeding and affection I was able to introduce her safely to Ginny and Bill. She became everyone's darling even though the Africans all called her Memsahib Makofe – Mrs Clout – as her delight was to sit on the roof of the Landrover and dish out a cuff to whoever went by. She loved to ride there when the Landrover was moving.

I often had to go to undignified lengths to persuade Henrietta to play the simplest scenes, like running from left to right across the set, or simply sitting still in the sun to await "Joy's" return to the house. To achieve the former I only had to lie flat on the ground, out of sight of the camera, to induce Henrietta to rush over and rough up my prostrate form. To dissuade her from leaving her seat in the sun for a place in the shade I had to sit in

Opposite: Action cameras! To get the lions moving fast in the heat of the day was impossible until I lay flat on the ground, when they rushed at me only too swiftly.

a small pit, covered with artificial grass, through which I shoved, and twiddled, a shaving brush to attract and hold her attention.

Henrietta had only one drawback, which made continuity difficult – she had a floppy ear. But we usually got the angle right so that if another lion flunked any scene we could always bribe Henrietta to finish it off, as she had a passion for Skipper sardines (no other would do), hard-boiled eggs and tinned cream.

The ideal likeness for Elsa was a lioness called Mara. She had been privately raised, was now fully grown and arrived with glowing testimonials. But when Ginny went in with her on her first day she had a bit of a shock. Mara had spent a few weeks at the orphanage and had felt terribly deprived of human company. She gave Ginny an enormous embrace and started to groom her with her very pink tongue. When Ginny looked down its rasp had removed the whole of the front of her jersey.

When we took a football out of her compound Mara grew threatening and I discovered that when she was young she had been given toys of her "own". I warned Bill to be careful. The next day he tried his luck and to my alarm Mara rose up on her hind legs, embracing him with her forepaws. She was purring and licking his face (thank God for his beard) but also flexing her claws. Try as he would Bill could not get to the gate, as her pet sack was lying in front of it and she would not risk Bill pinching it. Seeing the anguish on Ginny's face I arranged for a ladder to be let down near Bill, and he managed to climb it while we distracted Mara with the lure of some meat.

As I was determined to get Mara over her dangerous possessiveness I began to sleep by the wire of the cage, and when she began to relax took the camp bed inside for the night. In the end she produced some of the loveliest scenes in the film.

There is no doubt that the most spectacular lion on the farm was Ugas. His name meant Prince and he was as impressive as he was enormous. His mother had been killed by Somalis and he was looked after by a policeman in Wajir until he was nine months old; then he was given to Steven Ellis, the warden in charge of the Nairobi Park. As he had free run of Steve's house until he was fully grown he was completely at ease with people, believing them to be lions, or vice versa. He had also given numerous visitors the fright of their lives when the object they believed to be a lion skin rug rose nonchalantly to its feet.

Although I knew the story of Ugas' life I still found him formidable. I was therefore extremely impressed that when the time came for me to introduce him, Bill wandered up to Ugas without turning a hair. But if you have slipped through the Japanese lines in disguise, while suffering from bouts of malaria, and have harassed the spearhead of their troops in the jungle, perhaps a lion seems a little less daunting. Nevertheless, Ugas, who was now fully grown, weighed more than 400 lb, caused the springs of the Landrover to sink with a groan and gave the director palpitations when he playfully took the head of Mireille – a newly joined trainer – in his jaws.

Even if Tom McGowan and his friends had no faith in the African lions, Bill and Ginny never lost theirs. More than that, they derived obvious delight from the exuberant pleasure Boy and Girl showed on their walks in the mornings. One of the reasons that lions so often grow dangerous in cages is boredom. I noticed how all the lions in the film came to life as soon as they were free and could pick up a scent: they got as much satisfacton from smells as readers do from books.

There was very little advice I needed to give to Bill and Ginny: never stare at a lion; do not raise your voice; move slowly; and in moments of tension stand still and hold your ground – if you value your life don't turn your back and retreat. The Travers seemed to pick up the skills they needed by instinct and quiet observation.

Apart from this, nothing else went right for the director. The location, in the lee of Mt Kenya, was less perfect than predicted; the weather was appalling. This led to the prospect of the already expensive schedule slipping back whenever it rained or a cloudy afternoon wrecked the continuity of an outdoor scene begun on a sunny morning. Communications broke down. The tracks to the different film sites became quagmires. The roads to the nearest town, to the fleshpots of the Mt Kenya Safari Club, and to Nairobi itself, were often awash.

I didn't often go into the bar at the farmhouse, but when I did it was like going into the mess of a disgruntled regiment. There were complaints of leaking roofs, deteriorating food, no entertainment to while away the long wet hours of waiting. A rift was growing in the company between those who still maintained the circus lions were capable of taking the leading role and those who saw that salvation lay with the African lions. The director was caught in the crossfire.

At this moment an event occurred which I thought would deal a death-blow to the whole enterprise. One afternoon, not long before the first day's filming was due to start, Bill and Ginny took Boy and Girl out for a walk on the plains. They seemed more excited than usual, when they leapt from the Landrover, and Bill realised they had spotted a group of Thomsons's gazelles. Bill and Ginny watched as the young lions went into the motions of a serious, creeping, stalk. The unruffled gazelles grazed on, keeping their distance.

After a bit Boy and Girl looked round reproachfully at the human

spectators sabotaging their efforts. With concerted grunting, pawing and nudging they persuaded Bill and Ginny to drop to all fours and join in. But after half an hour they were getting no closer to their prey, and Ginny, who was beginning to ache, stood up. In a flash of frustration Boy pounced on her. Together they crashed to the ground and Bill heard Ginny's leg crack, like a dry stick breaking.

Both Bill and Girl ran over and the chilling minutes which followed seemed to stretch to eternity. This had become a game for the lions once more but Bill had to get them off Ginny, and safely into the Landrover, to prevent an even more serious accident.

It took all his courage, strength and ingenuity to entice them away by trailing his shirt, and then to make them stay put, with the remains of some titbits. Slowly and tenderly he lifted Ginny up and into the car for the painful journey to camp and the much longer one down to hospital in Nairobi.

*   *   *

Just at this precarious moment Joy arrived at Naro Moru after the most exhausting of all her world tours. She took one look at the rooms in the huts and the farmhouse and decided to pitch a tent beside mine.

Her role specifically excluded her from any involvement with the perform-ance of the actors or the lions; she was here simply to verify the well-being of the animals. She was, of course, fascinated by the lions and she was touched by the hyraxes brought in to play the role of Pati Pati, who had acted as nanny to Elsa and her sisters. The more alert hyrax, which had spent hours on Ginny's shoulder, nibbling rose petals, in preparation for her scenes, had begun to languish in her absence, but could still be cajoled into life with a quick swig of gin – which was just as well as a fondness for the bottle was written into her part.

Apart from this there were now two cheetahs in the company, with whom Joy spent some time, as she was hoping to adopt one herself; there was a pair of warthogs required to play in an important early scene – one of them was splendidly perky: and there was a buffalo which seemed very out of place and lonely on its own, unlike a young elephant called Eleanor who was relaxed and playful. It was going to be Eleanor's job to be chased by "Elsa". The little orphan elephant had been brought up by Daphne Sheldrick, the wife of David, warden of Tsavo Park, famous for its eleph-ants.

The poor buffalo was at the centre of the most unpleasant and short-lived drama of the movie. It had been acquired to make one of those terrifying

Opposite above: The film company were taking no chances with most of the unit, who stayed in their cages. The actors, trainers and lions were "free" to mix outside or inside the wire. *Opposite below:* Ugas was normally very good-natured, but took an instant dislike to one of the trainers and showed it.

charges for which buffaloes are justly notorious – but it had been badly miscast. Like Ferdinand the bull it preferred sniffing flowers, and the young Samburu herdsman employed to look after it always slept in its pen.

As the moment for filming the charge grew closer the producers in the field grew desperate. One day Bill and Ginny brought me a message from Tina, the dresser, who had a heart of gold, to say that in order to drive the buffalo into a frenzy the company was squirting Harpic up its arse. I was so outraged that I burst into the production office and told them that unless they desisted at once I would call a press conference, give the reasons and dissociate myself from the film entirely.

The first response was red-faced, gobbling and defensive. The second was to shoot the buffalo, in the hope of quickly and quietly removing the cause of offence. Unfortunately for the company, Bill and Ginny, who were much upset by this irrational solution, had picked a white arum lily, growing by a stream, and placed it on the buffalo's corpse. It caused quite a stir.

The film executives were livid. They told the Travers they were going to phone their agents in London and institute legal proceedings for this act of defiance. "Go ahead," said Bill. "As soon as you do that I shall ring up the *Express*, the *Mail* and the *Mirror* and offer them the photographs I have taken of the whole episode."

Luckily Joy was away when all this took place. She always observed scrupulously her undertaking not to interfere in the performance and refused to drag anyone else into a great fight she was having with Carl Foreman and Tom, who wanted to give the film a happier, and totally artificial, ending by having "Joy" scoop up "Elsa's" cubs in her arms, when they made their first appearance. It was a crass and quite unnecessary perversion of the true story, and was directly opposed to Joy's philosophy of interfering as little as possible in Elsa's free life.

*   *   *

No one would have been surprised if Ginny had refused to come back to play in a film with a cast of unpredictable lions, who could only be restrained from violence with a bullet. But one of her previous films, *Carve Her Name with Pride*, had been about Violette Szabo, a heroine and martyr of wartime resistance, and perhaps something of Violette's dedication now fortified her own ice-cool courage, which I had so often seen put to the test by the lions. Perhaps, too, the fact that she was playing with her husband, on whose love, courage and support she could utterly rely, made it less difficult to return – and save the film from crisis even before shooting had started.

Boy and Girl were as thrilled as everyone else to see her back. Girl leapt on the roof of her car as she drove up, and Boy thrust his head through the window and licked her face. But the next day, in the compounds, the lions shied off the strange white plaster leg she now disported, Boy ran off with her crutches, and Ugas rushed backwards and forwards in what was clearly bewildered distaste. In a few days the wardrobe mistress cleverly adapted Ginny's safari trousers and boots to hide the plaster, and filming could begin.

Carl Foreman was fully aware of the two factions which had grown up over the circus lions. He had also rumbled the sinking morale and lack of confidence in anyone's ability to restore it. He therefore flew out and, in a few days at the Mt Kenya Safari Club, laid down clear guidelines that would settle the circus issue once and for all. Like an able commander he brought all the grievances to the surface, resolved the legitimate ones and disarmed the rest with ridicule, reason or charm. He met Joy's furious opposition to the proposed ending by insisting that the scene should be shot both ways and the matter decided when the film was finally edited. While Carl was in Kenya, the High Commissioner, Malcolm MacDonald, arranged for him, Joy and the Travers to be received by President Kenyatta at the State House in which he had lived himself as Governor General. He showed Joy how he had lined the walls with her tribal paintings which Jomo Kenyatta had left in place when he had become President; they are still there today. His missions accomplished, Carl flew back to England to plan a new film, *The Young Churchill*.

The circus lions, Astra and Djuba, were to be given an immediate chance to prove themselves in front of the cameras. Astra's scene was the one in which Elsa made her first kill — a warthog.

Tom McGowan chose the bouncier of the two pigs in the compound, and it gave a memorable performance. At first it was intimidated by the sheer size of Astra, but after a little it became curious, and then cross. It turned and butted Astra in a series of counter attacks, until the old lioness retreated in dudgeon. The scene was kept in the film, and the warthog awarded its freedom. It was Mara who provided the kill in the end, just as it was Mara who had to take over a tree scene from Astra. Astra fell out of the branches within a few minutes, and refused a second attempt.

Djuba was so uncooperative that she only appeared in the scene where I have to shoot Elsa's mother — she played the corpse. Her cubs, Elsa and her sisters, were played by three tiny lions flown in the day before from Haile Selassie's royal collection in Addis Ababa. I think this was the point when the African lions won the day. Tom McGowan took a deep breath and decided to make a film in a way that had never been attempted before.

He had my sympathy. We knew that our lions would perform naturally with Bill and Ginny in some situations, but we could not guarantee even the simplest shots first time off. If "Elsa" was meant to sit like a sphinx on the Landrover roof, in an African village, she would be down and after a chicken, not once but two or three times, as the camera was turning. It was fun for the lion and the spectators, but hell for the director and the chickens.

Little Elsa, who played most of the simpler scenes with Ginny, had to be endlessly and ingeniously coaxed merely to sit, to walk or to run. But she rose to the occasion when she had to romp with the hyrax, or alert "Joy" to a spitting cobra.

Girl and Henrietta alternated through several difficult sequences. Girl simply couldn't see the point of chasing Eleanor, the elephant, out of the bush and into the camp. On the other hand, Henrietta, who was fond of a game, could not resist teasing Eleanor, and tripping her up, which she did, in front of the cameras, six times. The lionesses' roles were reversed when it came to a scene in my bedroom, played under the arc lights. The glare was so strong that even Skipper sardines would not lure Henrietta in. We therefore left her outside in the cold of the night while I went to sleep. The stratagem worked, and after a bit Henrietta burst in and, before she could jump on me, spotted a blue jerry under the bed, which she slid round the floor till she dropped from exhaustion. This went on each night until a week later Bill took my place. In the final version Girl completed the scene by nipping Bill's bottom, on which someone had thoughtfully smeared some of her favourite bone marrow.

Another bedroom scene ended less amusingly. Elsa was supposed to flop down beside me and go to sleep, while Joy wiped my brow, fevered with malaria. By now the director was getting impatient with so many retakes and gave Girl a sedative to make sure she dropped off at once. Instead, it left her confused, and she took hold of Bill's arm in her mouth, as if she had no idea who he was. It was a horrible moment. Although a vet was always available during filming, and constantly consulted, much less was then known about animal drugs and there were several unhappy incidents. It was extremely distressing for Ginny to have to play the death of Pati Pati with a hyrax which was actually dying. The dose of the drug was excessive and the poor little animal died in her arms as the cameras were turning.

We therefore always tried to tackle our problems with natural solutions. For instance, the lions were nearly always too frisky to go straight on the set in the mornings, so we would give them a romp on the plains before shooting and exercise them with footballs, with coconuts tied on to sticks and, most successfully of all, with highly coloured balloons that floated away on the wind, and burst with a satisfying pop. It was as unwise to walk the lions too long as it was to start them off too fresh. At the end of a very long day Mara, like an overtired child, flung all 300 lb of herself at Bill and dislocated his shoulder.

Mood was another important element which the company was loath to take into account with all the other delays. Towards the end of the filming Ginny had to play a long and loving embrace with the lioness she knew best – Girl. But she sensed something was wrong. She was uneasy herself, the day was cloudy and cooler, the scene was set under a tree with its mysterious rustle and swaying, and the noise of a stream was a further distraction. Although it was one of the simplest shots in the film she asked Bill to come and stand by. For the only time in her life Girl turned on Ginny, took her by the arm in her teeth and firmly forced her face down on the ground. Very slowly and quietly Bill and I had to move in to break up the clinch that was no longer loving.

At about this stage in the filming there were a number of new arrivals at Naro Moru and I made several new friends. The first was a cheetah presented to Joy, so she could prepare it for release in the wild. It lived by her tent and from now on came everywhere with us. Joy renamed her Pippa, for the phonetics were easy for calling out loud in the bush. She was a beautiful creature and gave Joy continuous interest and pleasure.

The second was Monty Ruben, whose father Eddie owned the transport company responsible for the receipt and despatch of all the film that we used. Monty had become especially interested in films and had worked on Kessel's *The Lion*, which was shot in Kenya with a Hollywood lion called Zamba. As a publicity stunt Monty had taken him out to the Nairobi Game Park for a photographic session with the African lions. The photographers were late and to fill in the time he walked up to the guards at the gate and said: "This morning I found one of your lions in the streets of Nairobi: it's in the back of my car over there. Would you like to come and let it out?"

To his everlasting regret the guards simply strolled over, took one look at the lion, shook their heads, said "It's not one of ours," and wandered back to their post.

The third was Marchesa Sieuwke Bisletti, with her lioness Sheba, and Sheba's three newly born cubs which had been brought in to play Elsa's cubs for the last scenes. Unfortunately Sheba was upset by her new pen and so many unfamiliar noises and smells. She leapt over her twelve-foot wire after dark, to the alarm of the population on the farm. By now the village of huts had grown almost to a town, as each of the Africans had brought in their families, and the army of technicians had swelled with the multiplication of problems. Some of us reached for our torches, and others went straight to the bar. It was Monika who finally ran Sheba to earth.

This incident was the last of Tom's nightmares. He had reached the end

Above: Mara was a very powerful lioness. Overtired after a long day's filming, she flung her 300 lb at Bill and dislocated his shoulder.

Opposite above: Girl, doped with a tranquilliser, did not seem to recognise Bill, the friend and companion of her morning walks.

Opposite below: "Mood was important. Ginny sensed something was wrong." Girl suddenly grabs her and Bill has to move in fast. Reality, not part of the script.

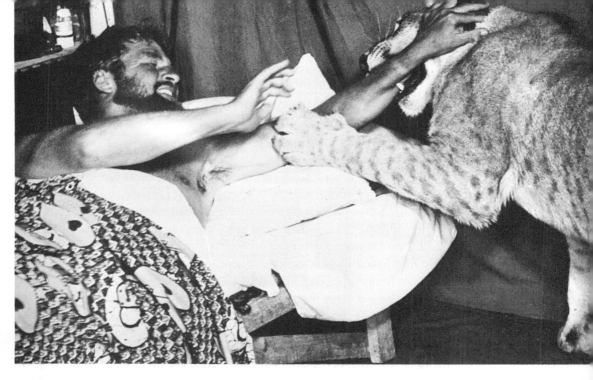

of his contribution to the picture. It had been substantial; he was universally liked for himself, and he was respected as the first begetter of the film whose coils had wound out of his grasp; but his departure brought a sense of relief.

The fourth arrival, James Hill, the new director, won everyone's immediate respect by confessing he knew nothing whatever about lions, except that they were very frightening, and by demonstrating his professional skill as a film maker. Although he directed all the final, and some of the most telling, scenes in the film he arrived just after one which I particularly admired.

Joy and I had once taken Elsa to the idyllic white sands of Watamu, where she had loved to play on the beach and swim in the sea. For the film we now took Mara and Girl down to that beach, but Girl seemed not to recover from the heat of the journey. We thought she was ill until I realised she was missing her brother Boy. The moment we fetched him she once more behaved like a carefree and happy star.

Mara played the shots in the waves and the breakers; Girl took the games and the walks on the sand with Ginny. These were for me some of the loveliest moments in the film.

Everything went perfectly at Watamu until one day Mara spotted a tiny figure in the distance, darting behind a rock. It was Joy, who had brought Pippa down to the coast, whom Mara did not know well, and who had excited her curiosity. She ran up to Joy and gave her an inquisitive pat, but Joy slipped on the coral, Mara's claws came out and Joy had a long laceration, needing a great many stitches. She never blamed Mara, but it reminded us all that playing with lions was not unlike playing with fire.

Probably the two most dramatic scenes in the film are those in which Elsa is challenged and attacked by another lioness, and in which she is courted by the lion whose cubs she finally bears. Astra was given a chance to redeem herself in the fight and gave a splendid performance. She and "Elsa" were each trained to think of the ground on which their confrontation was to take place as their own patch of territory. They were then suddenly released on it simultaneously and their instincts took over. Each instantly flew at the other in a spectacular display of aggression. The fracas did not last long, and we did not need to separate the combatants with the fire hoses we had ready, but it made excellent viewing.

Mara and Ugas were chosen for Elsa's courtship and nuptials. They gave a beautiful and stirring performance. They managed to provide each of the ritual phases – attraction, suspicion, approach, snarling rejection, growling demand, acceptance, domination, and purring, post-coital abandon.

If consummation itself was missing it was probably just as well. When he finally shot the first bedroom scene Tom McGowan insisted on exchanging a waste-paper basket for the blue jerry in the interests of "good taste". There

Girl loved the beach but hated the water – and there were a lot of swimming scenes in the script. Even Virginia McKenna could not persuade her to go in the water.

was no way the company was now going to show the act of procreation!

After nearly a year of our lives the moment had come to film the final scene – in which Elsa brings her six-week-old cubs to meet Joy and me, for the very first time.

TAKE ONE: Sheba and her cubs emerge from the bush. Bill and Ginny respond with delight, and he places his arm round her shoulder, as the lions settle down in the camp.

TAKE TWO: Sheba and her cubs emerge from the bush. Bill and Ginny respond with delight, and she bends to scoop up the cubs in her arms.

"The final decision about which ending we use will be taken in the cutting rooms, in London, by me," Carl Foreman had said.

*   *   *

Ten months before we had set out to use the art of the film to imitate the nature of our past life with Elsa. But the imitation now took over our future.

Bill and Ginny had succeeded against all expectation in reproducing, with the lions in the cast, the kind of relationship Joy and I had had with Elsa. I, too, had made friendships with some of the lions – in the case of Ugas, Boy and Girl as close as with Elsa. Quick in her animal sympathies, despite her special commitment to her cheetah, Joy was as concerned with the future of the lions as the Travers and I.

Just one example of the trust which the lions gave us was an incident out training, when Girl had stalked a gazelle. She suddenly exerted her speed, made her first kill, brought it back and laid it at Ginny's feet. Having developed trust like this, and seen how the lions revelled in freedom and rejoiced in unfettered companionship, it felt like betrayal to let them go back to captivity. Until I began my work on the film I had no idea of the range of lions' personalities – or the individuality of their response to each other and people.

We fought to save as many as we could, but the film company had far exceeded their budget and grimly set out to sell or to auction every vestige of property remaining – knickers, notice boards, lanterns, lorries and lions. Seven of the lions went to the Marquis of Bath at Longleat in England. Four lions went to Detroit Zoo in America; two to Paignton Zoo in England. Henrietta, who had arrived in such poor condition, was summoned back to a world without chickens, lions, elephants, or sardines – the zoo in Uganda thought a film star would bring them reflected glory. Little Elsa, like Mara, was destined for Whipsnade – but Mara's previous owner lived in Kenya and we hoped to persuade her to change her mind. We also hoped to save Ugas from going back to life in the Nairobi Orphanage. We had still heard nothing in reply to a letter we had written to the Scots Guards about Boy and Girl. One by one the lions were slipping through our fingers.

The battle to save at least some of the lions drew Joy, me and the Travers closer and closer together. It was because of this issue that Carl told Joy he wished he had never let her near the filming. To recover her peace of mind Joy took Ginny over to Meru for a few days, to show her the range where Elsa had lived, borne her cubs, and finally died.

The day before Bill and Ginny left they came to say goodbye and touchingly gave us their personal jeep to help us in our work with Pippa and any lions we might save. The parting came as a wrench, and I really had no idea if I would ever see them again. Joy's feelings were so powerful that it's best if they are left to a letter she wrote Ginny and Bill the next day.

> After you left I found it difficult to move, feeling such pain and emptiness inside me. What can I say to describe how I feel? You will know it without my going into superlative thanks.
>
> But you will not know a strange coincidence. When I wrote the words on Elsa's photograph I had an impulse to add "God Bless You" – I hesitated, and then did not write it. But after you had left I read my little guide, *Daily Light*, which has a few quotations from the Bible for each day. There I read: "I will not let thee go, except thou bless me".
>
> So Elsa is there all the time and watches and acts. It seems so pre-destined that you should have become such an integral part of her while filming and bringing her spirit across . . .
>
> How was your flight with the children, and arrival home in the darkened cars? Last night I went out of my tent and saw the moonlight on Mt Kenya. It was glorious and still. I thought of you and wondered if this mountain will hold you as much as it does some of us here?
>
> There is a comic opera counterpoint to the moonlit mountain. F. is trying to catch "her Grace" red-handed, and nightly sneaks round the camp trying to get evidence for a divorce.
>
> We miss you more than you can imagine. It is so strange we could only really be friends in the last few weeks as I had to suppress my feelings for all those ghastly months before. Love, lots and more, and thank you for all you have done.

I quote this letter as it reveals several aspects of Joy's feelings and character. She was amused by gossip and dished out a number of nicknames which tended to stick. She was also a genuine romantic and not merely sentimental, which she could be too. More importantly the letter illuminates two other things.

The first is the gratitude, admiration and growing affection she felt for Ginny and Bill. We both realised that there were probably no other stars in the world who could, or would, have played our roles as they did. If the film was going to succeed, theirs would be the credit.

The second is Joy's conviction that somewhere and somehow "the spirit of Elsa" was at large and directly influencing events in her life and mine, not to mention the animals we subsequently cared for – and indeed others in danger all over the world. Her belief in Elsa's guiding presence armed her with a virtually irresistible resolution for the rest of her life.

Just as Joy and I were beginning to fear that we might, in the end, save none of the lions from captivity we had a letter from the Regimental Sergeant Major of the 2nd Bn. of the Scots Guards, Campbell Graham. He and Sergeant Ryves had thought over the future of Boy and Girl very carefully, and reached this conclusion:

> After considerable discussion with Ryves we have decided to give you our permission to release Boy and Girl. We have been around looking at some of the first class zoos and we are not impressed. We both wish you luck in the enterprise, and hope you will keep us in the picture now and again, up to the time you leave them to themselves.

This was the origin of a wave on which I have been carried ever since. At the time I had no inkling of where the decision might take me, and only had thoughts of finding somewhere to release the two lions, which would also provide a home in the wild for Joy's cheetah.

By a stroke of good luck, an old friend, Ted Goss, had taken over from Larry Wateridge at Meru. He had originally gone there as Game Control Officer, but recently – largely thanks to a generous donation from Joy's Trust – the Meru County Council had felt it was worth their while to declare it a National Reserve. Ted became the first warden of the official Reserve.

Now, in April 1965, I went up to see him and he not only gave me a magnificent welcome but pointed out a very good site for my camp, at the foot of a hill called Mugwongo. As lions and cheetahs don't mix he suggested a separate camp for Joy, about twelve miles away, that was close to a stream, a track and his own headquarters.

When I got back to Naro Moru it was no more than an echoing shell – the film makers fled, the furniture gone, the village of huts almost empty. The last of the lions paced up and down in their compounds, unaware of their fate. I could not bear to say goodbye to funny Henrietta, or my beloved Mara or our principal, Ugas, whom I hoped we might still be able to see in Nairobi, though I didn't fancy the sight of him in a cage.

As we prepared Boy and Girl for their journey to Meru, and Joy gathered together all she would need for Pippa, we wondered if the film would be a towering success or a dreadful fiasco. There was, however, one piece of good news: Carl decided to keep faith with the ending – Elsa's cubs were reprieved from a human embrace.

When the date for the release of the film drew closer, Carl again experienced a renewal of faith. He put his name to a small book about making the movie, in which he seemed to recant his previous despair. For he wrote:

> Making *Born Free* was certainly the greatest adventure of my own experience in films. The people who made it were joined together by a fanaticism that overcame everything . . . the film's purpose was to tell the simple, true and charming story. I think it succeeds.

I thought so too, but whether the critics would, or whether people would pay good money to see this true, though hardly simple, story I had no way of judging.

Chapter 7

The Chance of Freedom
1965–1966

My little camp under Mugwongo Hill in the Meru National Reserve was built of palm thatch and surrounded by a six-foot high wire fence. It was partitioned to provide the lions with a separate enclosure – a pointless idea, as I was woken on the first morning by Boy sitting on my chest and Girl licking my feet.

I felt a surge of elation as I left the artificial world of Naro Moru for the last time and drove north to Meru. Once more I would be free to live out in the open – away from the farmhouse, the huts and the compounds; away from the relentless intrusions of a schedule and budget; away from the suspicion, frustrations and anger of a company quite often blind to the extent of their achievements.

In the back of my Landrover Boy and Girl settled down as the road opened up spectacular views. The rolling grassland of ranches gradually gave way to the rusty brown of the bush. In the distance mountains hung in the haze like a backdrop. The grey clouds of Naro Moru were replaced by little white puffs and a hot sun blazed out of a blue sky.

At Meru we would be close to the old Northern Frontier District, and frontier it was still. Shifta (armed gangs of Somali poachers and raiders), infiltrating the more peaceful herdsmen, frequently made themselves felt. One village was said to be inhabited by a mixture of Shifta and police, who occupied it diplomatically, on a time-sharing arrangement. Unaware of these threats to their safety, giraffe, zebras and gazelles picked their way through the scrub. I was coming home.

As soon as I reached the reserve I called on Ted's headquarters at Leopard Rock. Tall, fair-haired and with a friendly smile, he gave me a warm welcome and greeted Boy and Girl like old friends. He told me that Giles Remnant, who had joined me as an assistant during filming, had everything ready in camp.

Although two other reserves had been reluctant to accept us and Joy with her cheetah, Ted Goss had not hesitated. He was genuinely interested in my attempt to build and launch a man-made pride in the wild. He also felt that the experiment would attract valuable attention to the needs of conservation generally and of Meru in particular. I was aware, however, that since the success of *Born Free*, professional hunters, scientists, conservationists and game managers had been divided about the value and wisdom of rehabilitating lions. Ken Smith, who had been with me when we found Elsa, continued to back me. But I suspected that other wardens, men of the highest professional skill like David Sheldrick, Daphne's first husband Bill Woodley, and her brother, Peter Jenkins, were sceptical to say the least.

Meru Reserve covers about three hundred square miles: it is ideal game country. Mugwongo Hill, for which I now headed, is covered with green scrub and rusty-coloured rocks. It rises above the surrounding plain like the uneven twin humps of a Bactrian camel. The plain, across which I approached it, is watered by three rivers and a number of streams fringed with palm trees, acacias and thick green undergrowth. There was an abundance of game and Boy and Girl grew keenly alert to the enticing sights and scents round and about them.

My camp, in the shade of a tall acacia, hung with the nests of Layard's black-headed weavers, was in relatively open, red-earthed bush, with a lush green swamp nearby; Joy's would be more shaded, under palms, and stood twelve miles to the north on grey or black cotton soil; a dozen miles to the south-east Elsa had lived, mated and died in the riverine bush.

After my abrupt awakening on the first day, I took Boy and Girl for an early morning walk, as a form of self-protection, to work off some of their excess energy. It became a daily routine in which I learnt almost as much about the country as they did.

There was game all round us. A noisy and interfering old elephant whom we named Rudkin, after the production manager on the film, would sometimes bluster through the swamp before resting in the shade of our tree. At night he would poke his trunk over the wire and browse off the bushes inside it. Later he took to stealing the tomatoes we grew.

In fact the swamp was an irresistible draw for most of the animals. It was a favourite grazing ground for a big herd of buffalo; eland, which are the largest antelopes, weighing nearly a ton, and with beautiful, spiralling horns, frequently gathered there; while waterbuck and Grant's gazelles would come down to drink every evening. Reticulated giraffe, their rich chestnut coats patterned with a network of cream lines, browsed sedately on the acacias and thornbushes. Families of zebra roamed freely across the plain.

At first Boy and Girl were pretty indiscriminate in what they stalked or attempted to ambush: they chose Rudkin, a rhino, some ostriches and, on several occasions, myself. They were especially impudent on cool, wet mornings. At first they had no success in stalking more suitable prey which were well practised in evading the wild prides already established in the reserve.

During our first week I heard lions roaring in the night, and on one of our early walks a rumbled warning from the rocks at the foot of the hill, when I was about ten yards away, alerted me to a lioness and her cubs. Although Boy immediately began to mark territory he did not roar, as he was still far from sure of himself in this unfamiliar landscape, already occupied by potentially hostile strangers. Nevertheless, before long he and Girl would have to come to terms with them. I had originally expected to establish my lions in a couple of months but it was soon clear it would take much longer. They badly needed the support of others like Ugas, Mara and Little Elsa if they were to hunt successfully and hold a territory in the face of the local competition. But Mrs Grindley, the original owner of Mara, had decided that life in a zoo would be safer than taking a chance on freedom. She was backed by an expert on lions, Charles Guggisberg, who thought that neither Mara nor Ugas would have a hope of holding their own in the wild. I learnt that both Mara and Little Elsa were definitely destined for Whipsnade: and I wondered then, as I wonder now, whether safety is really more important than freedom.

I would simply have to find other lions to join Boy and Girl. A single lion can seldom protect a pride for long against outside contenders; and Girl would need other lionesses to help her kill and raise her young. Looking back, I always regretted not keeping Elsa's sisters. It had made her rehabilitation far more difficult. She had been lucky to find a lone male in the protection of the bush by the river and had succeeded, single-handed, in raising her three cubs there. But I do not think she would have managed it in more open country, or without Joy and me to provide her with an occasional kill.

I gave up confining Boy and Girl after the first few nights, so when I was woken by angry growls at 2.30 one morning I shone my torch on the roof of the Landrover, which they had adopted as their sleeping quarters. I was just in time to see them leap down and race after the lioness and her cubs. Boy soon returned cheerfully, though with a scratch on his nose, and insisted on climbing on to my bed. A few nights later there was a further fracas and I woke to see no less than twelve lions walking past camp. They were females with their cubs, and although Boy was happy enough to see them off, Girl fled into the darkness.

A week after that, the boot was on the other foot. My sleep was shattered by some fearful growling and my torch picked out the figure of Boy, cringing on the ground, with the fierce and imposing figure of Black Mane, lord of the local pride, standing over him. Boy's instinctive reaction of rolling on his back in submission saved him from serious damage.

I tried to discourage the lions from sitting on top of the Landrover and built a platform for them just outside the camp fence. I even considered wiring up the Landrover roof so I could dislodge them with a shock. In the end I settled for thorn branches, as I did not want to put them off the cars entirely, in case one day they strayed and had to be brought back to Mugwongo. So far Boy and Girl had remained contentedly round camp. I found great happiness living in the bush, with the two lions – not to mention Giles Remnant and a bottle of White Horse – for companionship. Life

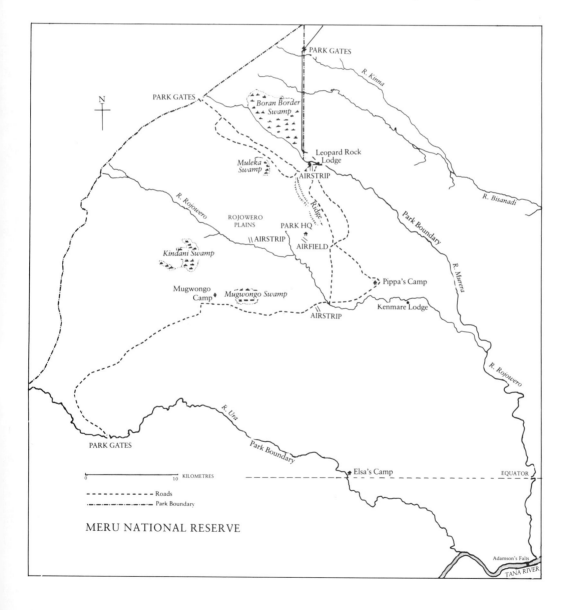

MERU NATIONAL RESERVE

seemed perfect with a moon rising in a cloudless sky over the palm trees, and no man-made noises to mar the beauty of the nights.

*   *   *

Joy left Naro Moru, with Pippa, a week after us. Lions and cheetahs, and for that matter leopards, are incompatible on the same ground. They hunt more or less the same prey, and if they come across each other's young they kill them, sensing the potential competition. Joy and I had therefore accepted separate camps as inevitable. Hers was near Ted's headquarters at Leopard Rock where she had permission to keep a small flock of goats to feed Pippa until she had learnt to kill. I was allowed to shoot a limited head of game for the lions.

Joy thought Pippa's full education would take at least a year and she hoped to stay and observe her for longer. She wanted to wait while Pippa mated and raised cubs, and with luck even witness the birth of a third generation. Her motive was not just curiosity. At that time very little was known about the breeding of cheetahs, and if not immediately endangered, their status was vulnerable. Since founding her Trust, Joy had talked to leading conservation organisations and was specially attracted to schemes for breeding endangered species in captivity, so that they could be restored to their natural habitats once these had been safe-guarded.

Joy planned to keep detailed records of Pippa's progress, and also felt she should explain to everyone involved at Meru what she was up to. Although the Reserve was run by Ted Goss as an employee of the Game Department, it was actually owned by the Meru County Council. The council therefore invited her to show our own little film about bringing up Elsa and her cubs. Four hundred people turned up to see it in the new Council Hall, and it went down so well that the council told us we could stay at Meru for as long as we liked.

I was thankful that as a Reserve Meru came under the jurisdiction of a County Council. Had it been a National Park it would have belonged to a much more rigid organisation whose Director was Mervyn Cowie, and I knew he was opposed to my work. Joy and I were entirely dependent on the good will of the council and Ted Gross. In her early days at Meru Joy relied tremendously on Ted to help her with the cascades of mail which continued to come in, not only from the public, but from conservationists and scientists studying the larger cats.

Joy had been one of the first donors when the council was looking for funds to set up the reserve and now Ted lent her the services of a delightful Meru ranger we called "Local", as we could never master his real name.

He had an excellent sense of humour, was hopeless with the many women in his life but, as I discovered when he had once helped us with Elsa, he was a brilliant tracker. Joy later described how he would feel the whereabouts of an animal "in his heart", as he would put it. This may have been no more than an unconscious evaluation of all the evidence collected by his senses and sifted through his experience, or it may have been the kind of telepathy which we frequently observed in the lions and cheetahs themselves, and for which I believe a scientific explanation will one day be found. Studies of giraffes have produced evidence of similar communication between parents and young. It has likewise been noticed among elephants.

Stanley, also from the Meru tribe, a pleasant boy in his early twenties, was engaged to look after the goats and Joy's camp – with this help she could spend more time with Pippa, carry on her writing and prolific correspondence, and even begin painting again. I have always felt that his devotion to the animals in his care contributed to his final tragedy five years later.

*   *   *

I was much less conscientious about my letter writing than Joy, but I did keep up my diary and honoured my promise to Bill and Ginny that I would send them reports on the lions, who were about to take a significant step forward. I had deliberately kept them short of meat in order to encourage their hunting instincts. At first they did no more than guard what I gave them from the more impatient scavengers like hyenas, jackals and, of course, vultures. But after some weeks Girl killed a baboon that did not get off the mark fast enough when it tired of baiting the lions.

A week later Girl disappeared for thirty-six hours. Boy was even more fretful than I was and set up such a howling at 11.30 at night that I followed him off into the bush to look for his sister. Instead he led me to a freshly killed eland in the swamp. As I swung my torch round it picked up a pair of glowing eyes in the reeds. I doubted if they were Girl's, particularly when I repeatedly called her name and the eyes did not move. To settle the matter I threw a stone at them, whereupon a lioness launched herself at me. I raised my rifle towards her, but it turned out to be Girl after all. She had gorged herself on the carcase of the young eland, and it was clear from the spoor that she had killed it herself after it had caught a hoof in a bush and broken its leg.

Some days later I took Boy and Girl, together, in search of game. Zebras go around in families, which remain in close touch even when they join a mass migration ten thousand strong, and on this afternoon it was a family

Once a lion decides to share your tent with you there is very little you can do about it.

The six-foot wire fence round my little camp at Mugwongo Hill failed to keep our lions in or the wild ones out.

which attracted Girl's attention. She stalked it perfectly, brought down a large foal with a charge from behind, and quickly shifted her hold to its throat; it was dead within a few minutes. Two weeks later she managed to kill a fully grown cow eland single-handed. Both performances were carried out with expert efficiency, while Boy, in the manner of most males, contributed nothing to the chase.

If my lions were not going to starve when I left them, I was still worried by the menace of Black Mane and his pride. Luckily Joy came back from a visit to Nairobi just then to say that the National Parks were changing their minds about Ugas, and might let us have him after all. He was a massive lion, hated his confinement in the Orphanage and was beginning to be branded as dangerous. Ted Goss and I went straight down to Nairobi to pick him up.

To my sorrow Mara was still in a compound with him, waiting to be flown to Whipsnade. Both lions greeted me affectionately and it was heartbreaking to leave Mara to her imprisonment.

Ugas' first act when he got to Meru was to cuff Boy several times and so assert his dominance; fortunately he treated me with deference and affection, and constantly brushed his head against my knees in greeting. His second initiative was to chase Black Mane away as soon as he saw him and although he continued to do this, and sometimes got a bloody nose for his efforts, he made his point, sprayed challenges on the surrounding bush and gave splendid voice at night. He was always something of a clown, and once squirted Joy backwards with the most perfect of aims.

By day Ugas showed he had by far the best nose among the lions, but being a male was idle about hunting: he also seemed to prefer my company to that of his own kind. It was genuinely affecting, though tiresome, when he discovered how to bring down the wire stockade to reach me, by merely standing on his hind legs and allowing gravity to do the rest. Then Boy and Girl insisted on sharing his meals, rather than continue killing, and I felt their education was making less than no progress.

I described all this to Bill and Ginny and told them about our recent plagues. The rains had brought out millions of beetles, flying ants and other insects of horrible appearance, which roasted themselves on our lanterns. One night we had to despatch twenty-six large black scorpions that had taken refuge in the warmth of our mess hut. In the morning two fan-tailed ravens came to gorge themselves on this feast before taking a tub in the lions' drinking trough.

More sinister than the insects was a plague of serpents. My cook was an eccentric character, who played an eerie home-made flute improvised from a length of hose-pipe, and sported ingenious gaiters adapted from the crinkly

sleeves in which our White Horse whisky bottles arrived. We were puzzled
when he ran over to tell us that a big snake was having a fight with a little
animal in his hut. He was quite right. A red, spitting cobra had a baby rat
in its mouth and was thrashing about trying to dislodge the furious mother,
which had a fast grip on its neck. Only when the cobra slithered through a
hole in some netting did the rat lose her hold. By then the baby was dead.

Joy also suffered from snakes – a night-adder, cobra or boomslang had
to be killed or evicted from her camp almost daily. The famous wildlife
photographer and maker of superb television films, Alan Root, who flew
up to see her, had always been fascinated by snakes, as by most of nature's
curiosities. He had lost part of a thigh to an irritable hippo which he was
filming underwater at Mzima Springs. On a kopje, or rocky outcrop, in the
Serengeti he jumped off an overhanging rock to find out what had killed a
jackal lying dead on the ledge below; the leopard responsible, which had
been hidden by the overhang, removed part of his backside.

Now he enthralled Joy, Local and Stanley, by catching a big female
puff-adder with a stick, grasping it by the neck, and milking its fangs of
venom with the aid of a glass. After he had put it down and let it go Joy
discovered there had been no film in her camera and asked for a repeat
performance.

If a puff-adder is relaxed and you are as experienced with snakes as Alan
was, it is normally possible to grab it quickly with your hand just behind
its head. But this snake was now worked up and it caught Alan's index
finger in mid-air. At first he did not seem too concerned as he had already
milked quite a lot of the venom and he did not want to upset Joy, who was
very excited.

"Sit down, Alan," she said. "You need some tea. I will make you some
hot tea immediately." "Bring some tea for Bwana Root at once," she called
to Stanley. Then, when it came, she told Alan: "I will get you some glucose;
you must have a lot of glucose in you," and stirred in at least four spoonfuls.

Alan now felt Joy was more shocked than he was, so he said, "Joy, I
think you had better have the first cup yourself" – and she downed it in
one. Meanwhile he had quietly applied a tourniquet to his finger, which
began to swell alarmingly.

Joy therefore went to the refrigerator and got out some anti-venom. But
Alan was reluctant to take it as he had been obliged to use it some years
before and knew that a second dose could be even more dangerous than
the venom itself. It was a nasty predicament as he now realised he was going
to be far too unwell to fly himself to a hospital.

As it happened there was another pilot at Leopard Rock who offered to
fly him to Nairobi. On the way he was so much worse, vomiting and passing

out, that he decided he would risk the anti-venom after all. By the time he reached hospital he was so ill that he could not explain the full course of events and he was given a second dose of anti-venom. It nearly killed him.

At his last gasp he managed to blurt out that his mouth felt like a battery and his tongue a copper electrode. The doctors instantly diagnosed the trouble, reversed the treatment and just managed to keep him alive with oxygen, anti-histamines, adrenalin and cortisone. He haemorrhaged internally; his limbs swelled to an enormous size and were covered in blood blisters. When it looked as if he would have to lose his arm the hospital in Nairobi rang up Professor David Chapman, a snake-bite expert in South Africa. "For God's sake don't cut it off," he said. "I will come straight up. He may not be able to keep his finger, but I think I can save his arm."

By coincidence the patient in the next room was Ionides, the world's greatest snake expert, who was himself dying. *He* explained what had happened. A puff-adder can turn its head back on its neck at an angle of 180° and must always be caught with a stick; if it is milked its fangs immediately fill with a more concentrated venom; and the tourniquet which had been applied to Alan's finger should not have been used. A puff-adder's venom contains a mixture of virulent substances, one of which dissolves the tissues of its victim and is irreversibly damaging if concentrated round the bite by a tourniquet.

Thanks to Professor Chapman's intervention, some skilful surgery in London and Alan's own guts, his hand was saved and his brilliance as a cameraman remained unimpaired – though his already depleted body did now lose a finger too.

Another snake casualty was Ugas. He came in one evening with a swollen and obviously painful eye. For a few days he dodged every dark branch and leapt aside from sticks in the grass, so I reckoned the culprit must have been a spitting cobra which aims at the eyes of an antagonist. In the end his eye obviously hurt him so much that I asked Ted Goss to send for Toni Harthoorn and his attractive new wife, Sue, who was also a vet.

Ted was pleased to have the chance of meeting Toni, anyway. Ever since he had taken on the creation of Meru as an official reserve he had thrown himself imaginatively into its development, opening up new roads with a bulldozer paid for by Joy's Trust, creating a "wilderness area" which you could only enter on foot, and providing a four-seater boat in which to explore the rivers.

Now he was anxious to bring in six white rhinos from Zululand. If Ted could bring off the tricky translocation, involving nicely judged doses of tranquilliser, they would be a unique feature of Meru and a rare sight in

Kenya. Toni, with whom I had carried out the early experiments at Isiolo, was now one of the top experts in Africa on tranquillisation.

When they got to Mugwongo Toni and Sue quickly sedated Ugas, diagnosed his eye as infected but intact and prescribed a series of painful injections for me to inflict on Ugas's backside. At one point Sue, who normally has a natural affinity with animals, presumed on Ugas's good humour and approached him too closely before he had got used to her. I had to warn her that if she had tripped, or been knocked over, his instincts would almost certainly have asserted themselves and she would have become just so much meat to him. Otherwise Ugas remained peaceful and only once made as if to crush my arm when I plunged the hypodermic needle into him.

Bill Travers now responded to my bulletins with two of his own. The first was an alarming account of how he too had been in the wars – almost literally. In his last film, *Duel at Diabolo*, he had to lead an escort of u.s cavalry into a redskin ambush. Unfortunately when the clash came, in a dry river bed, the production team had not watered the sand. The Indians rode at the wagons and their escort, which were completely invisible in a cloud of thick dust. A mounted brave at the gallop cannoned into Bill and broke the bones of his leg into fragments. Surgeons were trying to hold them together with steel pins. Coming events cast their shadows before them.

Bill's second piece of news excited Joy enormously: *Born Free* had been chosen for a Royal Film Première at which the Queen would be present.

Recently Joy had moved her camp close to Kenmare Lodge. Lady Kenmare, and her daughter Pat Cavendish, had built this as a base for visitors to the reserve and, like Joy's camp, it was close to the Rojoweru River with its waterfalls, palms, giant fig trees, scented shrubs and constant flutter of colourful birds.

Pat Cavendish had once owned a lioness called Tana. It had spent much of the time with her near Nairobi, but by the time Tana was three years old she had got on the neighbours' nerves when she began to bounce out at them on their early morning rides. Pat therefore decided to bring her to Kenmare Lodge and, with Ted Goss's permission, release her in Meru.

I wished I had been told this beforehand as Tana was set free without any preparation for life in the wild. At first she seemed to survive on the local cattle and Pat Cavendish gladly paid the claims for compensation. But as the claims grew suspiciously frequent recompense was made less willingly, until news of Tana's supposed misdemeanours dried up altogether. It was assumed that the Meru herdsman had balanced the books once and for all.

Joy had brought her natural flair to making her camp on the Rojoweru attractive and she took great care, as always, that it would be suitably decorated for Christmas. My assistant Giles Remnant had been replaced by a young Indian, Arun Sharma, who had a great fondness for animals and acute curiosity about their behaviour. When we arrived on Christmas Eve we found Joy had wrapped up parcels for both of us, and for Local and Stanley. There was a cake, a tree and we toasted Pippa who had mated and was expected to have cubs in March. Arun Sharma and I privately drank to another expected arrival. Sieuwke Bisletti had promised me four young lion cubs to fortify my pride – and they would soon be with us.

If not a white Christmas, it was in many ways a bright one, though I knew that Joy was grieving for a little leopard cub she had been given but which had died from a faulty innoculation at a local clinic.

✳   ✳   ✳

Early in January 1966 I was woken by the unwelcome sound of a car outside my hut at two o'clock in the morning. It was Joy. When I asked her what on earth she was doing she answered with some asperity that she had just been woken by the equally unwelcome sight of a large lion standing in front of her tent. Luckily she had kept her head and recognised the intruder as Ugas: please would I go and fetch him immediately.

Ugas had no doubt been straying in search of females. He badly needed them if he were to settle and mature. Girl, who had just come into season for the first time, certainly did not treat him as a worthy suitor and rebuffed him so fiercely that he was once knocked backwards into the water trough.

Sadly Ugas's eye never quite healed and now looked decidedly worse; when I saw him bellowing with pain I asked Toni and Sue Harthoorn to come back and, if necessary, remove the eye. As they discovered it had recently been pierced by a stick they did take it out: Boy and Girl lay quietly, a few feet away, while they operated. But in a short time Ugas was fully recovered: he fought, hunted and courted the ladies with undiminished success, though I noticed he constantly turned his head to maintain a field of vision on both sides. No longer in pain, his usual good nature reasserted itself and he was particularly playful with the four cubs when they arrived from the Bislettis.

To celebrate my sixtieth birthday in February Joy drove over to me with what she called a *caky*, in her pidgin Swahili, all trimmed with chocolate icing and candles. Her present to me was a refrigerator for the lions' meat, so that my own could be kept a little more hygienic. Joy also brought Bernhardt Grzimek with whom we had much to discuss, about his work and about ours: his fund-raising was becoming more effective than ever (over the years he has helped me more than any organisation) and as a film maker he was particularly interested in the prospects of *Born Free*. Joy had just received an invitation to go to London for the première at which she would be presented to the Queen. I would stay behind, partly because I disapproved so much of the way the film company had disposed of its lions, partly because the arrival of Pippa's cubs was now imminent and one of us should stay near her, and partly because I did not like to leave the four new lion cubs.

The reason why Arun Sharma and I had toasted these cubs at Christmas under our breath was that Joy disapproved of my taking them on: they were only four or five months old and I would have to stay with them for another year or two. Her own plans for Pippa were fairly long-term but she did not like extending our separation in different camps. She also disliked subsidising the cost of my keeping my lions from the royalties of *Born Free*. This made life very difficult on my own modest pension.

Happily Ugas, Boy and Girl took to the cubs immediately, played undignified games with them and kept them company on our walks. The young male, Suswa, was strong and energetic: one morning he leapt from the platform on to the roof of the hut and fell straight through on to my typewriter. His sisters, Shaitani, Sally and Suki were just as lively: when I investigated the source of what looked like smoke coming out of my hut I found the three of them in a cloud of feathers, tearing at the remains of my pillows.

A few days after Joy flew off, bound for the film premières in London and New York, I cabled her that Pippa's cubs had been born safely. To my amazement a week later an aeroplane circled my camp and dropped a message that Joy was on board. She had been overwhelmed by the film and its immediate box office success, although it had not appealed to the critics, one of whom assumed that the lions had been deprived of their teeth and claws!

She was now even more moved by the way in which Pippa welcomed her into her new family. In fact the cubs survived for only two months, but Pippa immediately came into season again and a second litter was born in August. They were christened Whitey, Tatu, Mbili and Dume; their adventures are described in Joy's book *The Spotted Sphinx*.

She and Stanley spent hours each day watching over them and keeping Pippa supplied with goat's meat. Stanley grew deeply fond of them.

When I next wrote to Bill and Ginny I told them how I had put on a black bow tie for the last time in my life to see the Nairobi première of the film. I congratulated them from my heart on what they had achieved, for I genuinely believed the success of the film was due to them: it was a belief shared by Joy. My letters also included accounts of the lions' latest exploits.

Boy was larger and broader than Ugas, and although Girl had begun to flirt with Black Mane and another wild lion, she was also impressed by her brother.

My letters sparked off a quick and surprising response from Bill. He said that following the excellent notices in America and the world-wide box office success of the film, he and Ginny had been asked countless questions about what had since taken place and about Joy, me and the lions. He wanted to make a documentary to answer them and to show that our relationship with Elsa was not a fluke: animals, even as formidable as lions, are capable of developing friendships which can survive release in the wild if they are based on the right combination of understanding and love. Joy and I thought the idea was a fine one but rather doubted if the government, or the parks authorities, would agree to it. Bill said he thought he could find a way of convincing them of the value of such a film to the country and to its wildlife.

*   *   *

The lions had grown increasingly independent. In June Ugas mated with a wild lioness and in July Girl mated on two separate occasions with Boy. He had to fend off the attentions of the wild males who loitered round Girl, but they always gave way when they were on his territory. Boy and Girl were now three years old, and would lead the four Bisletti cubs on successful hunts for oryx and eland.

A season of continuous drama opened in September. The first episode featured the Shifta. I heard a few shots after dark, and Joy arrived to say the Somali raiders had attacked a village nearby: she begged me to spend the night in the safety of her camp close to the park headquarters. As, at that moment, my lions were outside feeding off a zebra, and would have been a sitting target for the Shifta, I decided to stand by with a loaded rifle. Luckily the Shifta kept away.

The local buffalo proved rather more dangerous. They are the heavy cavalry of the African plains, and although lions find them excellent eating, they have three very effective forms of defence. The first is their massive horns which meet in the middle, creating a bony mass which only a very precisely placed bullet can penetrate. The second is the tactical skill with which a herd quickly gathers in a circle to face attack. The young, the weak, and the old are protected within, while it is impossible to breach the phalanx of lowered heads and horns from without. The most dangerous buffalo is the lone or wounded one. Not noted for their intelligence *en masse* – their defensive circle is probably instinctive – a single buffalo deploys as its third defensive aptitude a combination of angry courage and low cunning.

I had failed to get a zebra for the lions one day so on the way home I put in a shoulder shot at a buffalo. It was badly hit and disappeared into a clump of tall grass where one of my trackers, who had shinned up a tree, pointed it out to me. Although I advanced cautiously, it came at me fast, first appearing four feet away. There was no time to fire an aimed shot, so I pulled the trigger in its direction, saw the buffalo knock the rifle in the air and felt its horn hammer me in the ribs, throwing me to the ground. It missed as it tried to hook me with its horn, but trod on my foot and gave me a black eye. It then lay down ten yards away.

The tracker bravely came to my rescue, helped me up, and gave me my rifle back, just as the buffalo rose to its feet. Fortunately the effort was too much for it and it dropped dead.

With the help of my tracker I just made it back to the car which was about a mile away. But I was determined not to lose the meat I had shot so we returned to collect it before driving the seventeen miles back to camp.

There I radioed to Joy who arranged for a plane to take me to hospital in the morning. During the night I found the pain was only tolerable if I sat propped up at a table.

I was in hospital for several weeks, with cracked ribs and a broken bone in my foot. Meanwhile Arun Sharma kept a close watch on Girl, who had two cubs at the end of October. She moved them from lair to lair, and often left them for a whole day or night while she hunted or fed. When I returned a week later she allowed me to come right up to the cubs. She extended the same privilege to Boy, but the Bisletti lions, who were most intrigued by them, had to keep their distance.

One cub soon disappeared and I assumed was taken by a leopard during Girl's absence. The other, Sam, I had to adopt when Girl left it exposed to the hyenas and jackals prowling round the camp. Sam's adoption precipitated a third drama.

Simultaneously Girl seemed to come into season again which struck me then as being most unusual as Sam was still tiny and needed her care. Normal or not, Girl excited jealousy, and Boy and Ugas suddenly launched into a really spectacular fight for her favours, rising to their full height on their hind legs and swiping tremendous blows at each other with both paws, any one of which could have removed half a human face. Finally Ugas gave way.

When the fight subsided I asked Arun to come and look for Sam, who had been scared off by the violence. As Arun passed Girl and Boy the latter got up, made for him with a growl, and slashed him with his claws. I instantly went for Boy and hit him hard on the nose with a long stick, shouting to Arun to get inside a car. Boy retreated but came at me a second time, looking really nasty. Again I hit him with all my might, between the ears. Thank God his adrenalin, or hormones, began to ebb and his unprecedented aggression evaporated as quickly as it had erupted.

While Arun recovered – his gashes responded to penicillin treatment – I asked Terence to help me as my ribs were still giving trouble. Since he had built our house at Isiolo he had been working as an assistant Game Warden at Tsavo and then in the Northern Frontier, at Marsabit and Isiolo. Much of his work was in crop protection and he had acquired a reputation for producing maximum results with the minimum killing. He preferred to use a very light rifle at close range in the dark, and was once seen standing stark naked over the corpse of a buffalo with his gun in his hand. Pyjama trousers trailed from his ankle: the cord had untied at the critical moment.

Christmas, when it came, was what you might call a black one, and I fear that Terence must have found us gloomy company. Joy was desperately worried about Pippa's cub Dume, her favourite, who had been found ailing and taken to Nairobi for treatment. When she went out to look for the rest of the family on New Year's Day she found they had not budged from the spot where Dume had been removed from them. Sadly he died in Nairobi. I have since heard of a similar case of two cheetahs in South Africa who waited over several days for the return of a brother who had died and whose body had been removed.

The year ended just as badly for me. I had grown very fond of the little cub Sam, and after feeding him with bottles of milk and Farex would hand him over to Ugas and the Bisletti lions, who loved playing with him. At night he slept in a box by my bed.

Just before Christmas I was woken at 3 a.m. by a noise which sounded as if one of the lions was trying to get into the compound; it was rattling the wire. As I got up and went towards the door at the back of my hut I glanced down at Sam's box and it was empty. Outside I saw a lion by the light of my torch, only a few feet away, inside the wire. He was on his hind legs trying to force his way over it. Sam was in his jaws.

I shouted at the lion, thinking he was Boy, but when he turned, with a growl, I realised it was Black Mane. I rushed back for my rifle, but by the time I got outside again Black Mane had gone leaving Sam behind him. The poor little chap lay gasping in a pool of blood. In a few seconds he was dead, from a bite through the neck.

I have never before told the rest of the story in full because, if I had, it would have meant the end of everything I was doing at Meru. Equally not to have acted as I now did would also have risked the end of my work there.

Boy and Girl, brother and sister, with their cub Sam.

When Girl abandoned Sam I adopted him, but the wild lion Black Mane took him from my hut in the night and killed him.

Red-hot anger rose inside me when Sam died, for I felt it was a most unnatural murder. I got in the Landrover and dashed towards some roaring coming from the hill. There I found Black Mane and Girl together – mating. They disappeared at once into the darkness, but the roaring began again, closer to camp. I was bent on execution but would not risk shooting at the wrong pair of glowing eyes, nor was I prepared to carry out the sentence in front of the other lions. I therefore quietly followed Girl, Black Mane and a second wild lion until dawn, when Black Mane wandered away from the others. I shot him through the shoulder to the heart and hid his body from the tell-tale vultures. By the time I got back to Girl she was already mating with the second lion.

Some may find the execution of Black Mane unforgivable. But once he had felt so much at home in my camp that he dared to climb into my compound and take Sam, neither my staff nor I would be safe again. What is more, no young cubs born to our lions at Mugwongo would be safe either. At Meru I had been able to prove what I had always suspected after our experience with Elsa: it is easier and more humane to release lions in the wild if they are given their freedom in groups and not singly. But I still had not been able to watch lions raise their cubs from the moment they open their eyes until the day they produce young of their own. Until I did there would be gaps in our knowledge of how best to restock parks and reserves with introduced lions.

Chapter 8

A Chapter of Accidents
1967–1969

By the beginning of 1967 Boy, Girl and Ugas, who had been much more pampered than the human actors during the filming of *Born Free*, were as independent and wild as any three lions born and raised in the bush. But with the New Year came a subtle change to the background of their lives – one which had much more serious implications for me. Meru ceased to be a Reserve and was gazetted as a National Park.

This distinction and its consequences became so critical, and in the end such a threat, to the lives of the lions that I had better explain it. The National Parks were the cream of Kenya's reserves: they were like islands dotted round the country and within their boundaries no one might live or graze stock. They were run by a board of trustees, with a chairman, and administered by the Director, until now Mervyn Cowie, under whom they were staffed with wardens in charge of each park – themselves supported by rangers.

The rest of the game in Kenya came under the Ministry of Wildlife and Tourism and its Game Department was administered by the Chief Game Warden – the post once held by Archie Ritchie. The game wardens under him were either in charge of a general area – for wildlife is no respecter of boundaries – as I was at Isiolo, or in charge of a Reserve, as Ted Goss was at Meru. By and large the rules of the Parks were more stringent than those of the Reserves, which were usually County Council rather than National concerns.

I waited to gauge the effects of this change in our status at Meru. Mervyn Cowie, the original Director of National Parks, had just been replaced by Perez Olindo. I had no way of knowing how he would view my activities but I had my suspicions and, to make matters worse, Ted Goss was no longer there to advise or shelter me if lightning struck from above. Some months before he had been removed by a dramatic accident.

One morning Ted had tried to immobilise an elephant by shooting tranquillising darts at it. He hit it twice, with little apparent effect, and went off to get more darts, leaving a game scout to watch over the animal. During this time it became perceptibly drowsy.

When Ted returned it was still standing, apparently docile, in the grove of doum palms where he had left it. But when he approached from the front to fire another dart, it summoned its senses, charged and then chased him. The scout let off several shots without stopping or turning the elephant, which caught up with Ted, knocking him over with its leg or shoulder, and Ted found himself looking up as it knelt to gore him with its tusks. Luckily they missed him by a whisker, one actually tearing his shorts.

The elephant then stood and to avoid its trunk Ted pushed himself under the animal, working his way as far backward as possible. At that moment two things happened. The elephant trod on Ted's thigh with one of its hind feet and the game scout fired a shot. Ted could see blood on the elephant, which was now standing still, but realised that a fatal shot would drop the beast on top of him with inevitable results.

He therefore called out to the scout to hold his fire and very slowly, clutching on to tufts of grass, pulled himself back from between the elephant's legs. The scout then killed the animal with a brain shot.

Ted said that at first he felt only a deadening numbness from the shock, although his thigh had been smashed. Despite developing complications he

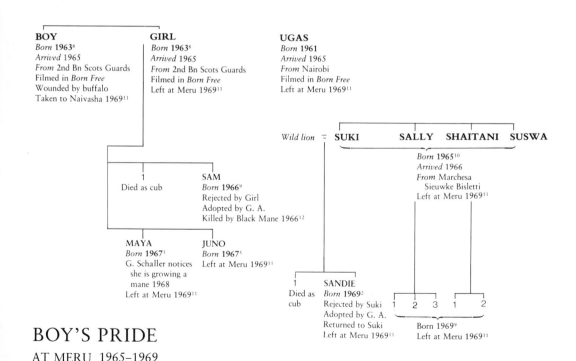

BOY
Born 1963[8]
Arrived 1965
From 2nd Bn Scots Guards
Filmed in *Born Free*
Wounded by buffalo
Taken to Naivasha 1969[11]

GIRL
Born 1963[8]
Arrived 1965
From 2nd Bn Scots Guards
Filmed in *Born Free*
Left at Meru 1969[11]

UGAS
Born 1961
Arrived 1965
From Nairobi
Filmed in *Born Free*
Left at Meru 1969[11]

Wild lion = **SUKI**   **SALLY**   **SHAITANI**   **SUSWA**

Born 1965[10]
Arrived 1966
From Marchesa
Sieuwke Bisletti
Left at Meru 1969[11]

1
Died as cub

SAM
Born 1966[9]
Rejected by Girl
Adopted by G. A.
Killed by Black Mane 1966[12]

MAYA
Born 1967[5]
G. Schaller notices she is growing a mane 1968
Left at Meru 1969[11]

JUNO
Born 1967[5]
Left at Meru 1969[11]

1
Died as cub

SANDIE
Born 1969[2]
Rejected by Suki
Adopted by G. A.
Returned to Suki
Left at Meru 1969[11]

1   2   3

1   2

Born 1969[9]
Left at Meru 1969[11]

BOY'S PRIDE

AT MERU 1965–1969

probably kept himself going, until he was placed in intensive care, by concentrating on endless practical details. The scout did not know how to drive his Landrover back to headquarters, so he had to give him instructions for each change of gear; the Flying Doctor had to be alerted and brought in; and most importantly – to him – he had to tell his staff exactly how to look after the six white rhinos which had recently arrived from Zululand.

Although in the end, by sheer will-power, Ted recovered the full use of his legs, his convalescence stretched from weeks into months and he never came back to Meru. While we waited to hear the outcome of the accident I considered the best way to secure my position, as I had received a letter asking me how soon I would be able to leave the lions. Help came from an unexpected direction.

Bill Travers had been working hard on the outline of the documentary film about the work Joy and I were doing at Meru. He realised that official permission would be necessary, and had prepared a persuasive brief pointing out how the documentary, following the international success of *Born Free*, would convince the world that the scenery and wildlife of Kenya were, in reality, no less beautiful or prolific than as portrayed in the film.

Bill knew that the British High Commissioner to Kenya, Malcolm Mac-Donald, was a passionate naturalist and photographer of animals and birds. He therefore asked him if he would take the brief out to Kenya and present it to the Government. Malcolm MacDonald promised to do this as soon as he arrived in Nairobi: landing at midnight he took it straight to the Attorney General. In a very short time the document was passed to the Minister for Tourism and Wildlife, Mr Sam Ayodo, who in turn gave it to the new Director of National Parks, Perez Olindo, indicating his approval.

When Bill arrived without warning at Meru he silently set up a movie camera outside Joy's tent on the first morning and filmed her unawares as she rose and called to Pippa. He then came and tried much the same thing on me. As it happened the lions were not in camp, and Bill questioned my good will when I sent him off to film a lion, peering round a bush, which I thought might be Ugas. Luckily it was Ugas, and he deigned to recognise Bill after a couple of years.

It took a little longer to find Boy and Girl who were off on a honeymoon. They were far too besotted by sex to acknowledge Bill at first, and Boy was really aggressive, as lions are when a female is in season. Later they calmed down and greeted their old friend warmly, however much they had grown or filled out in the meantime. The filming got successfully under way after this sticky start. Bill had asked Monty Ruben to help with all the practical arrangements and from now on he became a firm friend and staunch ally in the battles ahead.

In March I went to see the Minister, Sam Ayodo, in Nairobi, who was both kind and very interested in the lions: he was also surprised that his department had not passed on to him the reports I had been writing regularly. When I explained frankly that my principal aim was not scientific, but concerned with the freedom of the lions, and that I was calculating on their value to Meru as an attraction for tourists, and hence a source of income, he reiterated his backing.

Some weeks later, when the documentary was largely shot, I was puzzled to find authority blowing simultaneously hot and cold on my hopes of staying at Mugwongo. On 20 May the minister sent for me and told me he thought I should receive financial backing for my scheme to bring tourists to see the lions. This was at complete variance with Perez Olindo who, only the day before, had virtually put me on notice to leave. This contradiction gave me food for thought.

If they are honest, all successful hunters and game managers, like politicians, priests and soldiers, need a touch of the showman. Lyn Temple-Boreham had fed and watered lions in the Maasai Mara so that they responded to his call when he wanted to impress influential visitors with the importance of protecting them. Mervyn Cowie had done the same thing outside Nairobi when he was fighting his campaign to establish National Parks in Kenya. Joy, also, had been only too delighted to supply Elsa and the cubs with meat and to show them off to Billy Collins, David Attenborough and Julian Huxley. It was only later, after the Parks were established, and after Elsa and her cubs were world famous, that Cowie and Joy had undergone a change of philosophy. The battle I was fighting was not simply for my seven lions, and it was far from over.

Although Joy had originally provided me with a Landrover, and still contributed to some of my costs from her royalties, she had resisted my taking the four Bisletti cubs. She had since kept up continuous pressure on me to give up the lions and my separate camp, and to join her so that we could rehabilitate leopards together, once her cheetahs were settled on their own. Her position was uncannily like that of the Parks authorities.

Bill's arrival to make the documentary shelved the difference of opinion but quickly precipitated another. The idea for the film was his, it was basically financed with his money, and its aim was to show what had happened to the cast of *Born Free* lions – though it was to include Joy's work with Pippa, too. But the moment filming started Joy realised that the limelight would fall on the lions. She tried to insist that she took over the finance and that she and Pippa, as the natural successor to Elsa, should take over the leading roles. When Bill, quite justifiably, declined her requests she was outraged, withdrew from the film and refused to see or speak to him again – and she kept her vow.

Had our camps not been a dozen miles apart life would have been intolerable, but although our relations were strained they never snapped. When a flooded bridge collapsed under my Landrover in the middle of the night, and I had to walk several miles through the rain and darkness to seek her help, Joy came unhesitatingly to my rescue. Nevertheless when she heard of my scheme to bring tourists out to the lions at Mugwongo, her reaction was unequivocal: either I dropped the plan or she would cut off all further funds and withdraw the Landrover.

Shortly after that I heard through the grapevine that the Parks Board were planning to transfer their headquarters from Leopard Rock to Mugwongo – but Olindo had given instructions that I was not to be warned in advance. That is when the penny finally dropped.

Joy had first met Olindo several years before in America and had been much impressed by his quick mind and serious concern for wildlife. When he had become Director of National Parks, he had naturally expressed his gratitude for her financial aid to Meru and other reserves. Furthermore, he was anxious not to lose her support by sanctioning activities of mine that she found anathema. It looked as if my bacon was cooked: an official letter arrived from Olindo telling me I would have to leave, and Joy said that she would stop the Trust money if any visitor, including Bill's cameraman, ever came near the lions again. The film went on. The money stopped.

*   *   *

At times like these I was thankful to have the lions for company and my determination to finish the film was an excellent antidote to anxieties about the future. In February Girl had mated with Boy, while Bill was still filming, and her cubs were due in the first or second week of May. My letters to Bill record the outcome.

May 12th
Sometime after midnight on 9th I heard Girl roaring at the back of the camp. I got up to look for her. Later Arun Sharma, Korokoro (my tracker) and I spent all morning looking for her without success. Next morning Korokoro again went up the hill and found her close to the place where she had given birth to cubs last October. Later we went up the hill together. Girl got up to come and greet me: she had two little cubs. They must have been born the day before.

Poor little things, they have been deluged with rain each night. Girl is absolutely wonderful in her complete trust and I am sure there would be no difficulty in taking film of them.

June 4th
So far Girl is being a very good mother and never leaves the cubs. She has moved them nine times. Boy, also, has taken more interest in his family this time. In fact for two days he would not allow me to go near the cubs. Both are females, which is interesting when, by the same father, the first litter was two males.

June 20th
Girl is at her 12th lair. It is a perfect place for a lion's den. Huge boulders with innumerable nooks and crannies. The retreat they have chosen is a long cave, too narrow for Girl to enter. When she wants the cubs she has to stand outside and call.

Arun Sharma took as much pride and pleasure in Girl's cubs as I did, and longed to follow each stage of their growing up. But he had applied to go to Mweka, the college of wildlife management, and he was called away to begin his course just as they started to venture out from the safety of their rocks. I was really sorry to lose him, as he handled the lions with great understanding.

July 9th
The cubs are just two months old and yesterday Girl brought them to camp. It was a splendid sight with all the other lions present. The cubs are not a bit scared of any of them, including Ugas, who is very affectionate. They just treat Boy as a convenient object for their games, and to pull to pieces. They grab him by the mane and tassel of his tail, and although they pull and worry he never protests.

August 12th
Girl always fetches the cubs to the kills we provide before eating herself. On the 4th she disappeared in the morning leaving the cubs asleep in their hideout among the rocks. In the afternoon she returned and called them, and without pausing in camp, hurried off in the direction of the swamp. Boy seemed just as mystified by her behaviour as I was. We followed. Boy took up the scent and in a few minutes led me to a tree under which Girl and the cubs were tearing at the carcase of a young giraffe. Girl must have killed it about noon and hurried back to camp to fetch her cubs. As if to celebrate Boy and Girl and the cubs had a tremendous game, chasing each other round and nearly knocking me over.

September 7th
The cubs are in fine condition and often come into camp. They even take up the roaring chorus when the lions are together; while they are all going at once it fairly makes the camp tremble.

This was one of the most heart-warming moments I had experienced at Meru, and I was all the sadder when Ginny wrote and told me what had happened when they had shot the final sequence for the film in England.

They had gone down to Whipsnade to contrast the life of Mara and Little Elsa there with that of the lions at Meru. When they approached the cage Ginny had called them, and although it was more than two years since she had seen them, they rushed over to her, pressing their noses against the bars and moaning. The cameraman had been so sceptical about the chances of the two lions responding to Ginny that he was not ready to film their pathetic greeting. However, after Ginny had recovered her composure she called them a second time. Once more they ran over to her familiar voice. Both lions had rub marks on their bodies, Mara's eyes looked septic and Little Elsa's leg had a fresh and open cut.

With the documentary completed I felt rather more secure in my dealings with the Park Authorities, for it vindicated all we had been doing with the lions. Bill suggested sending a copy of the film to Perez Olindo, but I felt it would be wasted effort as he himself must be resenting the support I was getting from the Minister and Joy was still adamantly opposed to my staying. Olindo, who visited the park on several occasions – once to collect a cheque for £8,000 from Joy for its running expenses – never came near me or the lions. Indeed in October he wrote again asking me to leave and to suggest a date. His line was at odds with every single visitor, who expressed delight and amazement at the lions – not because they were once tame lions and were now leading a completely wild existence, but because they could live like that while retaining their trust and gentleness towards human beings.

At long last, in the week before Christmas, the Minister put down his foot. I was to stay at Meru, the lions were to stay at Meru, and the park headquarters were not to move to my campsite on Mugwongo Hill. The film had saved the day.

Over Christmas Joy and I agreed not to rake over the embers. During the previous year, with the help of her financial adviser, Peter Johnson, she had bought a small stone house in an attractive position on the shores of Lake Naivasha. She felt we would need it in our retirement, and we planned how we would move all our possessions into it during the coming month or two.

While I was away I would have to leave my camp in charge of my godson and new assistant Jonny Baxendale, son of my old friend Nevil, with whom I had traded in goats, prospected for gold and crossed Lake Rudolf in the improvised canoe. Tall, blue-eyed and fair-haired, he was always cheerful and very much his father's son.

My pleasure in Jonny's arrival was tempered by the tragic news that just before Christmas his predecessor, Arun Sharma, had gone off duck shooting near Mombasa, swum out to retrieve a bird, got into difficulties and been drowned. I was personally very upset and it was a real loss for the Game Department who had agreed to take Arun on when he left Mweka. The cost of the move to Naivasha turned my mind to money, and I had a hard look at my precarious finances. It gave me a shock.

For the only time in my life I found there was more in the kitty than I expected. During the evenings I had been writing a book, *Bwana Game*, which was to be published in the coming year; I could rely on a reasonable advance and royalties from it. Columbia wanted to make a sequel to *Born Free* and wished to employ me again as the technical adviser on their lions; they offered me a salary. Bill Travers not only assured me of a handsome income from the documentary we had been making, *The Lions Are Free*, but now asked me to make an appearance in a feature film about one of Daphne Sheldrick's orphan elephants at Tsavo. The title of the film translated the young elephant's Swahili name, Pole Pole, as *An Elephant Called Slowly*. Many years later Pole Pole was to play a tragic but inspiring part in the crusade against the exploitation of animals.

*   *   *

In fact 1968 turned out to be the most peaceful of our years at Meru; after the machinations of the previous one it was an anticlimax; and compared with what was to follow, in 1969, it was blessedly uneventful.

Joy was preoccupied with her cheetahs. At the end of March, about a month after we had moved all our permanent possessions into the new house on Lake Naivasha, Pippa had four cubs. They disappeared after a fortnight and Joy was inclined to think they had been taken by hyenas. However, Pippa immediately came into season and in July again had four cubs.

Joy and I were fascinated to see how the breeding of big cats is so sensitively regulated by the fortunes of their young. If the latter thrive, and while they are being nurtured, their mothers do not come into season. Almost the day after the bond is broken, for any reason, they are ready to mate. This seemed to explain Girl's amorous outburst so soon after Sam was born. One cub had died and I had adopted Sam which left her metabolism free to come into season and hence interest Boy and Ugas.

Joy was also interested in the way Pippa's older cubs had completely cut adrift from her, even though we occasionally saw them in occupation of different parts of the territory in which they had grown up. The relatively early separation of the young from their mother is just one example of how cheetahs and lions are quite different in their social behaviour. Joy had been

Boy, Girl and Ugas, all raised in captivity, soon learned to kill zebra, eland and buffalo once they were released at Meru.

Boy, Girl and the Bisletti cubs used my Landrover as a vantage point and unfortunately there was no way of stopping them.

doing some lovely paintings of the cheetahs, and when one of the latest cubs was killed by a lion she found her grief was assuaged by sketching its beautiful body.

Meanwhile Girl's two cubs were growing apace. I had wanted to call them Monika and Ruth, but Joy nearly burst a blood vessel, as she had been irritated by an interview which had given Monika all the credit for training the lions in *Born Free*: we therefore christened them Maya and Juno. Even this was not quite satisfactory.

When the two cubs were about a year old, George Schaller, who was making a study of lions in the Serengeti, came to stay with me and noticed that Maya was starting to grow a mane. The young lion was definitely changing sex and began to develop male genitals. I had noticed this phenomenon once before, in the Serengeti, where I had seen a young lioness begin to grow a mane.

I enjoyed Schaller's visit very much and learnt a lot from what he told me, and from his book *The Serengeti Lion* in which he eventually published his findings. We talked quite a bit about the personalities of the lions and their different forms of self-expression. I always wish he could have had time to take and analyse the data I had collected over the years, and the rudimentary diary I still keep on the lions to this day.

Girl and her cubs were constantly seen in the company of the three Bisletti lionesses, keeping themselves to themselves; whereas the Bisletti lion, Suswa, stayed closed to Boy and Ugas, who were always away in search of romance.

When it came to a hunt all the lions joined in. The Bisletti lions had mastered the art of killing zebra and had then graduated to the large eland. Now the pride seemed to specialise in buffalo kills. It was a thrilling but dangerous game to harry the herds of a hundred or two in the hope of separating a more vulnerable splinter group. Even so I arrived one day to see that fifteen buffalo had got Suswa cornered in a small thorn tree. He was teetering on a slender branch and would have fallen among them if I had not rescued him with the Landrover.

Their best chance was with a lone buffalo and I once came on Boy and the four Bisletti lions by the river, attacking a huge bull. In a few minutes they had it down. Immediately Boy got a hold on its muzzle and hung on, pinning its head to the ground and choking it, while the rest seized a grip wherever they could. In about ten minutes all was over, and so began the remorseless dissolution of the great animal. Provided the kill was large enough I could always step in and cut off some meat to stow in the refrigerator, but if ever there was too little to go round I would keep well away. Meat is too often a flashpoint with lions.

In December the heavens opened: we had fifteen inches of rain in one week and I thought the lions would grow webbed feet. That year it was a wet Christmas.

*   *   *

The year 1969 opened with deceptive tranquillity. Jonny Baxendale had settled into our lives admirably. Occasionally he would help Joy with her cheetahs, and he was fascinated by the range of curiosity and knowledge about the big cats she revealed when they spent the evening talking in her camp. Joy liked him, too, although she deplored his occasional nights away from Meru in search of entertainment. He also got on excellently with the lions – so well, in fact, that after one of his nights out, while sitting among them in the shade of a tree, he fell asleep. An hour or two later he awoke to find the lions all staring at something on the road nearby. He stood up, dressed only in his shorts, and found himself being goggled at by four tourists in a very small car. They turned round and fled.

Jonny also kept on friendly terms with the new Park Warden, Daphne Sheldrick's brother Peter Jenkins, who took over after two others had held the fort while Ted was in hospital. Peter must have known of the controversy surrounding the lions and probably harboured his own doubts about them. Nevertheless once or twice he came and had a drink with Jonny and me in camp, bringing with him his wife Sara, his seven-year-old son Mark, and their baby daughter. Boy and Girl, as lions always are, were intrigued by the children. On one occasion Girl became so worked up, pacing up and down outside the wire, that Jonny asked if the children could play inside the hut.

Suki was the first of the Bisletti lionesses to mate – I suddenly came across her in the long grass with a wild lion. They were not much more than ten or fifteen yards away and were so engrossed with each other that I stopped to watch and turned off the engine. The only trouble was that when I wanted to move on I found that my battery had gone flat and the starter would not work. Five times I made towards the starting handle and on four of those occasions the wild lion drove me back into the cabin. At the fifth attempt, very much looking over my shoulder, I swung the engine and made my escape.

Jonny and I witnessed another incident with Suki in the long grass, when she and Girl were lying by the remains of a kill. Suddenly they jumped up and pounced on some intruder. When I went to investigate I found them clouting a leopard which was lying on its back, striking out with its claws and growling like mad. After a little while the lionesses got bored and they all went their separate ways, with only a few scratches for their pains.

Joy wanted to know all about the confrontation when Jonny described it to her. She had no fear of lions or leopards – nor for that matter of virtually anything else, including people. Jonny once arrived in her camp to find her bawling in very bad Swahili at her cook, who was approaching her furiously with a carving knife. As on other occasions Joy's communication problem had raised the emotional temperature to danger level. Only two things held any terror for her, Jonny maintained: elephants and punctures.

Joy was never one to let either grass or primroses grow under her feet. She was very content with her cheetahs, and they occupied most of her time, but when Perez Olindo offered her a pair of leopard cubs she leapt at the chance of fulfilling the dreams that had twice ended so unhappily. Before setting off to Nairobi to collect them she called in at my camp to persuade Jonny to drive her. He refused, as he had business of his own in Nairobi, and no doubt had pleasure in mind as well: his timetable was unlikely to coincide with Joy's. To disarm her disapproval he said he would follow her down to Nairobi – in case she got a puncture. Joy promised to send me a message after she had collected the leopard cubs so that I should know when to expect her back.

That night a message was brought to my camp. It came from Jonny. Joy had gone round a corner, swerved to avoid two men walking in the middle of the road and driven her Landrover into a ravine.

Miraculously the car was caught by some bushes half way down the slope, with another two hundred and fifty feet to go. Joy was pulled out alive, but her bleeding right hand was shattered – the tendons cut and bones broken. A local chief emerged with a crowd from a bus just behind, called for its first aid box and poured iodine over her wounds. This was the scene which greeted Jonny when he drove round the corner some minutes later.

He took Joy straight on to hospital in Nairobi. I could imagine her despair as she contemplated what all this would mean: she would have to give up the leopard cubs, she would be handicapped with the cheetahs, she could no longer type her diaries, letters and books, and she would probably never paint or play the piano again. The prospect was appalling.

While Joy was in hospital for the next month Jonny and I had our work cut out in the bush. We took it in turns to help Local and Stanley bring food to Pippa's cubs. Then Suki gave birth to two cubs by a wild lion and we tried to keep pace with her as she moved them from lair to lair in the rocks as Girl had. It was work which I enjoyed and I felt further contented when I was told that Perez Olindo had appointed me to assist Peter Jenkins, on an honorary basis, with a nominal salary.

On her return Joy was moved by the welcome she got from Pippa and her three cubs. But when I took her to see Suki and hers we found that one of them was missing. It must have been stolen and killed by a leopard, perhaps even the one that had taken Girl's cub. Almost immediately Suki began to lose interest in the remaining cub and so I adopted it.

I could see Joy was enchanted by Sandie, as we called her, and she swiftly won her trust by playing with her for much of the day and by giving her tit-bits and milk. I was just about to suggest that Joy should take over Sandie entirely when Suki, who seemed to be in season again, came into camp at night, spotted her cub through the wire and began to call for her. In the morning I therefore handed Sandie back, and they went off merrily to join Suki's sisters and Girl, who were now consorting and mating with three large wild lions just outside the camp. Suki, however, now that she had taken back Sandie, immediately ceased to be in season.

After a month back at Meru Joy had to go into hospital for an operation on her foot. While she was away a very frightening episode occurred.

Jonny Baxendale had gone off in the morning to try to shoot a zebra outside the reserve for Suki and Sandie. By the late afternoon he had not succeeded and called in at Peter Jenkins' headquarters to collect our mail, only to find that Peter was out and had it with him.

Just as he was reaching the fork where the roads from Joy's camp and mine converged, Jonny noticed Boy, a long way from his normal territory. As we had not seen him for several days he stopped – and inevitably Boy hopped on to the roof. Jonny was contemplating calling on Joy for supper and he knew that she hated the lions sitting on our Landrovers. Having failed to entice Boy off his lofty perch, he sat on the bonnet himself and opened a bottle of warm beer.

At that moment, from the direction of Joy's camp, Peter Jenkins drove up in his new Toyota with half doors and open windows. With him were Sara and the baby; Mark sat on the front seat between them. Peter drew up some yards away, and switched off the engine. They began to chat as Jonny went over to collect his mail and the children grew a little restless.

After a few minutes Boy stepped down on to the Landrover bonnet and peered into the Toyota. Jonny felt a sudden twinge of apprehension and murmured something about backing off. Peter replied he did not think he would wait for the lion to scratch his paint. Just then, as silent and effortless as a shaft of light, Boy shot off the bonnet, passed Jonny and was thrusting his head through Peter's door of the Toyota.

Somehow, with his head and body forced back against the seat by Boy's massive shoulders, Peter managed to switch on the engine and, as Boy's paw stretched out to pull over Mark's head, the car jerked into gear. Meanwhile Jonny who had punched Boy in the ribs and pulled at his tail without any effect at all, ran for his rifle. He saw the car leap forward in a spurt of dust and Boy's hind legs dragging beside it. When Boy's forequarters fell out of the Toyota, seconds later, he expected to see Mark pulled out too, and his telescopic sights were already on the lion, only twenty yards away.

As Peter's car sped off to Leopard Rock Jonny hesitated to shoot Boy without first finding out if he had done any harm. He therefore left the lion and went straight to Peter's quarters. Mark had only been scratched on the head but had a deep and unpleasant bite on his arm. When Jonny asked if he should shoot Boy, Peter said he would like to see *all* my lions dead, and was obviously unable to concentrate on anything except getting Mark to hospital as fast as possible.

The next morning I went with Jonny to apologise to Peter and Sara, to enquire about Mark and to ask Peter again if he wanted me to shoot Boy. Peter answered that the decision was not his: he would refer this episode, and the whole issue of my lion rehabilitation, to the Director of Parks, with the strongest possible recommendations. He and Sara displayed the most admirable courage, calm and courtesy, both now and later, in everything to do with the accident.

Mark had a very nasty bite on his upper arm. Boy's teeth had sunk into it but mercifully they had severed neither an artery nor a tendon, and the bone was unbroken. Peter had driven him straight to a mission hospital where the wounds were stitched and dressed. Apparently they were not given enough time to drain, so they turned septic and gangrene set in. Peter and Sara then had to take him to Nairobi where further surgery and treatment helped his complete recovery. I was profoundly distressed by the family's ordeal.

Official repercussions were not long in coming. Boy must be shot; Girl, who was ten miles away at the time, and Ugas, must be shot; I must leave Meru; all the lions must leave Meru with me; the lions could not go to any other National Park, yet could not leave the country. Anger, prejudice and the fear of popular feeling animated a series of contradictory orders.

In the middle of this confusion Joy, who had come back just after the incident, returned to hospital for a third and major operation, to graft a tendon from her leg into her hand. She would be away for five months in London.

In my naivety I did not realise the heat of the opposition which had boiled up against me in the National Parks. They would not consider my suggestions for moving the lions to remote and unvisited parts of Meru or the other parks: they decided to allocate an area near Mugwongo, within the existing orbit of the lions' hunting grounds, for safari camps, which was certain to precipitate a crisis; and they attempted to post me, in my honorary capacity, to Marsabit which was two hundred miles away.

Furthermore, without a word to me, they sold Sandie for £85 to a well-known and highly respected animal trapper in Nairobi, John Seago, only a few days after I had found her suffering from a bite on the head, inflicted by one of the wild lions. I refused to hand her over in a state like that, and as soon as she was strong enough to survive on her own she conveniently "escaped" and thus evaded life in a zoo. John was good enough to sympathise when he heard the full story.

During these commotions I had several stormy interviews with Peter Jenkins and Perez Olindo and I carefully sifted the issues in my mind. I understood the contentions that lions are not yet endangered as a whole, in the way rhinos are, and that their rehabilitation is not yet a matter of life and death for the species; that my lions were less frightened than wild ones of people and so might be more intimidating to tourists; and that my activities interfered with the natural life of the Reserve.

On the other hand I believed that the Parks themselves – with all the animals inside them – would be threatened unless people paid to come and see them. *Born Free*, especially the film, had stimulated a great wave of interest in wild animals and their freedom. Scores of people had written to me to say that *The Lions Are Free* had made an extraordinary impact on television audiences in America where it had been given no less than three prime-time network showings to many millions of viewers. All this was bound to lead to an increased number of tourists coming on safari. I knew from my own experience that even veteran conservationists and hard-headed professional photographers could not resist coming straight out to see the pride at Mugwongo when they visited Meru.

There was no evidence that my lions were a special danger to man, except possibly to my staff and me, who were exposed to them twenty-four hours a day. Joseph, the assistant warden, had brought out some visitors to see the lions in a dilapidated Landrover. Boy and Girl had immediately jumped on to its rickety roof which collapsed, creating a jumble of lions and sightseers. The only danger was to the latter's dignity, which was quickly rescued by their sense of humour. On another occasion, after Girl had begun to kill really large prey, and Boy to battle with his rivals at night, we had returned to camp to find the two lions playing with and posing for a party of eight young men. They were soldiers of the Welsh Guards on leave from Aden. Quite against park rules they had got out of their car, but none of them was scratched. Lions always take a dangerous interest in children but even Mark Jenkins would have been safe if the Toyota had not stopped so close to Boy.

It is true that the presence of my lions clashed with the natural range of the wild ones. But against this, seven lions, who had faced the certainty of life in a cage, were living in complete freedom. Had I been prepared to confess to the killing of Black Mane I would have claimed it was more than justified – by the benefits to other lions, by the additional observations of lion behaviour it allowed us to make and by the making of *The Lions Are Free* which could not have been shot at Mugwongo had he been at large.

None of my arguments cut any ice whatever with the Director and the warden. I had been reminded on several occasions – it was unnecessary – that the lions did not belong to me. I was therefore amused to discover that they did not belong to the National Parks either: they were the property of the state. This produced Perez Olindo's only concession: a political one. Shooting the lions would create such dreadful publicity for Kenya and its parks that I need not destroy them. I must destroy instead their trust in human beings. As soon as I had done so I was to leave Meru. However, as Joy was in hospital, and as I was in charge of her approved cheetah programme during her absence, I could stay till she returned. It was now September; she herself was told to leave by the end of the year.

Joy should have continued her physiotherapy in London until October, but it seemed to be doing little good and she was restless to see the cheetahs again. Pippa's first surviving offspring were healthy and roaming their self-appointed territories, while Pippa had just been seen actually killing a small Kongoni antelope to feed her three youngest cubs. Joy's delight at their reunion was short-lived.

A week later Pippa was found with a broken leg. In a further three weeks she died after surgery in the hospital of the Nairobi Orphanage. Joy buried her up at Meru beside one of her cubs. After her devastation at Pippa's death this act seemed to restore her calm, clarity and purpose. We were shortly to need them.

As the first stage of my separation from the lions I was ordered to quit my camp. Joy had never approved of its existence and now she warmly welcomed me to hers. From there we saw smoke go drifting up into the sky as they burnt the huts that had been my home for more than four years; we watched it silently and with some emotion together.

A few days later I was in Peter Jenkins' office discussing the future of the lions. Just then Joy burst in to say that she had found one – she was not sure which – lying under a bush, fearfully emaciated and with a porcupine quill sticking out below its eye.

We all three set off together and as soon as I saw the lion I knew it was Boy. He tried to drag himself away, but he could only go a few paces; then let me draw out the six-inch quill. Peter said that nearly all the lions he had been obliged to put out of misery were suffering from septicaemia or starvation due to porcupine quills in the face and mouth.

In Boy's case it was obvious that the main damage was to his right foreleg: it was limp, useless and as debilitating as a broken right arm to a man of action. Peter and I looked at each other for moments of almost unendurable suspense. I could imagine everything that was running through his head – the anguish he had suffered for Mark, our honest but furious disagreements about the presence of my lions in the reserve, his understandable resentment when public or political pressure had obliged him to grant me or the lions one reprieve after another. He had brought his rifle with him and I felt that this time he would use it.

Slowly he looked at each of us in turn and then he quietly said that Boy was to be shot or removed from the park. He suggested that we should radio for a vet to come and assess Boy's chances of survival if he were moved. It was a generous, and no doubt costly, verdict.

That night I slept out with Boy as he was too ill to move although he wolfed down a goat I gave him. The following day Toni and Sue Harthoorn flew up to give him a preliminary examination under an anaesthetic which I injected just before they set to work. They found his right upper foreleg was broken, as if by a buffalo horn or possibly a car fender, and that he had a hernia too. On the other hand they felt he had a good chance of recovery if given time to convalesce, and Peter Jenkins allowed us three weeks in which to prove the case.

That night Boy was still so dopey that I stayed out with him again. For mutual support we propped each other up, my back to the side of his head, to stop it flopping on the ground. For additional support I had a rifle and a half-bottle of whisky. There was plenty of time, in the darkness, to reflect on the past and the future. Girl, Ugas and the Bisletti lions were totally independent. The lionesses among them, with Juno, who was nearly full-grown, and Sandie, who was eight months old, had joined the three wild males to make up a formidable pride, entrenched at Mugwongo. Ugas and Suswa had gone whoring after strange women, thereby losing their first territory but no doubt finding another. If Boy was going to survive an operation on his leg I gradually decided there was only one place to which I could take him – the new house at Naivasha. Safely there, I would seek a new home for him.

It would be several days before the Harthoorns could make all the preparations for the operation, so I moved Boy into the old compound at Mugwongo, built a makeshift table, prepared a block and tackle to hold the ends of the bones apart, and put up an awning. Meanwhile, in Nairobi, Sue searched successfully for two thirteen-inch steel pins, with which to reinforce the leg, but in vain for an undamaged humerus on which to model the repair work. Of the tens of thousands of lions shot by man in Kenya not a single skeleton had been preserved. The Harthoorns would have to work from the X-ray of a lioness made at Bristol in England.

As we prepared for the operation at dawn, Toni told me to keep my fingers crossed for cool, cloudy weather and no wind to carry dust into his work. We were a scratch team. The Harthoorns' pilot nobly stood in as anaesthetist; Joy and her assistant handled the antibiotics and disinfectants; I worked the pulley; and two rangers turned a hand to whatever was needed.

When Boy's skin had been shaved and his shoulder cut open Toni found that in the past two or three weeks since the accident the ends of the bone had begun to fuse again. The surgery was not only a nervous strain but very tough physical work. As time went by a second fracture was discovered. It took half an hour to excise the sac of the hernia and restitch the wound with wire.

It was six hours before the operation was completed. It must have been one of the most ambitious ever undertaken in the bush. The treatment of the hernia particularly held my interest as I had just had the same thing done to myself!

Just as they finished the clouds parted and the sun came beating down in its full force. Sue and I talked about the interminable drought as she and Toni stretched out under the shade of the big acacia. The seasonal rains were weeks overdue but I told her she need not worry and that the weather would soon break. The black-headed weavers were building their nests and it was an infallible sign.

It was a week before Toni and Sue could come back to see their patient. By then he was eating a goat a day and, although he disliked putting his foot to the ground, he could rise on his hind legs and stretch his right forepaw up a tree to knock meat off a branch. I also had to confess that he had already started to climb on to the Landrover roof and jump down again. This worried them intensely, though I was more concerned that Boy had taken to nibbling my toes at night.

As Toni and Sue now put Boy's chances of recovery at 90 per cent he would have to be quickly removed from Meru. Jonny Baxendale, who had left me, very kindly took time off to build a wooden cottage for me in the garden at Naivasha: beside it he made a compound for Boy.

Bill Travers had felt that we should film Boy's treatment and recovery as fully as possible, so a cameraman and Mike Richmond, the sound recordist for *The Lions Are Free*, had flown up with the Harthoorns and their pilot Paul Pearson on their latest visit. Paul, Sue and Mike were all to play crucial parts in the airlift that was about to take place.

In the meantime the bush telegraph had been at work. The rest of the lions frequently came to gaze at Boy through the wire and we discovered

Boy must have been in terrible pain after the operation…but I never worried about him, even if I turned my back to put meat up a tree in order to test the use of his leg.

that Shaitani had produced two cubs and Sally three; they were all fit and bouncing. The seven lions had more than seven cubs between them – just how many more had been sired by Boy and Ugas I would never know.

At this inconvenient moment the skies opened and several times Paul Pearson and Jonny Baxendale were prevented from getting through the clouds to Meru. However, the Russian Ambassador and two minions made it by road, bearing the incongruous gifts of vodka and caviare. Joy and I thanked them and were able to introduce them to Maya and Juno who gate-crashed the party.

Then on one dark afternoon Paul made it. Sue turned up at my camp with her instruments and some ampules of sedative, asking if Boy and I could be ready to pack up our lives at Meru – for ever – in half an hour, before the clouds closed in.

On that last, nightmare day Joy was as sad and moved as I was. Although Girl had drifted away from Boy for a year she seemed to sense she would never see him again. While we lifted his drugged body, wrapped in a blanket, into my Landrover she jumped on to the pick-up. No bribes would entice her down, so there was nothing for it but to drive her to the airstrip too. We needed every available pair of hands to load Boy's 450 lb dead weight into the aeroplane.

Luckily, on the way to it, Girl spotted a young giraffe. In a flash she had sprung down, stalked it, bowled it over and taken lethal hold of its throat. As soon as she was engrossed in feeding we lifted and heaved her brother's limp body into the back of the plane.

Chapter 9

By Lake Naivasha
1969–1970

As we took off I was too disturbed by my last view of Meru, and by the sight of Joy's tiny figure still waving from the edge of the airstrip, to worry about Boy.

Sue sat next to the pilot and kept bending over Boy's massive head, just behind her. I sat on the floor at the back of the little cabin, beside Boy's tail. I wondered what would happen if his drug began to wear off, and felt slightly anxious. Sue also looked uneasy and I asked her if anything was wrong.

"Boy's gums have gone blue, and he is starting to pant. I don't know if his heart can stand this after the anaesthetic, and all the blood he has lost. How high are we, Paul?" she asked the pilot.

"About 12,000 feet. I will take her as low as I dare," answered Paul, "but I am afraid he will have to stick it a little longer." Sue gave Boy a shot of adrenalin as we began to skim over the top of the forest in which I had hunted the Mau Mau. The trees looked like a carpet of broccoli, laced with silver ribbons where streams ran down through the gulleys or froze in a waterfall. A few spirals of smoke drifted up through the canopy.

At last the escarpment dropped steeply away beneath us as we reached the Rift Valley and Paul could take the plane lower. Our views stretched ahead into the distance on either side. Boy's breathing grew easier. Ahead of us, through a heat haze, we could make out the grey-blue waters of Lake Naivasha, roughly circular and about seven miles across. The nearer shore was pinkish, not with the thousands of flamingoes which cluster on some of the other Rift Valley lakes but with miles of mauve water lilies. Paul made for a small island, near the opposite shore, shaped like a crescent. To the east we looked down on the ranch where the Bislettis had bred the lions for *Born Free*, and the four that had come to us at Meru. But we turned west and followed the shore towards Elsamere.

Below us white pelicans flapped slowly through the sunshine while others swam sedately on the lake. A herd of lethargic hippos looked up at the little plane carrying a comatose lion over their heads. We soon spotted the airstrip where we were to land. It lay between Jack Block's house and Alan Root's where he kept his own plane, a hot-air balloon, his collection of snakes, an aardvark, and a number of other exotic animals adopted on his filming safaris.

We had arranged to buzz Elsamere as a signal for Mike Richmond to come out and meet us. After working with us all on *The Lions Are Free* he was more or less immune to the idiosyncrasies of lions and the people who live with them. As we flew in over the promontory on which the house stood, I could make out my own small cottage under the trees and the enclosure next to it, which had been put up for Boy.

There are many attractive houses around the lake. Most of them are built in colonial style of stone, or like Elsamere, white clap-board, with corrugated iron roofs. Just beyond us lay Diana Delamere's Djinn Palace, its crenellations and white Moorish dome standing out like sore thumbs. On the opposite shore I could see Colonel Rocco's pink palazzo, roofed with thatch. His talented daughters, Oria Douglas-Hamilton and Mirella Ricciardi, two more women to record the image of Africa, had grown up here.

As we circled the strip I wondered how on earth we would get Boy out of the plane, as he was still dopey and no improvised stretcher could be got through the small door. We would have to manhandle him into the Volkswagen van, but I very much doubted if we could manage his dead weight alone. Luckily a passing African, who worked in the carnation fields up the road, immediately agreed to help. He was quite unsurprised at being asked to lift an unconscious lion out of an aeroplane and into a truck. Bill had arranged for his cameraman, Dick Thompsett, to be here and catch it on film. He was too tied up with his cameras to give us a hand.

I climbed through the sliding door and held Boy's head as the others shoved his shoulders and then his hindquarters up into the Volkswagen. Mike drove us the three miles along the white road to Elsamere and when we arrived took us straight to Boy's pen, parking so that the sliding door gave on to the gate. Boy had still not stirred and since it was beginning to get dark I thought it would be best if both he and I spent the night in the Volkswagen.

Mike and Sue brought me a rug, some sandwiches and a bottle of whisky, for which I was very grateful. Before long I lay out on the back seat and went to sleep. But all night long I was disturbed as Boy worked his jaws and his tongue as if something were stuck in his throat. I was thankful he was beginning to show signs of life, but less so when he began to toss his head and grimace in the confined space of the van. Finally he began to chew the seat two inches from where I was lying. The door was on the far side of him, and I did not fancy stepping over him while he was clearly in pain and still confused by the drug; so I eased myself up on to the ledge at the back, over the engine, and curled up. I preferred the discomfort to those unpredictable jaws.

In the morning Nevil Baxendale turned up with an old tent as a shelter for Boy and food for me. It was a very kind thought, although it was nearly another twenty-four hours until Boy could get out of the van. He spent much of the time chewing one of Mike's cushions, and otherwise vandalising the Volkswagen. It took Stanley and me a long time to make it respectable again.

For the next night or two I pitched a tent near Boy's wire, to reassure him if he grew fretful. I also started to take stock of all the things that needed doing at Elsamere and to work out a routine to keep him quiet in his unaccustomed confinement.

There were about fifty acres of land which went down to the edge of the lake. Our frontage was free of the papyrus along the rest of the shore so that it was clear for boating and fishing. The house stood in a belt of aboriginal forest which had been spared when most of the rest had been cleared for building or farming. After we had moved in Joy had extended the original stone house and put sliding glass doors and windows along the full length facing the lake. On the other side, between the house and the road, which was hidden by a rise, lay a simple garden and untouched bush. My cottage stood here among the trees.

On the far side of the road, which circled the lake, lay farms, market gardens and the carnation fields. Beyond them was ranching land and, further still, natural bush rising into a rocky gorge known as Hell's Gate. This higher ground was quite unspoiled, even though it contained a number of steam springs which were scheduled for development, and supported plenty of game including giraffe, zebra and various different antelopes. Leopards had been seen and tracked in the gorge which was ideal country for them. Lammergeiers, giant bearded vultures with the largest wing span of any African bird, hovered over the ravine and nested on the cliffs. To get at the marrow of the bones they scavenged, they dropped them from a great height on to the rocks below. Joy longed to buy this land as a reserve and had already begun to talk to the government about it.

None of the larger animals crossed the road and came down into Elsamere. But little grey dik dik, tiny antelopes with dainty hoofs and horns, who mate for life, often darted about the garden in pairs. Occasionally I saw a bushbuck, a shy antelope about three feet tall, which has a single, gruff bark like a dog. Joy had told me to look out for the beautiful black and white colobus monkeys which loved to eat the flowers and leaves of tall

Elsamere, the house Joy bought on Lake Naivasha. The colobus monkeys and eagle owls lived in the trees; otters and hippos came up on to the lawn.

Joy with one of the eagle owls: she heard of one which put a rhino to flight.

acacias, and I sometimes heard or spotted them high above my head. Otters came up from the lake at night, to Joy's great delight – but the hippos who came too were not so welcome.

Joy was obsessed that they would ruin her garden, though so far it was hardly worthy of the name. She regarded it as a matter of urgent priority that I should put up a little latch gate to the vegetable patch that was otherwise surrounded by a few strands of wire. A hippo can weigh over two tons and I thought it unlikely that my gate would keep one out, but duly obliged. The hippos continued to make free of the land, including our vegetables, until we put down some logs at the top of the bank. Despite their size hippos cannot raise their feet very high off the ground and our barrier worked like a high brick wall. Nevertheless a few did make their way round the edges and I always carried a torch in the dark to avoid a collision.

In the mornings I would wake to the cheerful and imperious cry of the fish eagles who had staked out their hunting and nesting areas along the shore. They are aggressive birds, even driving away their own young, once they are fully fledged, to protect their fishing waters. They attack any bird rash enough to fly through their air space with food in its beak or its talons, be it pelican, eagle owl, or the goliath heron which had adopted a mossy tree stump just above the lake as its look-out point. Tiny malachite kingfishers darted down from the papyrus in search of minnows and all manner of birds flaunted their presence with their plumage or their song. There are more species of bird resident round Naivasha than in the whole of the British Isles.

Although I had Stanley to look after Boy there was very little time to go up into Hell's Gate or to watch the birds. Most of our stuff from Isiolo was still in packing cases and there was a lot of sorting, repairing and decoration to do. The water and electricity suffered from uncertain connections and the lawn needed levelling and a mower. I also had to find a place to take Boy when he was well enough to hold his own with wild lions: I knew Peter Jenkins would never allow him back into Meru and Perez Olindo seemed equally opposed to what I was doing. I could never keep him here indefinitely in an enclosure measuring 100 ft by 60 ft. I therefore wrote to a number of friends who might be able to help, explaining the kind of location Boy needed.

It had to be outside the jurisdiction of the National Parks; it must not be frequented by tribesmen and their herds; and it must be sufficiently arid and remote not to have been earmarked for farming or tourism. On the other hand, it also had to be large enough to carry a pride of lions and the game population to support them. Furthermore, to get lions in, it must be reasonably accessible to Landrovers; and if it were very remote it would be necessary to clear a small airstrip. In other words it was rather like looking for an iceberg on Lake Rudolf.

All the time Boy was getting stronger and at night he would keep us awake with his restless and unusual roar of three bellows followed by about thirty grunts. I have heard other lions make a good many grunts on occasion, but none to equal Boy's record of ninety. A friend who lived five miles away on Hippo Point said that he would listen to Boy's performance, and whereas I could never pick up any response to it he could hear the Bisletti lions, three miles further on, replying. It meant that Boy's roar must have carried a good eight miles. His forlorn solos made me more anxious than ever to find him a new home before he became too frustrated at Naivasha.

Just before Christmas the Harthoorns were due to take the pins out of Boy's leg but they had to go abroad and so their friend Paul Sayer, an excellent vet, came to do it instead. When he opened the wound he could see only one pin and spent some time searching Boy's leg in case it had worked its way out of position. At last he had to give in and stitched up the skin. It was only the next day, when Boy began to get over the anaesthetic, that I remembered I had heard him chewing something that sounded like metal a few days before. I went into his compound and saw the missing pin lying on the ground; it must have been there all the time. Happily he was back in form by Christmas Day.

* * *

It was now the end of the year and Joy was preparing to close her camp at Meru. She still kept in touch with Pippa's cubs. The younger ones would soon be mating, but her appeal to be allowed to stay and observe the next generation was turned down. I therefore drove to Meru to collect her. When I reached her camp Joy had gone out, hoping to get a last glimpse of the cheetahs.

I spent the day looking for Ugas, Girl and the rest of the pride and I found all the lionesses except little Sandie. They were on a buffalo kill. Although I had not seen them for more than a month they took my sudden appearance as a matter of course. While I was sitting with them Sally sauntered off to a small tree a few hundred yards away. When she came back after twenty minutes she was followed by the five little cubs.

They were now several months old and at first they peeped shyly at me through the long grass. Then, seeing Sally lying near me, they gained confidence and all piled on to her, jostling to get at her milk. Sally and Suki took it in turn to feed them. I had a feeling that Sally had brought them out of their hiding place deliberately to show them to me. I still could not see Sandie, but she may well have been sleeping off a heavy meal of buffalo meat in the long grass.

When Joy came back to camp in the evening she told me she had been less lucky and had not seen the cheetahs on this, her last, day. It made her extremely tense and unhappy and I could tell she also blamed me for the fact that she had been asked to leave.

Although Pippa never held the same place in her emotions as Elsa, she was nevertheless very deeply attached to her and she felt an additional affection and responsibility for Pippa's cubs once their mother was dead. It was a painful wrench to leave them. Joy was intensely frustrated at being thwarted from pursing her observations a stage further. She was always exchanging views and information about lions and cheetahs with the scientists she met, and she believed her records would one day be a valuable reference for anyone stocking reserves with animals bred in sanctuaries planned for the purpose. On top of this she was both angry and hurt at being told to leave Meru. This had been Elsa's final home, the park had capitalised frequently on its association with Elsa and Joy had made very generous grants towards its establishment and running costs.

There were other, more personal, reasons for Joy's deep unhappiness. Her right hand was still painful and virtually useless, which was an incessant irritation for someone so energetic. She could not play her piano, and now that there was time to paint she found she still could not handle a brush. She therefore arranged to have a third operation, while I continued to search for somewhere to settle down with Boy. This too upset Joy for she felt I should simply take him to his new home and leave him there.

Within a few days of Joy's arrival at Elsamere, it was clear that Boy would not be moving anywhere for some time. Instead of improving, his leg had got decidedly worse. Paul Sayer came down to Elsamere with Toni and Sue Harthoorn to examine him and as soon as they opened the leg they found that the bone ends had not fused – they had grown apart instead of together. As a result Paul decided to cut back the two ends of the bone and insert a pair of steel plates across the fracture to hold everything in place. The second phase of this operation took five and a half hours, so that poor Boy was under an anaesthetic for more than eight altogether. Even then Tony and Paul had been able to put in only one plate, as it was too risky to keep him out for longer.

That night and the following day he was barely conscious. On the second evening his breathing slowed, he grew cold, and his temperature fell a long way below normal: I thought he was a gonner. I tried talking to him continuously, and played tapes of lions roaring, but he simply didn't respond. So, in the middle of the night, I rang the Harthoorns, who advised relays of hot water-bottles, body massage and brandy. The treatment began to produce results, particularly the brandy which I squirted into his mouth with a syringe. By the morning Boy was able to get to his feet unassisted and after that he did not look back.

At the same time, I received a letter from Bill Travers about Boy. His own experience, after his collision during the filming of *Duel at Diablo*, had been very similar to Boy's. He wrote:

> It seems to me the authorities may reject your plan because there will always be, especially in old age, a slight stiffness of his leg. If the same applies to lions as to humans, then that is a distinct possibility because I have an eleven-inch steel rod threaded down my left leg, from the knee to the foot, which replaces the marrow and holds together all the various fragments of bone. But I have no real sensation below the knee. I certainly can't run as well as I could, nor do I have as much control. If this is the case might not Boy eventually become disabled and therefore there would be a danger of his becoming, in spite of himself, a man-eater? Perhaps one ought to consider whether a partly disabled lion wouldn't be more happy to survive in a large compound.

Bill then went on to suggest that as an alternative I should consider the rehabilitation of snow leopards, as he knew about my special interest in Indian animals, and that at one time I had been tempted to discuss with the authorities the introduction of tigers into a confined area of Kenya as a strategic reserve of the species. Looking back, Bill's warning about Boy was uncannily prophetic, but at the time I was determined to see him settled happily again in the wild and told Bill that this would have to take priority over the snow leopards or anything else.

Although the single plate was only held in place by four slender screws, it miraculously continued to carry Boy's weight. What he needed now was an open space in which to exercise and build up his muscles, for after a couple of months he still walked with an uncomfortable limp.

Joy continued to hope that by concentrated effort she could teach herself to paint again, but once more she was disappointed and her frustration reached a new level when she visited Meru with Stanley, to search for the cheetahs, and failed to find them. To add fuel to the flames, she heard that Billy Collins had been out to see two other authors then at Naivasha, Sue Harthoorn and Colonel Rocco's daughter Mirella Ricciardi, but had not called on her: she was always afraid that her position as a best-selling author might one day go into eclipse. It is human nature, in a situation like this, to vent your accumulated feelings on someone close to you.

She reached breaking point when I refused to drop my plan to take up one of the offers I had received to settle Boy in Botswana, Ethiopia, near

The fondness remained: beneath the surface the bond of shared experience was unbroken.

Tsavo or up by Lake Rudolf. She said our lives had become incompatible, she would divorce me, and her grounds would be cruelty.

It seemed to me that the proposition, the contention and the remedy were all three exaggerated.

It was quite true that after we had moved to Meru our lives had not been a bed of roses. Joy had disapproved of my attitude to the lions; I think she grudged me the independence of my separate camp; she was implacable in her anger that I had gone ahead with Bill in making *The Lions Are Free*; she held Boy, and hence me, responsible for her exile from Meru; and she had always regarded my smoking and drinking as extravagant.

But despite all this we still shared our deep love of living out in the wilderness and of the creatures there; our approaches to their conservation were often identical; we respected each other's devotion to the animals we looked after however different our motives; and there had never been a moment when we had not done everything we could to help each other in an emergency. Beneath the surface the fondness remained; and below that the bond of shared experience was unbroken.

As to my cruelty, this must have existed very largely in Joy's mind: she hated opposition of any kind and no doubt there were occasions when she found me exceedingly obdurate. Julian Huxley's wife, Juliette, was very fond of Joy, greatly admired her gifts and became one of her few confidantes. After Joy died, she wrote that for all her remarkable achievements Joy always remained, at heart, a child. I think this was true.

After much soul searching I told Joy that if she really wanted a divorce I would not contest it but that I was prepared to pay neither her lawyers' costs nor alimony. Life might become a little easier, but I was genuinely fond of Joy and it was sad that our marriage should break up like this after twenty-six years.

＊　　　＊　　　＊

Jack Block, who had a house just along the lake shore and was a director of the carnation farm, did much for my morale at this gloomy time. He was not only Chairman of the finest chain of hotels and game park lodges in Kenya but a dynamic figure in the World Wildlife Fund. Always keen to support animals, he offered personal help in financing the cost of keeping Boy. But before I could accept it another letter arrived from Bill Travers. The sight of the envelope raised my spirits as I never knew what outlandish enterprise he was not going to suggest next: a scheme for teaching elephants in Africa to handle timber in the way his friend Elephant Bill had trained them in Burma? Another exotic project in the Himalayas? Perhaps even a wild plan to rehabilitate Boy in India?

What his letter actually contained was a proposal even more preposterous. He said he had wandered into a shop in London and found a young lion there. Rather than let it go to a zoo or an English game park like Longleat, would I be prepared to release it in the wild with Boy? The lion was called Christian.

At first I thought the suggestion was a joke, but when I realised Bill was serious I told him just how many obstacles would be put in our way. One by one he proceeded to demolish them, on the telephone from London.

"We mustn't be negative, George," he said. "Christian is nearly a year old, he will make an ideal companion for Boy and help him win any fights for territory. It will also be a marvellous chance to see if lions which are bred in captivity have lost all their instincts. What is more, if we film the whole thing I'm sure the government will back it, like last time, as it will be terrific publicity for Kenya. I will come out to see you next week; in the meantime will you find out where we could take them?"

The more I heard about Christian the more the idea appealed to me. He had been born in a zoo in southern England and was a fourth-generation circus or zoo lion. His father had come from Rotterdam Zoo and he was therefore conceivably related to Elsa. When he was a small cub he had been put on sale in the pet department at Harrods, as was then permitted by law, where he was seen and bought by two young Australians doing their Christmas shopping. Ace Bourke and John Rendall had come to Europe in search of adventure, having just taken their university degrees. With their impulsive purchase they certainly acquired what they were looking for.

This was the end of the swinging sixties. Carnaby Street and the King's Road had gone into technicolour. Ace and John grew their hair, put on snakeskin boots and wore wolfskin jackets or purple ankle-length coats. When they got a job in a pine furniture shop at the World's End in Chelsea they took Christian to work there each morning. At first he was a considerable asset. As he sat in the window passers-by would do a double-take, and custom accelerated. At night he shared the boys' flat.

The problems started when Christian began to grow. They persuaded the vicar of the Moravian Church in Chelsea to let them play football in the graveyard and Christian became adept at the game, especially in tackling. At the shop, however, he became less of a pull: customers were distinctly apprehensive of an adolescent lion at large among the chests, dressers and tables. For much of the day he had to be shut in a basement store room, behind a table top over which he could peer but not leap.

One day Bill wandered unwittingly into the shop looking for a desk.

Simultaneously Ace and John recognised the George Adamson of the film and with the promise of showing him "something interesting" they coaxed him downstairs. The adventure for which the young Australians had come to Europe took a new turn as soon as Bill set eyes on Christian. They could not resist it when Bill asked if he might try to arrange for them and their lion to go out to Africa. Out in Africa I could not resist the challenge of taking on a lion from London.

I had not made much progress in the hunt for a new home for the lions by the time Bill arrived in Nairobi. I found I was still up against all the old prejudices in the National Parks, who thought that our quixotic plans were turning conservation, which was a serious business, simply into show business. My position was made worse by a vitriolic article in the press, attacking my work, by the distinguished writer and traveller, Wilfred Thesiger. Although he was a friend of Peter and Sara Jenkins, and understandably incensed by Mark's accident with Boy, I thought this public abuse was unnecessary.

But I also had some allies. Monty Ruben, who had so much experience of filming in Kenya and whom I had come to know well through *Born Free* and Bill's documentaries, had many good friends in government — so had Ken Smith who was now Senior Game Warden of the Coastal Province, which included Garissa, and in particular Kora.

With their support Bill and I went to see the government's special adviser on issues of this kind, which involved both conservation and the national image. Tony Cullen recommended us to look at several areas, but seemed to think that Kora was most likely to meet all the contradictory qualifications our unusual assignment required.

While Bill and I were searching for a home for the two lions, Joy began to write her second book about the cheetahs, *Pippa's Challenge*, and she grew increasingly enthralled by the birds and animals round Elsamere. She was infinitely patient with them, perhaps in contrast to her usual approach to people. By sitting silently for hours she came to know the reedbuck which nibbled the grass round her as she ate breakfast, the otters that came up in the evenings, and the serval, genet, and civet cats which prowled round, like the honey badger, at night. Her favourites were the colobus monkeys and the Verreaux eagle owls.

These owls are the largest in Africa. They have big, black eyes, the size of ping-pong balls, pink lids and white lashes. A well-known ornithologist, Leslie Brown, had spotted a pair which had adopted an abandoned fish eagle's nest in one of our trees. Joy kept a regular watch on it and was rewarded when the fledgling grew and took wing. At first he couldn't manage a hoot and only whistled, so she christened him Pfeifer (from the

German). While he was young his parents fed him attentively with regurgitated mole rats which they hunted to the great benefit of our lawn.

The aerial battles round the lake were continuous and, on the way home from shopping in Naivasha, Joy found an eagle owl lying on the ground with a damaged eye, apparently dying. It must have got the worst of a duel with a fish eagle. She asked for my help, so I wrapped it in a canvas sheet and put it in the car, but by the time we were back at the house Joy was convinced it was dead. I knew that these birds were skilful at feigning sleep or death and occasionally lured some of the small finches to a sticky end by this trick; I therefore shot a dove and put it in a cage with the owl. When we came back half an hour later the owl was lying exactly as I had left her, but the dove had disappeared. Joy's patient made a full recovery.

After some time the eagle owls raised another fledgling and when it was old enough to fly Pfeifer took over its feeding. The population of mole rats was soon exhausted and as there were very few snakes about, which they also regard as a delicacy, we put out chicken heads. This brought the predatory fish eagles, and once an augur buzzard, down in search of a snack at the expense of the young owls, but Pfeifer was staunch in defence of her sister – whom Joy called Bundu – and their food supply.

When Bundu grew up she displayed the same courage. Joy once saw her driving off a genet cat which tried to steal her supper of chicken heads. She proudly reported the battle and its outcome to Leslie Brown, who rather crushingly told her that he had once watched an eagle owl put a rhino to flight.

Over the years a kind of teasing friendship grew up between the owls and Joy's other favourites, the pair of colobus monkeys. They were very shy until one of them literally dropped into Joy's life; it fell a hundred feet from a tall acacia in the garden, landing a few yards from where she sat. Joy was naturally afraid it had hurt or crippled itself and could not bear to lose one of the monkeys, which were very rare round the lake – at 6,000 feet they are below the altitude of their normal mountain habitat. They are extremely attractive and, although protected, were relentlessly hunted for their beautiful black-and-white fur and their tails which were sold as superior fly whisks. On this occasion Joy need not have worried: the monkey picked itself up and was soon feeding happily in the tree canopy again.

Not long after this, Joy noticed that one of the monkeys was clutching something in its arms, and it took her little time to realise it was a baby. The family were inseparable and, though the father sat some way off, he played an increasing part in teaching the youngster how to climb and leap, and rescued him when he got into difficulties. We studied their feeding carefully and put out a few snacks; little by little they came to accept and trust us, particularly Joy.

It was after she had been to Nairobi for a few days that Stanley told her the father was missing. After a long search we found him motionless in the fork of a tree: one arm hung limply down. In consternation Joy asked Stanley and the other boys if they knew anything about the tragedy and they said that while we were away some shooting had gone on in the next property. Joy got the boys to tie three long bamboos together and when they succeeded in dislodging the colobus they saw he had been peppered with shot. We talked to the employers of the culprits, the police were brought in, the men confronted and their guns confiscated.

What particularly moved and upset Joy was the state of hunched shock in which the mother and her son, for several days, occupied the tree where the father had died. Her face had suddenly grown old and wrinkled. Slowly their spirits revived and as time went by Joy was given two more colobus. Over the years the family has flourished and multiplied. They and the eagle owls still live in the trees at Elsamere today.

When Joy was writing a book, painting a picture, planning an enterprise or travelling the world to promote her work, all would be well; and throughout our marriage I noticed that when she was able to express her affection for an animal and sense that she was being rewarded with affection or trust in return, it gave her peace of mind and provided her with a reassurance that she could not find elsewhere. Once more I was aware that her time among the animals at Elsamere, and the progress she was making with her new book, *Pippa's Challenge*, seemed to be restoring her equanimity. Her morale rose further, after a visit to Meru in July, when she found one of Pippa's older cubs, Tatu, with three cubs of her own.

By July the prospects all round began to look brighter. To my great relief Joy dropped her talk about divorce. She seemed resigned to my hopes for Christian and Boy – who was bursting with rediscovered energy – ceased to undermine my reconnaissance for a place to release them and turned her mind to the imminent production of a film of *Living Free*. Bill, Ginny and I had decided to have no part in it, and Joy was suspicious of the two men who had come out to Kenya to make the preliminary arrangements – she called them "the gangsters". Nevertheless she was drawn into talks about scripts and locations.

Then I had a windfall. A game warden rang up to say he had a two-month-old female lion cub whose mother had been shot: could I give her a home? This suited me perfectly because Boy and Christian would need at least one lioness to help them kill and as a mate. I went to fetch her, but since I dared not put her straight into Boy's enclosure she went into a small annexe. Next morning they were lying side by side, as close as the wire would allow. When I appeared Boy stood up and glared at me aggressively; he became quite agitated and even snarled at me, which he had never done before. In fact he seemed to be so protective of the little cub, Katania, that I immediately put her in with him and they became instant friends. To Boy's evident embarrassment Katania tried to find a teat on which to suckle. Normally a male lion would never be as tolerant of a cub but presumably his loneliness had mellowed him.

By the time that Katania was settled at Naivasha my searches had narrowed to the region round Garissa. Ken Smith, as Provincial Game Warden, had supported my approaches to the District Game Warden, the Provincial Commissioner and the District Commissioner. The District Officer arranged for me to meet the Tana River Council whose decision it was and held a *barazza*, or communal meeting, for the local residents. They all seemed in favour, probably as they saw the presence of lions and me, and the making of the documentary film, as a source of income and interest.

The Tana at Kora was about a hundred yards wide, sometimes more. It was now a deep red with soil which had been washed into it: when I first knew it, thirty years before, its waters had been crystal clear. The banks were lined with tall, leafy trees, shrubs and grass, all of which were bright green compared with the dry, brown bush which stretched in endless undulations, over the ochre earth, to the horizon. Only one feature stood out: a group of sandy-coloured rocks about two or three miles back from the river. The largest was shown as Kora Rock on the map and it rose four hundred feet above the surrounding country.

In the old days I had done many safaris here. It was well known as a hunting block, for the game was afforded excellent protection by the thick bush. The elephant carried particularly good tusks and there were plenty of giraffe and rhino, not to mention zebra and the lesser game on which lions so often depended for a living. From the air we could see no cultivation, no camels, cattle or goats and no tribesmen. It was tough country but it met most of our requirements and I quickly decided to make a formal application for it.

It was a stroke of luck for me that at that precise moment Ken Smith, who had put up a paper to the Chief Game Warden and Ministry of Wildlife and Tourism recommending my Kora scheme, was posted to the Ministry and found his proposal waiting on his new desk for approval. He immediately stamped it. I sent a message to Bill to bring Christian as fast as he could and had a celebration lunch at my old stamping ground, the Norfolk Hotel, with Monty Ruben, and Jack Block who now owned it.

Over lunch Monty told us that his father, Eddie, had just sold the family interest in Express Transport. His father had built his own waggons to hitch to his first team of mules; now he shifted anything anywhere, by sea, road, rail or air; he had over a thousand employees. Monty himself was becoming a director of the luxurious Mt Kenya Safari Club. I wryly reflected that Monty's and Jack's fathers had both come to Kenya with just a few beans in their pockets, exactly as I had. Now their two sons controlled the most attractive and valuable properties in the country. I had only two tents to my name – but I was genuinely happier than if they had been a couple of palaces.

I think Terence probably felt much the same, although he had invested his share of our mother's estate in building a house on the beach at Malindi. It was within easy reach of the big ranch near Tsavo where he had worked at cattle protection for the last few years. Now he came to my aid in making preparations for Kora. Past master at putting up camps and the construction of roads, he was out in the bush with a gang, cutting a track from the main Nairobi–Garissa road to the hill at Kora. He was then going to clear a way from a camp, at the foot of the rocks, to the river. I made a final recce from the air and when I spotted Terence in a sea of thorn bushes dropped a message telling him to cross his arms over his head for each day he thought it would take him to reach Kora. He signalled twice, so I went back to Naivasha to make the last preparations.

Within a very short time Bill cabled the flight on which he would be arriving at Nairobi with Christian, Ace and John. It would have been quite impractical to mount a convoy to take all three lions on the long journey up to Kora, so I left Boy and Katania, for the time being, in the care of Joy and Stanley. Once Christian was ensconced at Kora I would come back for them.

Joy saw me off and her last words were that I must renew my subscription to the Flying Doctor and get a radio transmitter so that we could keep in touch in emergencies. At the time I thought this was a little pessimistic: only later did I realise how wise she was.

Chapter 10

A Lion from London
1970

If you try to fly a lion from London to Nairobi you collect some funny looks. One of the District Commissioners I had gone to see about a suitable location for Christian's release stared at me in bewilderment. He said he thought I must be mad: there were already too many wild animals in his district, without adding to the stock of lions.

The airline did not believe Bill, at first, when he said he wanted tickets to Kenya for three men and a lion. Then they told him he would have to insure Heathrow Airport.

"How much for?" asked Bill, in equal surprise.

"Oh, it will have to be for at least a million pounds," they said seriously. "Just think what could happen if he got loose and ran amok among the passengers, or out on the runway." So Bill insured London Airport for half an hour, the time it took to film the loading of Christian into the plane.

At the airport in Nairobi Africans clustered round Christian's crate and the holding bay, where he was allowed out of it. At a year old he had weighed 170 lb on a pair of butcher's scales: tall at the shoulder and handsome, he was now growing a mane. He was stared at with mixed curiosity, interest and admiration. Many of the crowd who came to look at him had never seen a lion in their lives: they could not afford to go out into the game parks.

I found myself studying Ace and John with a mixture of similar feelings, for their appearance could have been described in much the same terms as Christian's. They were young, tall and good looking. If anything their manes were rather more advanced than Christian's. And, like him, the young Australians were a long way from home. Bill and I watched them with respect as they encouraged Christian, emerging groggily from his crate, and settled him in a corner with some food and water. For the next forty-eight hours they came out to the airport several times a day to keep him company and check on his condition.

It was touching to see how the young lion, who was obviously fond of both boys, would sometimes eye Ace and leap up to rub cheeks with him.

Opposite: On the eve of leaving the caravan in Bill and Ginny's garden at Leith Hill in England, Christian weighed 170 lb.

Ace sensed what was coming and braced himself for the assault with outstretched arms.

When Christian had recovered from the flight we took our Landrovers to collect him for the three hundred mile journey to Kora. He hopped into the back of mine after Ace and John, without hesitation. Bill, and the three friends who were making the film, followed in the other two trucks. The small convoy caused quite a stir when we stopped for petrol or to let Christian stretch his legs.

Rather more than half way to Kora Nevil Baxendale, at my request, had very kindly put up a camp with a small enclosure for Christian so that we could break the journey for a couple of nights. To mark Christian's first day on the real soil of Africa, Ace and John removed his collar. Then, after a quick supper, they shifted their camp beds beside his wire and fell fast asleep.

The next morning Christian pranced round Ace and John with a friskiness they had not seen before. They walked him up a low ridge beside the road, so that he could get a good look at his new country. All the other lions I had released had been born out here, in the wilds of Africa or at any rate in relative freedom. One of the reasons I had accepted Christian was to find out if releasing a zoo-born lion would be more difficult, because his natural instincts might have diminished or atrophied after generations of captivity.

As these thoughts were going through my head Christian suddenly went tense and froze. He had spotted a cow grazing in the bush. Very slowly indeed he sank to a crouch and circled downwind from the cow. Next, taking cover behind some bushes, he silently narrowed the gap between himself and his prey. In a split second he had ceased to trot round Ace and John like a pet dog and had adopted the techniques of a wild lion. I regretted having to drive the Landrover between him and his prey. But Christian was not to be easily turned from his purpose. He quickly started to stalk the cow all over again. Ace and John grabbed him and – for the first time in his life – Christian turned on them with a warning snarl. I knew then that I would have no more difficulty educating Christian than any other lion.

For the last few miles of the journey we let Christian follow the Landrover on foot, as the going was very slow and bumpy. He had to get used to the strangeness of the smells, the noises and the heat; the temperature on the Tana, in the middle of the day, was hotter than anything he had known before. At first he was very ungainly on the stones and rocks, and his feet were obviously very tender. There were a great many thorns underfoot and although he could get them out of his pads himself he usually looked helplessly at Ace and John until they removed them for him.

When we finally reached Kora Terence took us down to the river, where he had put up a temporary camp for Christian's arrival. It was proving very difficult to sink the posts of the permanent camp in the hard ground under Kora Rock and its completion was going to take another week. The river camp was a colourful introduction to African life for Ace and John. Almost as soon as we arrived Terence told us how his labour gang had been sleeping out beside the track and a crocodile had crawled over one of the men in its haste to get back to the river; it had scratched him with its claws in the process. Shortly after that John shifted a stone, as he set up his camp bed, and a large scorpion scuttled away under the rocks. I thought it was a trifle unfair of Bill then to produce the sloughed-off skin of a big python he had found in the bushes.

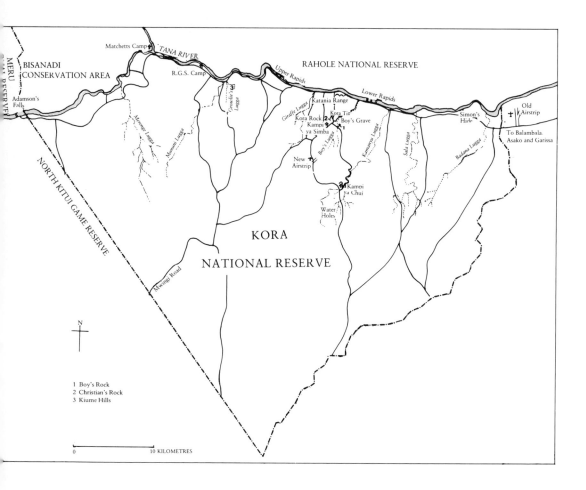

I told Ace and John to keep an eye open for the rather more attractive animals they would see visiting the river, and others, like waterbuck, which never left it. The baboons, territorial, noisy and provocative, were always hanging about there. So were the grey vervet monkeys with their scarlet and blue private parts. Many of the larger animals came down to drink in the evening or early morning – antelopes, zebra, giraffe and occasionally buffalo. I believed that in severe droughts elephants made their way to the Tana from as far away as Tsavo, two hundred miles south.

The Tana is certainly the most significant feature at Kora. It is the largest river in Kenya and at this point runs from west to east, five miles south of the equator. It forms the northern side of what is known as the Kora Triangle, the area I had been allotted for my new experiment with this strangely assorted pride of three lions. The river rises on the slopes of Mt Kenya whose snows, melted by the equatorial sun, perpetually feed it. Between us and the mountain there are seven hydro-electric dams which have almost eliminated seasonal flooding at Kora and have replaced it with a gentler pulse of their own. Deforestation, cultivation too close to the banks and overgrazing have produced the erosion which washes red-brown silt into the river. It clogs the machinery at the dams and is swept down to the coast. There it is deposited on the reefs, where it is killing one of the most exquisite coral gardens in the world.

From the air the river can be traced instantly by the bright greenness of the trees and shrubs which fringe it. The most distinctive are the doum palms with their slim, branching stems. They bear neither coconuts nor dates but rock-hard nuts enjoyed by elephants and baboons. There also flourish tall acacias, tamarinds, Tana River poplars and henna bushes from whose leaves comes the hair dye long used in Africa and now, I am told, fashionable in Europe and America.

If the river is the most significant feature of the landscape and the reason why we ourselves chose Kora, the most conspicuous feature is the group of hills known collectively as Kora Rock. Their tops are round, rusty and smooth: they turn pink towards sunset. The second largest, crowned with a boulder, inevitably became Kora Tit. Geologists do not agree on the precise origin of the rocks, though one theory is that they are richer in potassium than the land which surrounded them and so have resisted more effectively erosion by the rain and sun.

We had decided to pitch the main camp at the foot of these hills for several reasons. It would be easy to find from the air and gave us the advantages of a slight elevation – the occasional breeze and a view of the valley below. The rocks provided the lions with excellent look-outs – and when they came to have cubs, with lairs. Furthermore, if Kora were ever opened to tourist safaris, we would be two or three miles back from the track, which would inevitably become busy, along the river.

The most extensive feature of Kora is the thick thorn bush, known as *nyika*, which virtually covers the whole Kora Triangle. It grows out of an earth tinged with rust, for the meagre rainfall oxidises the iron in it as it is rapidly evaporated by the sun. The vegetation of the *nyika* is largely *Acacia* and several varieties of *Commiphora* bush, all of which carry formidable thorns. At one time the *nyika* stretched from the Sudan in the north to Tanzania in the south, and extended eastwards from Kora to the coast. It was impenetrable to the first Europeans who explored Mt Kenya and repelled even the pastoral tribes whose cattle fell victims to the sleeping sickness carried by its tsetse flies.

One evening walk to the top of Kora Rock, with Christian at our heels and sniffing at the bushes, was enough to show all this to Bill, Ace and John. The next day we were joined by Monty Ruben who was once more helping Bill with the production of the film. Having settled in this motley band, mostly expatriate, I set off for Naivasha to fetch Boy and Katania.

* * *

When I returned Terence had completed the main camp, up by the rocks: it was divided into two — one side for the lions and the other for Terence, myself and Stanley who had come to look after the lions and help cook. It was by no means the end of Terence's work for there were many miles of important roads still to cut.

There were some tense moments introducing Christian to the enormous Boy and tiny Katania. The Australians brought him into our side of the compound before we let him see Boy and Katania through the wire. Boy glowered at Christian who cringed behind Ace and John, while they themselves were awed by the size and strength of Boy. Katania, sensing trouble, withdrew to the far side of the pen. Just then Boy hurled himself at the wire partition with startling speed, strength and ferocity, and let out a thundering roar. The fence bulged dramatically, but held Boy's massive weight.

Christian was further shaken by this demonstration and pressed against Ace's legs. After a second formidable charge by Boy, Christian pushed John over in his eagerness for reassurance.

The following day I noticed that Christian and Katania were developing a sympathetic interest in each other, so I cut a small hatch in the dividing wire, through which Katania could slip in and out as a go-between. Although Boy disapproved of their consorting together, and made several dashes in their direction, he did so with less conviction than before. It was touching to see how gently Christian played with Katania and the tenderness with which they rubbed their cheeks together.

That night I thought I should take another relationship a stage further. I left Katania with Christian and let Boy wander about on our side of the fence as I wanted him, Ace and John to be completely at ease with one another. It amused me that when Boy chose to spend the night in their tent they were too prudent or flattered to argue.

The next evening, over sundowners, we once more discussed exactly when and how we were going to let Christian face Boy for the first time without a safety curtain of wire. Boy weighed nearly three times as much as Christian, so we decided it would have to be outside the compound, giving Christian the chance to cut and run if Boy roughed him up too much. Secondly we worked out a plan to lead them by different routes up to a meeting place on the large sloping rocks beside the camp. We would plant Katania there with them, hoping that, a miniature peace-maker, she would soften the belligerence of Boy's first charge. There was no doubt he would go for Christian — it was just a question of how violent the attack would be.

This was the crucial moment of the whole enterprise; if Christian were to turn tail and disappear into the bush — which I thought was extremely unlikely — the film would lose most, if not all, of its point and Boy would have to face a new and hostile world alone. We had already heard the local lions give voice at night.

The next day we began our preparations for the confrontation. On alternate mornings we took Boy and Christian up to the rocks where the open space would enable them to see each other approaching and give the camera an excellent field of vision. As soon as both lions felt at home there I decided to take my chance.

Ace and John went up first with Christian and left him sitting in the sun, while they stood well back in the edge of the bush. Then I led Boy and Katania up from a different direction. At first all three lions just lay down, about fifteen yards from each other, and Christian never took his eyes off Boy and Katania.

We waited like that for about twenty minutes and then Katania left Boy, who had picked a vantage point at the top of the rock, wandered slowly down to Christian and started to tease him. But today Christian, who was still gazing at Boy, felt far too anxious to play games and pushed her away.

That seemed to release a spring inside Boy. He came charging down the slope with a terrifying roar and lashed out at Christian with the full force of his gigantic pads. I thought Christian was bound to make a dash for it,

On the first evening Bill, Ace (centre) and John (right) showed Christian the river. It was a moment of tranquillity before the arrival of Boy who met Christian with a thundering charge against the wire that sent him cowering behind our legs.

with fatal results if Boy caught him. But once again Christian's instincts asserted themselves, as they would have in any wild lion that had the mind and the courage not to bolt. He rolled on to his back and lay there in a classic posture of submission – letting out a little howl of anguish that ended in a cross between a whine and a rattle. Honour satisfied, Boy cuffed him again once or twice but just a little less aggressively than before, and lay a short distance away.

Later, when all three lions had calmed down, we examined Christian and found that he had only one small cut on his foreleg. Boy's blows must have had tremendous force but he had kept his claws in.

After this confrontation all three lions were free to mix with each other whenever they chose. Once or twice they spent the entire night in Ace and John's tent. As Boy roared his head off, Christian was as bumptious as ever and Katania could not resist licking their faces or nibbling their toes; they must have had second thoughts about the pleasures of life in the bush. Nevertheless the high spirits of all of them remained unabated.

It came as a bit of a surprise when Christian was clearly off colour one day. I felt his nose and it was both drier and warmer than it should have been. It's not the easiest manoeuvre to get a thermometer up a lion's anus but I managed it and it confirmed he had a fever, almost certainly tick fever, which had killed Elsa. It was an unpleasant thought but fortunately I had brought the right vaccine and two days later he was better.

The time had now come to see how Christian would get on, for the first time in his life, without Ace and John. They decided that during this separation they would go off and have a look at the rest of Kenya for a couple of weeks. The film crew also left, having shot virtually all the footage that was needed of Christian in Africa. Suddenly the camp seemed quite empty.

*   *   *

Ace and John had cared for Christian as long as he could remember; they had romped, wrestled and played with him; and on the rare occasions he needed rebuke or punishment they provided them. In a word they had combined the roles of his mother, his brothers and his elders. Protection, feeding and self-discipline are all essential if a cub is not to die of exposure or starvation, or to stray into the jaws of a carnivore. The ragging and fighting with other young lions is almost equally important. It ensures that they bond and thus rely on one another in the hunt, and trust one another when it comes to a show down with rivals for mates or territory.

When John and Ace, on whom Christian had been imprinted as if they were his mother, left Christian for the last time he would have to transfer some of his affection and trust to me: even more importantly he would have to develop a really close bond with Boy, however late in life it might be for them. When young males grow up and, as often happens, are driven off out of their pride, their chances of survival increase considerably if they are accompanied by another lion.

I had always found with Elsa, and later filming *Born Free*, that one of the best methods of developing a relationship with a lion is to take it on daily walks. At Kora I set off on the three-mile walk to the river with Boy, Christian and Katania, at about 6.30 each morning. It was impossible for me to push my way through the bush with them for the shrubs, thorns and trees grew too close together. So I kept to the roads which Terence and his team of African labourers were opening up to the principal features. They used no machines but simply cut back the bush with pangas (like machetes). To clear the thorn branches, with their lethal spikes, they cut traditional implements – sticks with a fork at one end for pushing and a hook at the other for pulling. Then they levelled the ground with mattocks or heavy hoes. Occasionally they would have to crack a particularly obdurate boulder by lighting a fire over it before pouring water on the heated stone.

I noticed that both Boy and Christian seemed specially wary of Terence's labourers: it interested me, because during the filming of *Born Free* I became aware that although the lions seemed quite relaxed in the presence of Europeans, even strangers, they were instantly alert if an African appeared. In the end I came to the conclusion that it went back to the process of imprinting. Fundamentally all lions are suspicious of all humans, but the lions I had worked with had been raised by Europeans: the sight of a white man – or possibly his smell – seemed more acceptable than a black one. There were, of course, exceptions, such as Stanley, who had done so much to feed and look after Boy through his convalescences, but even he had to be careful.

Each day Christian grew a little more familiar with me. At first he would simply rub his head against my leg, in the lion's habitual greeting, several times a day. Then, rather more boisterously, he would bounce out and ambush me on our walks to the river. His relationship with Boy improved, too. He was always sidling up, to sit as close as possible to him and Katania. On our walks he would follow a few paces behind them and constantly imitate Boy's activities and even mannerisms; in return Boy grew increasingly tolerant.

Christian had enjoyed the river during his early days in the temporary camp. Despite his swim in the English Channel, Ace and John had to lure him into the Tana on the first day by plunging into it themselves. Like all lions Christian hated getting his feet wet and pulled a terrible face if he had to wade through a puddle, but once in deeper water he was an admirable swimmer. I was glad that my own camp was some miles away as there were a number of crocodiles on this stretch of the river, and I did not want Christian to swim across in search of adventure until he was more alert to the dangers of the new world.

When it began to get hot, at about eleven o'clock in the morning, I would sit down, light a pipe and take a cool drink from the thermos. The lions quartered the banks for interesting sights, sounds and smells. At first they would follow me back to camp for lunch: later I would leave them out all day and drive down at about five o'clock. If they were no longer resting where I had left them they would always come to my call.

Kora is so close to the equator that it always gets dark at about seven o'clock. Towards dusk I would prepare any meat I had shot for them; in the wild lions only make a kill once every few days, so I made a point of spacing out these meals at careful intervals. One of the advantages of Kora not being an official reserve was that the County Council allowed me to do this. Nevertheless I was criticised at Kora, as elsewhere, for taking the life of antelopes and zebra to feed lions which were supposedly free. I had several reasons for doing so.

In the early stages of training, the lions could not yet kill for themselves – they were too young, too inexperienced or there were too few of them; as they grew older it was important that they should not go wandering off on the other side of the river and take domestic stock if wild game eluded them; it was also essential for me, if I was to maintain my observation of them till the experiment was complete, to develop their sense of territorial attachment to the area round the camp. All wild lions win and hold a territory if they can and it is closely related to their hunting, feeding and breeding.

I was particularly careful only to give the lions a little meat each day and so the number of animals I shot was never greater than those that would have been killed if they had been a group of wild ones on their own. Once the authorities had approved my scheme I was not going to leave the lions to starve, or return them to captivity because they were slow in mastering the art of killing.

Although Christian and Katania were nowhere near ready to kill for themselves, we had a number of adventures on our walks when they suddenly picked up an unusual or exciting scent.

On one of our early expeditions I walked to the top of a large rock near the camp. Boy stopped in the shade half way up, but the others followed. Without any warning, Christian suddenly dived into a thicket and precipitated a most frightful commotion. The branches shook as if tossed by a hurricane and a few seconds later an enormous porcupine shot out, dashing away down the hill with Christian and Katania at his heels. Luckily some instinct warned Christian not to pursue the chase too closely and about twenty minutes later he came trotting back, blithe and unpunctured.

On another day all three lions paused to investigate some bushes which obviously held an interesting quarry. Boy stayed on the track, while Christian and Katania circled round the back, until Christian pushed his nose into the clump. I have never seen anything like what happened next. As if he had been flung by a spring, Christian was suddenly in the air, eight feet above the ground while beneath him, with the snort of a dragon, a rhino charged out of the bush. It made for poor Christian the instant he landed, and Christian fled for the camp with the speed of a greyhound. In those days there must have been a couple of hundred rhinos at Kora.

At night I would keep Christian, Katania and sometimes Boy inside the compound for safety's sake. Although we had not yet experienced a close encounter with the native lions we had seen their spoor and heard them roaring at night. It would be just as well to take their measure before letting my two younger ones meet them face to face.

It was not exactly in my own best interest to fence Christian in all night. Lions are meticulously clean in matters of defecation and extremely disciplined in the places they choose for this purpose. They have no such inhibitions about passing water; and Christian, who still craved human company most of the time, was forever drenching my camp bed. As wild lions behave in exactly the same way I could not be too angry and remembered that in the case of Elsa and her sisters this incontinence had a powerful disinfectant effect on their bedding. At first it was infested with bugs but after a bit the blankets and straw lost all trace of fleas and parasites.

No doubt one of the reasons for Christian's restlessness at night was that lions are nocturnal, and Boy conducted a lively dialogue with the lions that lurked menacingly, but invisibly, on the nearby ridges, rather like Indians investigating a lonely farmstead in the American West.

After a week I felt I had to stop mollycoddling Christian but was interested to see that at night he always went off in the opposite direction to the wild lions.

He had been away from camp for several days and nights on end when Ace and John returned from their tour of Kenya and the Serengeti. They had just begun to tell us about their adventures, and their visit to Joy, who had asked them about every detail of life at Kora, when Christian materialised from the bush. From his spoor I knew he had spent the time several miles off but somehow he had sensed the Australians' return. I had exactly the same experience myself, six weeks later, when I left Boy and Christian for a few days. They kept well away from camp until the moment of my return.

Christian's hours with Ace and John were numbered, and a day or two later they said goodbye. I felt a lump rise in my throat when for the last time Christian took one, two, three steps, leapt into Ace's open arms and licked him on either cheek. From the expression on the boys' faces I could tell just how much his freedom was costing them.

                              *   *   *

By the beginning of December the lions had begun to settle down properly. They had been here four months and knew their way about, staying away for several days at a time. I see from my diary that on 8 December they all left camp together and did not show up the next day. The following morning and afternoon I looked for them without success. Then, at about 4 a.m. on 11 December, Christian pitched up alone. This was worrying, as latterly Katania had been spending most of her time with him. I tossed him some meat and he disappeared into the darkness.

As soon as it was light I set out to follow him but soon lost his spoor. It took me until evening to locate him up on Kora Hill – and he was alone. At 2 a.m. that night I was woken by Boy roaring; he too was alone. Now I was really anxious about Katania.

The next afternoon I found the spoor of all three lions on the river bank; it was about three or four days old. I could see that Katania had been playing with the others, racing up and down the bank with Christian. Boy's tracks broke off at the edge of the water and I picked up his spoor again on the opposite bank. Going back over the prints very carefully, I saw Christian's emerging on the near side, on his own.

It looked to me as if Katania had followed Boy or Christian into the water and had tried to cross the river, but being so much lighter had been carried down by the current, and must have been taken by a crocodile before she could make the bank. Even at her age lions are excellent swimmers and I do not think she would have drowned.

Not only was it a great blow to me – for I had grown very fond of her and needed her as a female in the pride – but Boy and Christian were clearly uneasy; all the gaiety seemed to go out of them. Christian, particularly, missed someone to play with. It was imperative that I should get at least one or two more lionesses as quickly as possible even though I had seen Boy with two local ones the evening before the tragedy.

Crocodiles were the first enemies of my lions to raise their ugly heads at

Opposite: "Kora was a place of peace." The early days with Boy and Christian were some of the most enjoyable of my life.

Kora, though they turned out to be far from the worst. They lived along the river, basking on the mudbanks in the morning and evening, courting and mating in the silted waters, and scooping nests for their eggs, which they left to incubate in the sand. Three months later the mothers, hearing the cheeps of their hatchlings, would clear off the sand with their feet and ferry their broods in their mouths to a nursery safe in the reeds – that is if they had not already been spotted and devoured by monitor lizards or marabou storks, who were equally partial to the eggs.

Some time after Katania's disappearance I was sitting on a rock in the river close to where Katania had disappeared; it was one of the lions' favourite rendezvous. The bank was quite steep and dropped down to a stony beach that gave way to sand, rocks and shallows edging the main stream of the river. The riverbed spanned about 150 yards at this point. I gazed at Christian who was sitting nonchalantly on a rock by deeper water. As I looked, a log drifting towards him began to take on a suspicious, and then a sinister, shape. I realised that a big crocodile was stalking Christian and wondered how soon he would notice.

I always carry a rifle – or very occasionally a revolver – and I now raised it and slipped the safety catch. Christian was still unaware of the danger, so I fired. I suppose I could simply have shouted at Christian to warn him of the danger but sooner or later the croc would have got him or one of the other lions.

Quite unperturbed by his narrow escape, Christian walked back to the Landrover with me and jumped lightly on to the roof. It was something which I always discouraged at Kora, but he had seen Boy do it, and once he was up it was extremely difficult to dislodge him. I only hoped he would refrain from this habit in front of Joy, who was coming for Christmas in a few days' time. When I went down to Naivasha to fetch her I found a message from a colleague, Rodney Elliot, offering me two young lions for Kora. On Christmas Eve I sent a telegram accepting them.

At the end of the year I wrote to Ginny and Bill, telling them the latest news of the lions and trying to give Ginny a feeling of our camp at the other end of the world. I loved to sit up on the great rocks surrounded by the endless sea of thorns stretching to the horizon. They looked exactly as they must have for millions of years. So, too, must the rocks and hills have echoed to the roar of lions over hundreds of thousands of years, as they did today when Boy gave voice in the evenings. The puny efforts of man were almost invisible – fragments of half-buried stone-age tools, a few gravemounds scattered in the bush, the healed stumps of lopped branches along a lost trail, and down by the river a tangle of rusting girders to mark the crossing of soldiers in the war. Now it was a place of peace.

Chapter 11

The Shadow of Death
1971

The peace of Kora was quickly shattered. From the roars in the night I could tell that the menace circling on the hills was closing in. Sometimes Boy would go out to meet the challenge of the native lions, but at others the roaring took on a different note and I could tell that he was mating with one of the lionesses. When he came back nowadays he was tense and jumpy: I had not known him like this before, except in the presence of Girl when she was in season.

At the beginning of January, to my immense surprise, Boy forced his way through the gate, when Stanley was about to feed him, and bit him in the arm – not badly, but deep enough for Terence (who had decided to pitch a camp of his own by the river) to take him down to the nearest hospital to have it dressed. I was not alone in camp when they were away, for work was still going on round it, and Bill Travers had arranged for Simon Trevor, the cameraman who had filmed *An Elephant Called Slowly*, to begin shooting a second movie about Christian in Africa.

One morning, just after Stanley and Terence had come back, Simon and I were having a quick breakfast, at about 5.30 a.m., before setting off to collect Rodney Elliot's two young lions from Maralal. As we were finishing, Hamisi rushed in to say that Boy had got hold of Muga, one of Terence's labourers, just outside camp. There was a lot of shouting by the gate, so I grabbed a torch and an electric cattle prodder I had been given, and made for the noise. At first I could see nothing in the darkness; then I heard another cry about fifty yards away. As I moved towards it I could see Muga and Boy in my beam. Boy backed off as I yelled at him but crouched in the bushes looking extremely dangerous.

At that moment Simon drove out in his car with the lights on. He stopped it between Boy and me, leapt out and shouted at Muga, who was bleeding from the head and shoulders, to get in. The dazed man responded instinctively to the command from Simon who drove him into camp. Luckily Simon's wife was a trained nurse and although Muga immediately fainted she cleaned up his wounds. His shoulders were only superficially scratched, but his head had three puncture marks and there was a hole through his cheek.

When Muga was sufficiently recovered Terence drove him to Garissa hospital and, seeing several men waiting in the surgery, asked that Muga should receive immediate treatment. Twice the doctor refused, and when Terence expostulated he explained that two of the other men waiting had also just been attacked by a lion.

I could not understand what Muga had been doing on the track at that time of day, but they said that he had gone out for a shit. All the others had told him he was mad. The ground round the wire had not yet been cleared, lions prowled near the camp every night, and all the men had been repeatedly told to stay inside unless they had an escort.

"I'm not afraid of the lions," said Muga – and let himself out of the gate. A fortnight later I went to see him at the hospital, and found he had just been discharged as the result of a family tragedy. Two days before, his father had been given a lift to see him in hospital, but on the way home the driver was drunk and turned the car over. All six occupants had been killed, and Muga was arranging his father's burial. It would have been quite inappropriate to punish him for leaving the camp without permission, but I once more stressed the rule, and only later wished I had reinforced it with a penalty for disobedience.

The two young lions Simon and I had fetched from Maralal had been very wild at first. They had been kept in separate cages since they had been trapped a month before, and hated all the shouting as the crates were loaded on to my truck. The male was called Juma and the female I named Monalisa, as her face was scarred and she could only snarl on one side of her face. After a few days at Kora they began to grow calmer and to come out of their crates to take food; but Juma, especially, remained very wary.

On most nights we would be woken by the roars of the wild lions and in the morning could trace their movements from their spoor. They usually went around in twos and threes. In this thick bush, where game was difficult to catch, the prides were small, and young males would hunt together, after they had left their family. Lions everywhere adapt to the prevailing conditions. I have read that during the dry season the Kalahari lions lose condition, and are obliged to live singly, subsisting on very small prey like hares and even birds. On the other hand at the time of the great migrations of wildebeest and zebra, you see sleek prides of twenty or thirty lions on the lush plains of the Serengeti.

Although Christian showed considerable pluck when he went out with Boy, he was too young to be of real help when it came to a serious fight – which it soon did. Boy came in, just as it was getting dark, bitten or slashed

on his head, hind legs and scrotum, and with a deep wound on his back —
a bite on the spine is one of the lion's most effective techniques, paralysing
or crippling its adversary.

I sprinkled the wound with sulfanilamide powder, covered it with gentian
violet and tried to confine Boy to the enclosure after dark. The second night
he refused to come in, so I parked my Landrover close to him and went to
sleep on the roof. I woke with a frightful start, an hour later, as the car
suddenly swayed under the weight of a lion which had leapt up beside me.
As soon as I could find, and flash on, my torch I saw it was Christian. I did
not quickly forgive him for the shock — particularly as he refused to leave
me for the rest of the night. From now on I managed to keep Boy in at
night, but I began to let Juma and Monalisa roam as they pleased, although
the two lions who had attacked Boy out on the hill came down to camp in
the night and tried to get at him in his enclosure. I drove them away, but
shortly after I heard a call of distress from the thick bush not far away. I
rushed towards the sound with my rifle, but there was now complete silence
and I could not catch any glinting eyes in my torchlight. When I returned
to camp I was relieved to find Christian, but there was no sign of Juma and
Monalisa.

At dawn Christian and I went out in search of them. About three hundred
yards from the wire I found Monalisa: she was dead, bitten through the
neck. With murder in my heart I started to follow the spoor of the two wild
lions. It was perhaps fortunate that the trail petered out before I could catch
them. One of them had an easily recognisable roar and was now known as
The Killer.

It took Christian and me another three days to find young Juma, hiding
up on Kora Hill. He was unhurt, but although he was very nervous he
followed us willingly to camp. From now on Christian and Juma became
excellent companions, and remained in splendidly cheerful spirits despite
the constant threats of their rivals who bitterly resented our occupation of
Kora. On the other hand Boy was still in a very bad way. The bite on his back
had grown into a permanent swelling. He obviously needed professional help
and when the vet, Paul Sayer, examined the wound he found that a splinter
of bone had become detached from the spine and must be removed. The
operation took him about two and a half hours, by the time he had done
it and sewn up the other gashes. Boy let out a couple of protesting bellows
when the water in a swab was too hot but otherwise gazed into the distance,
not batting an eyelid. Paul warned me not to treat a deep wound with
antibiotic powder again as it could heal on the surface, leaving a septic
pocket beneath.

Simon Trevor had been filming all our day-time activities and Bill now

"Boy came in with a deep bite on his back. I sprinkled the wound with sulfanilamide powder."

While Boy recovered from the effects of the bite, Stanley looked after him as devotedly as he had at Naivasha.

decided to come out to Kenya to see how he was getting on. Simon met him in Nairobi. A few days later they organised the collection of two more lionesses from the National Park Orphanage, and all flew up to Kora. The newcomers were about the same age as Christian, eighteen months old, and I called them Mona and Lisa. Like Juma, they had been born in the wild and had grown very nervous from being gawped at in Nairobi, so I attempted to win their confidence by sleeping on a campbed next to their enclosure.

If Boy recovered soon from the wound on his back we would have the makings of a formidable pride. Boy himself was mature and experienced; Christian was growing fast into a large and confident companion; while Mona and Lisa were potentially a pair of fine lionesses. In about a year they would be ready to kill and mate. As a bonus I was given another little lion of about two months old. He had been flown up in a Supercub plane and so we called him Supercub. Mona and Lisa had been slower than the Londoner, Christian, to take to the wild, but Supercub seemed to be at home from the start.

It was hard work keeping an eye on my pride, and I often had no time for shooting game to feed them in the evenings, so that they would keep in touch with the camp. Instead, once a week, I bumped twenty-five miles down river to a village called Balambala and bought an ox. To add to our labours I still had to go on dressing Boy's back and giving it regular compresses of scalding Epsom salts, to drain the pus and bring down the swelling.

*   *   *

After six months at Kora we had experienced an almost equal balance of setback and success. Settling down in the bush, however remote, is much like acclimatising yourself to any other neighbourhood. You take stock of the good and the bad features; you adopt or adapt what you can, and endure what you can't.

From my lions' point of view there was a reasonable variety of prey and constant water in the river. They had a stronghold on the rocks if they could win it, and they had full support from me while they fought for it.

From my point of view the accommodation was excellent. Within the twelve-foot high perimeter wire we had a large mess hut, thatched with palm and open on the side that sloped down to the foot of the rocks. The other three sides were closed in with Terence's patent walling of wire mesh, covered in sacking and painted with several coatings of cement. There were window spaces to entice the rare breezes and an increasing number of perforations, at knee height, where guinea fowl who quickly attached

The eighteen-month-old lionesses Mona and Lisa were very nervous when they first arrived, but became used to me when I slept next to the wire of their enclosure and began to take them water. They liked to test their strength against my legs.

Unfortunately my skin was not quite as loose as a lion's and I was relieved when their friendly attentions relaxed.

themselves to us pecked for their grist. We had three or four similar huts for Terence, myself, our stores and any guests who turned up. Terence also built a shed for the trucks and tools just inside the double gates on to the road.

All the cooking was done under a thatch awning above the traditional fireplace of three stones. There was an unlimited supply of dead wood to burn. The food we could buy locally was simple: goat's meat, a few vegetables, eggs, rice and tea. As we did not eat game there was nothing to be had off the land except a little wild honey which the Africans particularly enjoyed. For decent meat, fruit and butter we had to rely on the goodness of visiting friends, hoping that they also understood our reliance on the restoring properties of gin and White Horse whisky. One calor gas refriger-ator was reserved for our supplies, one for the lions' meat.

There was no need to heat the water in our shower. By midday the sun had raised the tin drum, suspended from the branches of a tree, to an ideal temperature. The two-seater lavatory was our masterpiece. Two elephant jawbones we placed over a trench; they were not only more appropriate than any porcelain artefact but the perfect height, and fashioned by nature to afford human contours the maximum comfort. Terence, Stanley and Kimani, who had joined Stanley to help cook, fetch water, collect wood and keep the camp running, shared with me these castaway quarters, whose official address now became "Kampi ya Simba", Camp of the Lions.

Terence had extended our network of roads, so that we could follow the lions as they explored further and further afield. He had recruited his workers from Balambala and other villages outside the Kora Triangle. He still nurtured his unaccountable distaste for the lions but worked tirelessly out in the bush. To his delight he had discovered he possessed a new skill: he had suddenly developed the gift of water divining. Since every silver lining in his life has its cloud, he was also furious he had not put this talent to use all his life. From time to time he left Kora to go down to his house on the sea at Malindi. Although he had never married and was only one year younger than me, I rather suspect that the charm of mixed company also drew him to the coast.

If you live next to a factory you have to grow used to the siren which goes off every morning at six o'clock when the shifts change. At Kora it was pointless to resent the morning call from the ravens Crikey and Croaky – I could always recognise Croaky by his bandy legs. However, when they produced three really destructive offspring, Mad, Bad and Worse, who began to defoliate our books and play hell with our stores, even Croaky got fed up. He drove them out. I later came across them, miles up river, and they would mob the Landrover in the hope of scraps.

Again, if you live within the sound of a railway you have to accept that your days will be punctuated by the sound of clattering tracks. In much the same way the flock of guinea fowl at Kora let off their squeaky cackle at intervals through the day and night, stimulated no doubt by impulses of desire or alarm. Maddening as their noise can be, I must confess I enjoy their company and their glinting, iridescent plumage. While I buy millet to feed them, Terence grows exasperated when they flutter up on the table at breakfast, and persecutes them for days afterwards.

Although a young cub took to chasing the ravens, he never caught one. But Arusha, a lioness who joined us later, used to lure guinea fowl to their doom by pretending to be asleep. Having caught one of the idiots she shared it around. I have always thought it would be a dirty trick to start eating the guinea fowl myself and have tasted only one during my time at Kora. I saw it killed by a martial eagle, which swooped on it just outside camp. I managed to grab the bird before the eagle absconded with it. Martial eagles are large and extremely powerful. Terence saw one stoop on a gerenuk, which is quite a sizeable gazelle, and the blow from its talons must have penetrated the skull for the gerenuk was instantly killed.

We found ourselves providing hospitality for any number of different birds. The white-headed buffalo weavers nested in the branches of the acacias round camp, and soon took peanuts out of my hand. They build their nests at the end of the thinnest branches to deter the larger birds and snakes from getting at their eggs, and then put up palisades round the branches as additional protection. Several times I have seen the ravens frustrated by these devices from stealing the chicks. When the weavers have finished with the nests the flashy superb starlings seize their chance and move in.

Violet-backed sunbirds also flit in and out of camp. Their defensive tactics are less elaborate but just as effective. They built their own nest only a few inches from the hornets' nest in the tree by our shower and trusted to the protection of their neighbours' stings. The ingenious ways in which birds turn the behaviour of other species (including man) to their own ends never ceases to surprise and delight me. When they find a swarm of wild bees, honey guides give a distinctive chirp and flap their wings about, until someone follows them back to the tree, climbs it and cuts open the comb. Africans believe that no good comes to a man who fails to reward the bird with its fair share of the comb and the grubs which cling to it.

Our importunate guests come in all shapes and sizes. The agama lizards are both decorative and useful. At night the males are a drab grey, like the females; but when the sun gets up they take on brilliant reds, blues and greens. I suppose it is to attract females and advertise their territory; as long as it is light they can change colour in a couple of seconds. They are aggressive little things, with sharp, tiny teeth. They tend to lose their tails in battle with each other. However, they also put their darting, sticky tongues and mincing teeth to good use by eating the ants and termites that in turn like to eat the posts of our huts. Some visiting scientists were furious when a coucal flew down and made off with their favourite lizard. Their leader dived under a bush and pulled it alive from the throat of the squawking and furious bird. My own favourite spent a lot of time in the peanut tray and was known as Jimmy Carter. Some lizards were brave enough to stalk the flies that settled on Christian's coat.

The plainest visitors are the naked mole rats. They are hairless, as their name implies; their skin is a sickly pale and almost transparent pink; their eyes are squinched up; and their teeth are elongated into fangs for digging. They live largely on roots and bulbs just below the surface of the earth, where it is permanently warm and fur would be uncomfortably hot. They tunnel swiftly, in well-organised gangs, scraping the earth back down the line and at intervals throwing up mounds like little volcanoes. I have tried to tame them, but never succeeded.

On the other hand the ground squirrels quickly lose their fear; they are greedy, shameless and delightful beggars. I am sure early man must have shared his leftover seeds and nuts with them. Another vegetarian (though partial to the marrow of bones and tusks) was a porcupine who occasionally took a bath in the lions' water trough.

We have had a great many callers looking for leftover meat: a pair of white-tailed mongooses, a civet cat that ate from my hand until the jackals made life too hot for it, and Dracula the monitor lizard who was at least three feet long and looked like a miniature dinosaur. In the hotter weather he would retire to aestivate in the roof of the mess hut; happily his house training was perfect.

The only intruders we really object to are those that tend to bite or sting the hands that feed them, but unfortunately there is very little we can do to keep them out. Scorpions like to lurk in the cosy shelter of a shoe or sleeve that retains its warmth at night, while snakes too often find their way on to a shelf or pile of blankets.

If our accommodation was an asset from the beginning, it took a little time before we could really rely on our communication and support systems. Under Terence's supervision the roads improved with time and use. In our early years the drive to the nearest airstrip, twenty miles away, gave us one or two nightmare journeys in cases of emergency. Mail was irregular, to say the least, and had to be collected from Garissa, 100 miles and five hours' drive away. We were therefore often glad of the newly installed radio that

Joy had urged us to get. It meant standing by every morning and evening to find out if we were wanted, or to alert whoever we were calling, but in a crisis we could contact control at other times of the day.

In our first six months at Kora we were lucky not to have needed urgent help, but now we were on the air I could always get hold of Joy at Naivasha. It was also a tremendous comfort to hear that Ken Smith was moving to Garissa and that Kora would be in his specific district of the Game Department. I had been told that the local District Commissioner was in favour of my continuing here and recently I had been invited by the local County Council at Galole to visit them to pay the year's rent.

They insisted on a ceremonial handing over of my cheque for £750. Inevitably, the occasion was followed by a drink of tepid beer at the height of a boiling afternoon, after which I was obliged to stay on for an evening showing of *The Lions Are Free*, attended by all the notables of Galole, except those who had succumbed to the earlier celebrations. I was assured that if in difficulties the police at Garissa would come to my help.

Because Kora is a kind of tribal no-man's land I did not expect too much trouble from our neighbours. To the south-west were the Wakamba, who keep cattle and are expert carvers, although it is only their less good work, like little wooden animals, which finds its way to the souvenir stalls of Nairobi and the craft shops of Europe. They also have a reputation for prophecy: one of their elders grew famous for predicting the coming of the "iron snake" – the building of the East African Railway. Certainly Joy was impressed that one of their witch doctors foretold her final miscarriage. But perhaps the Wakamba are best known as hunters. They cleverly fashion their bows and arrows from the most appropriate woods, poison the steel arrowtips with a distillation of *Acokanthera* bark, and wrap the heads in leather to keep them fresh and effective (which they are). I suspected it was the Wakamba who, with the Somalis, were gradually destroying the rhino population of Kora and they soon gave me even greater cause for fury.

The Orma, to the east of our camp, were less of a nuisance. They live for their cattle and we were only likely to get across each other if their cows proved too tempting for my lions.

The third group who might prove a thorn in our flesh were the Somalis, over the river to the north-east. They are a very tough and resourceful people who straddle the frontier between Kenya and Somaliland. They make excellent businessmen in the city and are doughty fighters in the bush. They were supposed to remain north of the Tana but I knew that if there were a drought they would not hesitate to bring their cattle, sheep and goats down to the river, and would strip both banks of every shred of green stuff. They would give short shrift to the lions if they raided their stock; and would treat us the same if we tried to stand in their way, for they were always accompanied by groups of unscrupulous Shifta. In short they were the human counterpart of the local lions – and I prayed for rain.

Broadly speaking, apart from the local lions, our animal neighbours caused us few problems. The largest were the elephants, whom we sometimes saw in family groups of ten or twelve. They came down to drink in the river at night. Although the lions enjoyed harassing them, they never pressed home their attacks except occasionally to corner a young one, which was their only chance of making a kill. The lions were also respectful of rhino; again their only hope would have been to isolate a calf: more than once a lion has been found with its rib cage smashed by a rhino's horn.

Lions find it difficult to resist going for a hippo, and I have found the carcase of one killed by a native pride at Kora. But hippos are better left unmolested when they are grazing – which is when they are at their most dangerous. The hideous gape you often see when they are in the water is neither a yawn nor a threat. To put it bluntly, they fart from the wrong end and they are probably expelling the gases given off as they digest the 110 lb of grass they can eat in a night. They may wander several miles inland in search of fodder and if you get between them and the water, when they are on their feeding grounds, or the well-worn tracks to them – which are sometimes three or four feet deep – they will charge without mercy. Hippos can move surprisingly fast.

One of my rangers retired to a small island on the Tana to grow maize and vegetables. During a drought he heard tearing and munching just outside his hut in the middle of the night. When he went out to investigate he found a starving hippo eating his thatch. The hippopotamus ignored his protests and literally bit him in two. The distinguished naturalist, Hugh Cott, has seen a hippo standing by a pool with the two halves of a crocodile lying on either side of it.

Crocodiles have always fascinated Cott and in particular he tried to solve the riddle of why they swallow stones. He worked out that on dry land the stones usually represent only 1 per cent of their mass – but in water this becomes equivalent to about 15 per cent of their effective weight. He therefore concluded that they instinctively took the stones to steady themselves in fast flowing currents, and to give them better purchase when manoeuvring their victims in water. Their teeth have flexible settings and therefore lack strength. To make up for this weakness they leave the prey that they drown to rot under water. When a limb becomes loose they twist it off by spinning themselves over and over. Like hippos, the ears, eyes and nostrils of a crocodile are placed high on its head and face to give it the best use of its senses when the rest of the body is submerged. But unlike a hippopotamus, a crocodile is much more dangerous in water. It will nevertheless make an occasional foray up on the bank to snatch food. Terence once found the carcase of a female waterbuck which had been killed by a leopard about 250 yards from the river. It was clear from the spoor round it that a large croc had come up from the water and dragged it 200 yards towards the river, while the leopard followed, still clinging to its prey. One foolish young crocodile, about six feet long, was caught and killed by my lions when it strayed too far from the river.

The lions usually concentrated on more conventional quarry – buffalo, young giraffes, waterbuck, lesser kudu, and the long-necked gerenuk which thrive in the *nyika*. These, and dik dik, provided them with the excitement of the search, the chase and the kill which is the essential life of a lion. It was this excitement which we set out to find on our daily walks.

6 June 1971 started like any normal day. Boy had been away from camp for several nights and so as soon as it was light I took out Christian, Juma, Mona, Lisa and Supercub to see what we could find. They had a bit of fun chasing dik dik, and then we climbed Boy's Rock where I left them for the day. When I got back to camp at about ten o'clock I sat down to breakfast alone, as Terence was in Malindi and had paid off his labour force. Outside there was the sound of noisy drinking from the water trough, and Kimani, who brought me a plate of scrambled eggs, told me that it was Boy, who had just turned up.

Not long afterwards Kimani came back to clear the table, and as he did so we both heard terrified cries from the bush behind the camp. For a fraction of a second I was undecided whether to pick up my rifle or my electric cattle prodder, but knowing that there would be no time to come back if the trouble was serious, I seized a rifle.

I ran to the big gates and from there I saw Boy, 250 yards away, with Stanley in his jaws. As I rushed towards him shouting, Boy dropped Stanley and sidled into the bush about twenty yards off. Stanley was left sitting on the ground, covered in blood which was pouring from his shoulder.

I strode past Stanley, raised my rifle and shot Boy through the heart. Making certain that he was dead or dying, I turned back to Stanley, and yelled do Kimani to come and help me. He hesitated, as he was obviously scared stiff of Boy, but I told him to come quickly as Boy was dead and we must to something immediately for Stanley.

Together we helped him stagger a few steps towards the gates, before he collapsed. I then ran for my truck and drove him the short distance to my hut, where we laid him down. As I started to examine the wound on his neck, and the deeper one at its base, Stanley died. His jugular must have been severed and he had bled to death in less than ten minutes from the moment he had first cried out.

All that morning I tried to raise the police at Garissa on the radio, but was told by control that as it was Sunday it was extremely unlikely that I would get an answer.

I did not want the other lions to come back and find Boy's corpse lying by the track so I decided to bury him. With Kimani's help I lifted him into the back of the Landrover and drove off alone to a sandy riverbed we knew as Elephant Lugga, taking a block and tackle. I dug a grave under a shady tree, and with the help of the pulley slowly lowered Boy into it. It was a sad moment after all we had been through together. I had known him for nearly eight years, which was twice as long as I had known Elsa.

At first light next morning I went out with Kimani and dug a grave for poor Stanley, as I was determined to bury him if I could not get in touch with the police soon. But at ten o'clock – a full twenty-four hours after the tragedy – I got through. They were absolutely adamant that I should not bury Stanley and said that they would send a vehicle immediately to collect his body. It took them all day; at 5.30 in the evening it arrived with six policemen.

Despite the condition of the body in this heat, they began taking statements, and then insisted on coming out to Boy's grave, and opening it, to make sure that I had shot him. They did not leave until 9 p.m. by which time the lions, who had been out all day, had suddenly returned to camp, giving me further anxious moments.

Words cannot properly express the remorse I felt for what happened. Stanley had been warned over and over again not to leave camp when the lions were at large; he had seen Boy go for Muga as well as himself only a few months before; and he had been with Joy and me long enough to appreciate the dangers of life in the bush with us. He was good natured and loyal and however hard the work was had always been patient and cheerful. He had looked after Boy devotedly, especially while he was recovering from his operations at Naivasha and Kora. Perhaps he had relied too heavily on the trust which had grown up between them during those difficult times.

Piecing together what had happened, partly from Kimani and partly from the tracks on the ground, it seemed that Stanley may have taken it into his head to go and look for honey. When Boy had returned to camp and finished drinking, he must have noticed someone moving about on the other side of the camp and gone to investigate. Perhaps he did not recognise Stanley, or perhaps Stanley did not recognise him. At any rate it looked as if instead of standing his ground, which would have checked Boy, Stanley had turned and made for the safety of the gates. The lion would have found a running figure irresistible.

To my sorrow the police took Stanley's body to Garissa and buried him in an unmarked grave. He had no wife, and I would have liked to bury him at Kora, or otherwise at Meru, close to his family, who received the insurance money on his life. He was only twenty-eight when he died.

*   *   *

For the next few days I could not take my mind off the tragedy. Among the lions I had known Boy's temperament had been remarkably stoical. He had accepted his wounds, his injections, his operations and his travels with invariable tranquillity, just as he tolerated and came to accept the company of so many people – Bill, Ginny, the vets, Ace, John, the film crews, Stanley and me. So struck had I been by this that it had blinded me to the danger signals: the damage he had done to young Arun Sharma and Mark Jenkins at Meru, and to Muga at Kora, earlier this year.

I remembered now the letter Bill had written to me at Naivasha, eighteen months before, asking whether the pins in Boy's leg might not inhibit his movement or give pain, and so turn him into a man-killer. I was also reminded of Joy's frequent advice to let Boy loose at Kora and to leave him to fend for himself. She was nevertheless extremely sympathetic in the face of this horror. I thought of Thesiger's article too.

The first thing I did was to write a full and exact account of what had happened for the authorities, who were very understanding. The local papers and the *Daily Express* both offered extensive accounts of the accident, which inevitably carried a note of criticism. But over the next two months there was no violent reaction against either me or my work.

We were, however, faced with violence of another kind. At the beginning of August Mona, Lisa and Supercub disappeared into the bush and I was unable to trace them. After several days of searching I came across three Wakamba youths, watering a herd of cattle at the wells five miles away.

In answer to my questions they said they had seen three lions at the water a week before, and that one of them was smaller than the other two. As they added that the lions had killed three of their cows I asked them to take me to the remains. The cattle had certainly been killed by lions, but after careful examination I came to the conclusion that they were not mine. Two days later I followed the fresh spoor of three lions to a large thicket in which they were obviously hiding. To make sure they were not my lions I called "Mona", "Lisa" and "Supercub" several times, but there was no response: it convinced me they were wild.

After another two days Lisa and Supercub turned up in camp, but I never saw Mona, who had always been the least capable, again. I am sure that the Wakamba had killed her in mistake for one of the lions that had taken their cows. As the Wakamba had no right to be at Kora anyway, I asked the chief at Balambala to expel them, which he did.

After Mona's disappearance Christian, Juma, Lisa and Supercub spent most of the day with one another, often hunting elephants which suddenly appeared in numbers. Seeing them together convinced me of the answer to a question which had been nagging at the back of my mind for some time. Not long before his death Boy seemed to be behaving in an unnatural way: he began to chase Juma wherever he went. I now realised it was not Boy who was "unnatural", for Juma was not maturing as other young lions do and, in fact, looked increasingly feminine. I had taken "his" sex on trust, but every day it became clearer that Juma was a lioness.

When the pride grew tired of chasing elephants I tracked them down to a waterbuck, freshly killed by wild lions who must have been skulking very close and only kept away by my presence. That night I heard the distinctive roar of The Killer who had despatched Monalisa. There followed a tremendous squabble in which a string of lions shot past the camp. It was impossible to tell who was chasing whom. Later I was woken by the sound of a lion in great distress. When I went out to investigate I was met by Christian and Juma, who led me cautiously into the bush. As dawn broke Lisa limped towards me with blood oozing from her shoulder and hind leg. Though not permanently damaged she had been badly bitten.

I then started searching for Supercub and came across the spoor of a lioness and a cub, which were joined by the tracks of a male lion. A little further on I saw what looked like a young lioness lying fast asleep under a tree. As I drew closer I realised that the animal was dead, and that it was Supercub. He had been bitten through the neck in exactly the same way as Monalisa.

The lioness he had followed must have been one of Boy's wild consorts but she had not saved him from the wrath of The Killer. It was not unlike Black Mane's murder of Sam, which had seemed so unnatural at the time. It was coming home to me that a male lion may kill any cub he finds when he takes over a pride, or wins a new lioness for his harem, to remove the competition to his own progeny.

The effect of all these sudden deaths was that Christian immediately stopped roaring: he seemed to realise that discretion was the better part of valour. What is more, all three lions ceased to mark territory. Another consequence was that Bill wrote to say he and other friends of mine in England felt the reaction from the resident lions was so destructive I should find somewhere else to continue my work.

I replied that although I had lost five out of the eight lions I had brought to Kora, I was confident that, given a little more time and the reinforcement of a few more lions, I had learnt enough to make the experiment work even in this harsh country. Unfortunately just at that moment, when I needed all the support I could muster, trouble struck from a different quarter.

Wilfred Thesiger, who had been out on safari when Stanley was killed, now published another article in the *East African Standard*. In it he attacked my entire work at Kora, on the grounds that to rehabilitate tame lions is excessively dangerous and they will always be a threat to any human beings they encounter afterwards. His article was largely a compound of prejudice and ignorance.

Its prejudice against my work in general arose from the particular incident of Boy and Mark Jenkins, but it also grew from his own long-standing attitude to lions. Years before, in the Sudan, he had raised two himself and after nine months he had shot them. During five years there as a District Commissioner he claimed he had shot seventy more lions in the wild, which gave me an insight into his psychology. Lion control was not strictly part of his job, whereas it was of mine, and I did not shoot quite as many as that in all my twenty-three years in the Game Department.

The ignorance of the article was manifest from its inaccuracies. An old friend of mine, Syd Downey, one of the most respected professional hunters and later conservationists in Kenya, was asked by the paper to comment on them. He pointed out that Thesiger, who had no experience whatever of rehabilitated lions, implied that they were inefficient killers and incapable of integrating with wild lions – which was untrue. Downey also corrected two other misleading impressions – that wild lions do not suffer injuries while hunting and that they never take to man-eating unless they are damaged in some way.

There was one dangerous mistake in the article. It claimed that it was quite safe to sleep out in the presence of wild lions. It is true that they do not necessarily attack you; on the other hand plenty of people have been taken from their tents or their huts as they slept, including professional hunters.

Finally Thesiger's article alleged that I must have shot hundreds of wild animals to feed my lions and that soon there would be none left at Kora. I never shot on that scale and I had already begun to buy domestic stock to feed my lions. Over the years our presence at Kora has led to the increase of game and not its reduction. The only exception are rhinos, which have been poached almost out of existence all over Kenya.

Wilfred Thesiger is a distinguished figure with the very best interests of wildlife and of Kenya at heart. I therefore hoped that his misleading arguments would not overshadow the one positive suggestion in his article, which was that I should trap for release at Kora lions and other predators found attacking stock. In point of fact only the two original lions, Boy and Christian, had been bred in captivity; all the others had come to me either directly or indirectly from game managers as the result of stock protection.

If a man like Wilfred Thesiger, who had good friends in the Game Department and is an honorary game warden himself, could hold so many misconceptions about my activities, I would have to work very fast to get across to the authorities, and to the general public, the true facts about my work. If I failed, my days at Kora would be numbered.

Chapter 12
Christian's Pyramid
1971–1973

Exactly two years after he had left the pavements of London Christian was freely ranging ten or fifteen miles up and down the banks of the Tana River with Juma and Lisa. He had fulfilled his promise of becoming a huge and handsome lion – he must have been one of the largest in Kenya. Juma was a beautiful lioness, but still shy and unapproachable. Lisa was smaller, gentler and more affectionate. Oblivious to the fact that Terence and I – and for that matter they too – were still threatened with eviction, the three lions made the most of everything Kora had to offer.

For a time they were inseparable. Christian would come back scratched but undaunted from their frays with the wild lions. I found the remains of a lesser kudu they had killed together. Two days later I came across the story of a far fiercer battle. They had tackled a full-grown hippopotamus and, in the terrific struggle to get it down, the ground was furrowed and small trees were uprooted. The hippo finally dragged Christian to the very edge of the water where he had to let go.

Although the lions were almost adult, Christian retained all his mischief and curiosity. Now that they had started to kill for themselves they sometimes ignored the camel meat I put out for them. When a carcase has lain in the sun for several days it can blow up like a barrage balloon, and one evening Christian could not resist biting into such a grotesque object to see what would happen. He never did discover for the results were sensational. The camel exploded and the full force of the anaesthetic gas was discharged with an obscene hiss directly into his face. He lay dead to the world for five minutes. Lisa circled round and solicitously patted him, before he returned to his still dizzy senses.

In early 1972 when all three lions were about two and a half, Juma and Lisa matured: as a male Christian was about six months behind them. The lionesses began to wander off for two or three weeks, leaving Christian lonely and depressed. Quite soon he pulled himself together, increased the frequency and volume of his roars and began to mark territory in the full style of an adult lion, scraping the ground as he did so. When Juma and

Lisa next returned after ten days on the loose – in more senses than one – Christian went through the manoeuvres that normally precede serious mating, but it turned out that he was not yet up to the full performance.

In defiance of Christian the wild lions now began to chase Juma and Lisa, not to harass them but to importune their favours. I would see the two of them relaxing in a sand lugga or on the rocks with the wild lions; we grew familiar with several of them. Juma and Lisa both mated with the tattered and almost maneless lion we knew as Scruffy. They clearly preferred this disreputable and more experienced roué to their elegant contemporary Christian. It is often the way with lions – as it is sometimes with women.

In the nature of things Juma and Lisa were still sitting pretty. There is a presumption that a lioness will remain on her territory: and these two felt confident round our camp at Kora. The odds would be on them seeing off a female interloper; here they would fulfil their roles most successfully – familiar as they were with the best lairs for their litters, and the most likely hunting grounds when they had to provide for their mate and their cubs.

On the other hand Christian was at a distinct disadvantage. Not yet fully mature, he had no help in seeing off Scruffy and it was built into his being, after testing his strength, to give way reluctantly and seek out his destiny elsewhere. At times I would go out to give him help in his struggle as I feared for his life. At about three o'clock one morning I heard sounds of a running battle. I soon picked up Christian close to the camp and caught the glint of two pairs of eyes in one of the bushes. Christian charged into the thorns, there was a growl and he bolted out with a lion on his tail, which swerved in my direction as soon as it saw me. I fired when it was ten yards away; it turned to one side and dashed off. The pair of wild lions then came and invested the camp, making low, whinnying moans – which I knew were their deadliest threats – until I went out again and heaved stones at them. One of them sounded just like The Killer.

On another night I could not reach Christian, who was in trouble up on the rocks. In the morning when he did not come back I followed splashes of his blood until the trail was lost. It was forty-eight hours before he turned up, badly bitten and clawed on his face and forelegs – all frontal injuries that testified to his courage. I confess that for a short time afterwards I contemplated getting rid of Scruffy once and for all. I am very glad I didn't.

The period of gestation is 108 days and according to my calculations we could expect Juma's and Lisa's cubs sometime in November 1972. While we waited for them Scruffy roared and hovered round the camp until one morning I went out to find him and Christian sitting companionably together on Kora Rock. In a sense this was one of our most important achievements at Kora so far – the integration of our lions with the native ones. Nevertheless

Opposite: There is a presumption that a lioness will stay on her own territory. The odds would be on Juma and Lisa if it came to seeing off a female interloper. This fight between two lionesses was filmed in *Born Free.*

in Christian's case I felt the cessation of hostilities was more likely to prove an armistice than peace.

*   *   *

Up till now the dice at Kora had been loaded against me, but at last they began to fall in my favour. The lions were growing up and more confident; Ken Smith at Garissa was looking for ways to give me official support; and then Joy produced an ace – though sometimes I call him a knave – from the pack.

Recently she had advertised for an assistant to help her with the leopard project she was planning, but continuing hand trouble had obliged her suddenly to cancel it. She therefore passed me an application from a young man called Tony Fitzjohn. It was a godsend: it looked as if he could turn his hand to anything. He had grown up in England, and when he had left school had progressively qualified himself as photographer, chucker out for a night club, and instructor on Outward Bound adventure training courses. By the age of twenty-six he had sampled high life and low, and had knocked round Southern Africa in lorries and ships.

In appearance and temperament Tony was Christian's counterpart. He had a fine physique and good looks; he was fearless in dealing with lions;

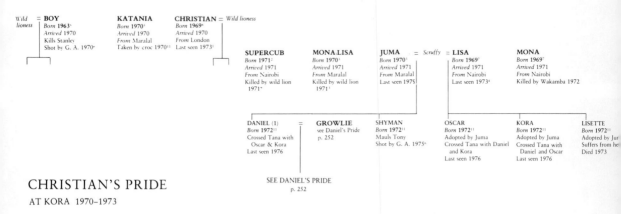

CHRISTIAN'S PRIDE

AT KORA 1970–1973

neither his energy nor his capacity for mischief were often restrained. Like Christian he had an unnerving habit of disappearing from camp without warning, for weeks on end, and of materialising again just as unexpectedly. There the parallel ended, for his dexterity with girlfriends was in a different league from Christian's, and I never once found Christian with a bottle at his elbow.

Tony was a master with his hands. To keep our truck on the road he could coax a tyre from the Game staff, a can of petrol from the army and life from an ailing engine, when any one of these would have been beyond the powers of Terence or me. Without him I do not know how I would have succeeded in staying at Kora, yet all I could offer him was a way of life, basic food, a few bottles of beer and a roof. I could never afford to pay him a penny.

Now I come to think of it he did have one other trait in common with Christian. When deprived for too long of company, particularly female, they were both apt to let off steam and there was no knowing what might happen next. In normal circumstances, Christian would have gone roving with other males of his pride – as Ugas, Boy and Suswa did at Meru – leaving the lionesses to their own affairs. But there were no other lions at Kora who wanted his company. He would roar in the night yet it produced neither companions nor girlfriends. Waking to his lonely roars, early one morning, I went to offer him companionship – and before long spotted him crouching, ready to ambush me.

It was one of his favourite games; he would jump up and greet me without any rough-housing. But today he rushed me, knocked me down and pinned me to the ground; I was totally helpless. With his great weight on my back, I could do nothing when he gripped me with his paws and took the back of my head and my neck in his jaws. One of his claws went in my arm.

Suddenly he let go. I was so bloody angry that I picked up a stick and went for him. He was off in a flash, realising full well that he had broken the rules. But he broke them again almost immediately, this time with Tony. While I was away, discussing our future with the County Council, Christian beat him up with his paws, knocked him down several times and then dragged him along by his head.

Tony saw red, bunched up his fists and punched Christian on the nose with all his considerable strength. Again Christian made no attempt to retaliate but sat among some bushes staring at a badly shaken Tony – and it takes a hell of a lot to shake him – reading a paperback in the Landrover, while they both cooled down. When we talked it over afterwards we realised that Christian had simply been working off his loneliness and frustration.

Tony seemed to think he had come off worse than I did because Christian

In 1972 Ace and John came back to see Christian. He was growing into one of the largest lions in Kenya, and was too large to leap into Ace's arms. When he sat on me I was helpless.

had some respect for my age and white hairs. He hadn't seemed very respectful to me.

*   *   *

Looking back, the struggles at Kora were as much a watershed for me as for Christian. Up till then I had been more or less continuously on safari for fifty years. My life at Isiolo was interrupted every few weeks by patrols and emergency calls to scotch the misdemeanours of lions and elephants.

Although rather different, my five years at Meru had hardly been settled. I had not actually been on the move but I was constantly worried that I would be made to get out. It infuriated me to leave Girl's pride and their offspring almost as much as it distressed Joy to be separated from Pippa's cubs just when they were about to mate and give birth to her grandchildren.

Age modifies human interests and behaviour in a number of ways. Two of them became increasingly clear in my early years at Kora. The first is that however much of our lives has been spent travelling, there is a growing satisfaction in staying put, not just for the obvious physical reasons but for psychological ones too. Novelty loses some of its charm; as our senses become less dependable, we derive security from surroundings which are completely familiar; as we go out less, in search of the people we most want to see, we make it easier for them to find us; as we begin to do less, we gather round us the symbols of who we are and what we have done.

The second is that however much we have lived from day to day, and for the day itself, we increasingly look back on the past and find in it guidelines for the present, in which we are less active, and the future, which we may never see – in other words we begin to live part of our lives vicariously, through younger generations.

Joy, who liked to plan things further ahead than I, foresaw both these needs when she bought the house at Naivasha and, having no children of her own, outlined a programme for Pippa and her descendants that would last her a number of years.

Unfortunately I could never have settled at Naivasha with its nearby road, the passing motor boats and a stream of tours from Nairobi; and I had been thrown out of Meru. Equally, I had been obliged to abandon Elsa's cubs in the Serengeti and the cubs in Girl's pride at Mugwongo. Contented at Kora with Christian, and with Juma and Lisa on the brink of breeding, I had found a place where I would be happy to settle and die. Sadly I was once again under notice to quit.

Knowing that if I really wanted to stay I would have to muster all my powers of persuasion, I turned to my friends for support. We invited the local Game Warden from Hola to visit Kora, with members of the Tana River Council; most of the council had never seen the lovely river scenery that Terence had opened up with his new tracks; they were deeply impressed. They were in need of my rent and they saw the presence of my lions as a future draw for tourists, and the revenue they would bring with them.

The local Member of Parliament, Mr Kase, who was Assistant Minister of Information and Broadcasting, came to see the lions and brought with him Mr Sigara, the District Information Officer. Mohamed Sigara was, by good fortune, the son of a Somali mzee or elder who had been very helpful to me with information about the Italians during the war. He and the other officials may not have been experts on ecology and conservation but, recognising the publicity value for the country and the growing interest of the local people, they immediately arranged press and radio interviews about my life at Kora. Mr Kase was, of course, aware that both the Minister of Tourism and Wildlife and the powerful Attorney General had supported my projects and the documentary films about them.

As if on cue, Bill Travers now completed his third documentary *Christian the Lion* in which I described Stanley's death but also tried to demonstrate the positive side of what we had achieved. At one level Bill's films had apparently made a very good impression on the Permanent Secretary and the Chief Game Warden who had such an influence on our destinies; at another Tony took great trouble to show the movies to school children, their parents and the police at Garissa. Meanwhile Ken Smith was advancing a case of his own, not only to allow us to stay at Kora but to classify it as an official reserve: he too found the films useful to his argument.

In her books Joy several times expresses the conviction that some of the more critical moments of her later life were swayed by the spirit of Elsa. I have no belief in the power of the dead to influence the living in quite this way. On the other hand I have observed that in my own life a principle of "fair exchange" seems to have operated more and more significantly.

One of my most unusual experiences has been to see my character taken over by Bill Travers. By assuming it in *Born Free* he was led into the life of the lions and thence into producing some of the finest wildlife documentaries of recent years; film production became a way of life for him. In exchange he helped make the Meru experiment possible, and when I ran into the worst of my problems I always found that his films eased the way. What is more, Boy, Christian and I each owed our existence at Kora to him. Whatever the physical differences between us, there was a continuous meeting of spirits.

Of course the first great exchange of my life was with Joy; more recently Tony and I had begun to enjoy the kind of reciprocal benefits that zoologists call symbiosis; and very soon Christian was to repay his adoption as handsomely as Elsa had.

This was in fact a critical time for Christian, as Juma and Lisa had taken over Kora, with their wild mate Scruffy and his friends. He had therefore gone up the river and occupied a particularly dense henna thicket as his stronghold. One of the reasons for his choice was that in the prevailing drought the Orma and Somali herdsmen had – against the regulations – brought their livestock into the Kora Triangle and the cattle made easy pickings when they came down to drink. We also had evidence that Christian had started to go over the river. Directly opposite there was a large area of open country, excellent for hunting, while if he went upstream he would find himself in the Meru Reserve.

We always feared the worst when Christian disappeared for any length of time, and sure enough after spotting some circling vultures, Tony and I discovered him sitting proudly on the corpse of a freshly killed cow. We quietly dragged it out of sight to avoid retribution from its owner. Christian's blood was now up in every sense. He had been driven from Kora Rock but he had made this stretch of the river his own; he had killed here; and at last he began to have a success with the local lionesses. Single-handed, at his age, he could not have taken over a pride, but there is often a lioness who comes into season and is prepared to go out and look for a mate. I never actually saw his consorts but I know he successfully mated twice; I heard one noisy honeymoon continuing for four days and nights with scarcely a break. Apart from the unmistakable sounds of his nuptials I could follow their spoor.

Although we had carefully hidden Christian's cow he did not get away with his thefts. Before long two Orma tribesmen stepped out of the bush one morning and stopped me to complain that Christian had again attacked their stock. Tony and I therefore accepted our responsibilities and spent an execrable night in our trucks near the Orma's cattle boma, occasionally firing shots to attract Christian's attention and waiting for some response that never came. I had just dropped off in the small hours of the morning, when I was woken by a rattling door and seismic upheaval; Christian had thrust his head through the window and was jogging the truck with impatience. He had been in yet another fight, was covered in scratches and wolfed down twenty pounds of meat in a very few minutes. When he jumped in the back of my Landrover hoping for more, I slammed the door and hurried him off to the camp with Tony following.

We were now approaching Christmas and when Joy got in touch to make plans, I told her about Christian's misadventures and the imminent arrival of Juma's and Lisa's cubs. She was delighted, as she had asked the novelist

Ralph Hammond Innes, and his wife Dorothy, to stay and longed to show them the cubs. I would have to send Tony down to Terence's camp on the river during their visit, as Joy was convinced he led me astray when we opened a bottle.

Joy had first met Ralph through Billy Collins, and had received valuable advice from him about the business side of her writing and of her Appeal. By now Collins Harvill had published her three books about Elsa, two about Pippa, one on the tribes and *Joy Adamson's Africa*, which reproduced a selection from all her sketches and paintings. Neither Billy nor Joy was a placid personality and from time to time Joy would rage at him, if he did not seem to pay her enough attention or raise her royalties in tune with her latest aspirations, and cut off all negotiations. But however low the barometer fell it always seemed to recover before her next book was ready to go to the printer.

The exchanges in Joy's life were no less fortunate than mine. Her recognition as an artist grew directly from Peter Bally's profession as a botanist – advantages accrued from this interest to both of them. A little later our marriage gave her not only Elsa, but the first of her books; they enriched my life, just as they did hers – if not in quite the same way! When it came to publishing there was yet another exchange. From Collins Harvill Joy derived all her wealth though she gave most of it away. In return Billy Collins received inspiration for a new list of books. Previously he had published none on Africa. Now, influenced by Joy's success, he commissioned guides to African birds, animals, game parks, snakes, butterflies and coral fish. He went on to publish important books by Jane Goodall and Hugo van Lawick on chimpanzees and wild dogs; by Iain and Oria Douglas-Hamilton about elephants; and by Mirella Ricciardi, whose *Vanishing Africa* recorded, in beautiful photographs, the tribes painted by Joy twenty years before.

Collins had published all Hammond Innes' best-selling novels, so that when Joy heard he was thinking of setting one in Africa she had leapt at the chance of repaying his kindness by asking him to Kora. She evidently thought that seeing a lioness and her cubs might even persuade him to write about conservation, so I warned her that wary Juma might be too shy, and Lisa's cubs too young, for us to get anywhere near them. I was right about Juma, whose cubs were born at the beginning of November, but just before Christmas Tony and I had an extraordinary experience with Lisa whose litter was born at the end of November.

We had gone to look for her latest lair when we heard Christian moaning in the bush, followed by a high, thin wail of a cub. When we crawled in to have a look there was Christian with a tiny cub, too small to be Juma's, though we were close to Juma's lair and Juma was nearby. We lifted the cub out of the bush but Juma would have nothing to do with it; and as Lisa was nowhere to be seen we took it back to the camp. We kept it warm and next day took it back to the rocks – and this time caught sight of Lisa. We called to her but she was utterly indifferent until she heard the mewing of the cub, when she immediately dashed down and carried it off to a crevice by the scruff of its neck. Although the two mothers kept their litters well away from the camp, they did not hesitate to join us in the evenings for a drink or a meal.

Joy, as always in the bush, made a glittering celebration of Christmas Eve, with a tree, candles, presents, a cake and champagne. On Christmas afternoon I said I would go up and see if Lisa and her cubs were relaxed and settled. I would leave the others a short way off and if she was happy, and I did not come back, they could follow one by one. Dorothy wrote an account of what happened next in her own travel book, *What Lands are These?*

He didn't come back, and I followed him, fascinated but slightly frightened. I didn't know how far he had gone. I came upon him suddenly, standing very still and looking fixedly towards some bushes. I stopped beside him and followed his glance. At first I couldn't see anything but the pattern of leaves and twigs. Then I saw movement – her pink tongue licking three very small cubs, clambering over her forepaws. She was about fifteen feet away, looking straight at me with amber eyes, an intelligent, perfectly aware look. My scent was probably familiar to her from camp, but it was George's presence which reassured her. From time to time he spoke to her, a quiet sound with which she had become familiar, "Lis-sa, Lis-sa". He turned to me and I remember his eyes were alight with pleasure and pride. "It's a wonderful example of confidence, isn't it?"

The others had gradually joined us. Lisa rolled on to her side and the cubs began to suckle.

When I had first arrived at Kora Joy had seriously considered the possibility of coming here to continue her work with cheetahs or to take on a leopard. Over Christmas I told her about a letter which I had received from the Tana River County Council expressing the hope I would stay on at Kora. I had replied that I would consider it if I could keep in touch with the lions and begin to rehabilitate leopards. There had been no answer but, not long after Joy left, a letter came from the Chief Game Warden, John Mutinda, to say that as long as I had permission to stay at Kora he would be happy to let me have any leopards his department might trap.

Predictably Juma continued to keep her cubs well away from us for a long time, although I knew Christian had been to see them. The affectionate Lisa remained as welcoming as ever. Juma's two, the first to be born at Kora, we christened Daniel and Shyman, for the latter was as shy and jumpy as his mother, while Daniel was happy and good natured. Lisa's three, Oscar, Kora and Lisette, had few distinguishable characteristics, but Lisette seemed less robust than the other two. At a very early age the two families began to intermingle and we saw just how advantageous it was to a pride when lionesses came into season and conceived simultaneously, as they often did. If one mother was short of milk, or injured – conceivably killed – her cubs had a chance of survival. There is always one mother to guard a nursery of cubs while others go hunting. This is the beginning of the bonding between contemporaries which can be so vital when lions have to make their own way in the world. Communal upbringing is another example of the economic protections built into a lion's genes. Such is the effort needed to raise young that a single cub does not justify the time, the energy and the potential stress involved: it is usually abandoned, as happened when Girl lost one cub and immediately neglected Sam. On the other hand the pooled activities of several mothers ensure that their resources go furthest.

At one stage Lisa lodged her litter at the four hundred foot summit of Kora Rock. The side nearest to the camp is sheer, and we watched with our hearts in our mouths as she climbed up and down its vertical face without ever putting a foot wrong. Realising that she would not risk a false move, the baboons would sometimes taunt her from a ledge only five or six feet away during her perilous descents. The baboons were not very popular with any of us – including Crikey and Croaky. One day I saw the two ravens dive-bombing them, to keep them away from their young, and actually hitting the baboons on the head. When Juma and Lisa did at last bring their cubs to camp in the evenings, Juma, whose two were darker and more heavily spotted than Lisa's, still kept us at arm's length – not that we ever intended to touch or handle any lions born at Kora.

Of Christian we saw less and less. One of his last dramatic performances demonstrated just how superior a lion's sight is to our own, especially in twilight or darkness. After he had adopted his stronghold by the river Tony and I were sitting with him as the sun set behind the doum palms and tamarinds on the opposite bank. It was difficult to squint into the water as the orange rays were reflected directly into our eyes, but Christian suddenly tensed and peered intently down at the river.

At first Tony and I could see nothing; then one or two dark objects – perhaps a log, a branch or even a crocodile – came floating downstream towards us. Even when they were just below where we sat, Christian continued to look across the river, and Tony at last made out a man waving from a small island on the far side. When we waved back he scrambled through the shallows and worked his way along the bank until he was opposite to us. He was dripping wet.

He called across, in a foreign accent, that he and a party of friends were boating down the Tana and two of them had just overturned. The objects which Christian had spotted were a canoe, its engine, a tent and some bedding rolls: he would swim across to get them. We told the man to stay where he was; it was now getting dark and with crocodiles about it was not safe to cross. We said we would rescue his equipment and fetch him and his friends in the morning.

They turned out to be an oddly assorted bunch to come on at the far end of the world – a Scotsman, five Greeks and a Japanese judo instructor. We found them marvellous value for a couple of nights, while they were convinced that Christian had saved at least one of their number from a particularly gruesome African death.

After the amphibious rescue operation we saw very little more of Christian. He seldom came into camp and only occasionally kept company with Juma and Lisa. He must have sensed that in the interests of self preservation he should leave the territory round Kora to the father of their cubs and go off in search of his own – possibly one less frequented than his riverside preserve. I used to count the days on which we had not seen him but in the end, when they reached ninety-seven, I gave up recording them in my diary. He had been so much part of our lives, indeed was almost solely responsible for our being here at all, that we felt a deep sense of sadness and loss; yet I was almost equally happy that he was exercising his freedom in a way that was wise.

In September and October I had to go down to Naivasha to look after Elsamere while Joy went to Russia as a guest of the Soviets. She very much enjoyed, and made the most of, her invitations to places like Hungary, Thailand, Japan and Russia, where conservationists discussed with her their crises and hopes.

After talking about her books in Moscow, Joy was flown to the Black Sea and asked to add her own graft to the Friendship Tree, which bore lemons, grapefruit, pomelos, giant oyas and tiny kumquats grafted on in the name of figures as famous as Darwin and Pasteur. Round its roots was strewn soil from the graves of Tolstoy, Tschaikovsky, Pushkin and Gandhi. Joy was then shown several of the one hundred reserves in Russia, including those specialising in the breeding of bison, brown bears and Przewalski's horse. At Askaniya Nova she was taken out on to the steppes to see improbable herds of zebra, wildebeest, eland and impala. The director had even crossbred zebras with horses, to produce zebroids like Raymond Hook's on Mt Kenya, though for what particular purpose I cannot imagine.

When Joy flew back to Nairobi she found the Russian ambassador and the representative of the Tass news agency waiting to meet her at the airport. She immediately brought them up to Kora to introduce them to the lions, though it seemed to me that they were just as happy eating, drinking and fishing. While we helped Joy celebrate her diplomatic triumph Terence, Tony and I had something much more exciting to celebrate. On 19 October 1973, Kora was officially gazetted a National Game Reserve. For the time being at least, our existence here, and that of the lions, was secure.

*   *   *

So far I had tended to think of Kora as five hundred square miles of unwanted bush – a tribal no-man's land – in which the lions could wander freely in comparative safety to themselves and others. I now began to think of it differently, as a landscape whose inhabitants, from the smallest microbe to the largest elephant, had evolved and interlocked over millions of years, but which were now being threatened with more rapid and disastrous changes than ever before.

The Kora Triangle lies, like an inverted pyramid, along the south bank of the Tana. The sun is directly overhead for twelve months a year; the average monthly rainfall is seldom more than an inch; sometimes there is no rain at all for several months on end. As you look down on the wilderness of thorns from one of the rocks, the first impression is of overwhelming desiccation and stillness. Nevertheless Kora is anything but dead. For three years I had watched its living pulse: the sudden burst of flowers after a sprinkling of rain; the recurring dramas of courtship, battle and hunt; the ebb of activity among the animals and birds as the sun rises to its zenith, and finally sinks into darkness; the flow as it stirs them to life in the dawn, and again as it cools towards evening.

But every week I began to learn more about its mysterious mechanism. Terence talked about the plants and trees as we walked down to the river or planned a new road; Joy and I were sent books on the natural history of Africa in the hope that we would offer some words of approval; all sorts of scientists came to poke at the scorpions and peer at the birds; knowledgeable, inquisitive and patient, expert film makers like Alan Root waited in hides with zoom and long-distance lenses, to expose the secrets of life that went on under our noses.

They all assured me that the sun was the key to the system of Kora and each of its parts, however basic or fragile, permanent or ephemeral. The

foundations of rock and soil had been flung off from the sun; rain, temperature and climate were precipitated and sustained by the sun; every moving
creature, from millipede to man, owed its animating current of energy
entirely to the sun. Even so there was only one line along which this powerful
current could reach us – through the lowest form of life, Terence's beloved
plants.

I could see the amazement on visitors' faces as they stepped down on to
the airstrip, or out of their safari trucks, and saw only a few wisps of
straw-coloured grass and the grey leaves of the trees and the thorn bushes
that looked drained of all moisture and life. But Terence said they were not
to be sneered at; the leaves of the grasses and plants, the shrubs and the
trees, all contained enough chlorophyll to absorb the sun's energy, to
convert, to use and to store it. It is true that our grasses at Kora are so
sparse and vulnerable that it would take ten acres of grazing to support a
single cow. On the other hand the ashen thorn bushes that appear quite
dead are perfectly adapted to the arid conditions.

Their hooks and spikes may not defend their branches from the teeth of
the browsers but the resins they exude protect them from fungi and insects
exploiting the damage. Terence knows their properties backwards – which
resins have been used for insecticides, fumigants, snake-bite, camel-mange,
embalming agents or myrrh. Some attract sweat bees, those maddening
little insects which hum round your ears and whose honey is almost the
only delicacy of the bush.

I have often heard Terence pointing out *Boswellia*, a source of the
frankincense which, with myrrh, was presented by the magi to Christ in the
manger; the sweet-scented henna bushes down by the river, whose leaves
crushed in lemon juice produce the orange-red dye; and, often next to them,
salvadora whose red berries are loved by birds and whose twigs are used
by Africans for cleaning their teeth.

Most typical of the trees in the *nyika* are the thorny acacias – above all
the flat-topped *tortilis*. By the river some of the *elatior* acacias are eight
hundred years old. Out in the bush the baobabs, whose bulbous trunks
hold water like sponges, can live to a thousand. My friend Malcolm Coe,
the zoologist, discovered that baobabs depend on fruitbats or bushbabies,
brushing through their branches, for fertilisation. Indeed most of our plants
and trees can reproduce only if their seeds are dispersed by animals or birds.

Ninety per cent of the energy harnessed by these myriads of leaves is
burned up in the process of growth, flowering, fruiting and seeding but the
rest is available for other forms of life to exploit. There is little enough grass
along the banks of the river to satisfy the impala, zebra, buffalo and hippos;
there is still less further inland. Yet there is plenty of nourishment on the

shrubs and the trees for the specialist browsers. The lowest shoots are nipped off by the dik dik. Higher up Joy's favourites, the lesser kudu, with their lovely spiralling horns and crescents of cream on their pale grey flanks, and the lumbering rhinos, make their mark. But the elegant gerenuk, with its long curving neck, will rise up on its hind legs to reach even higher.

The trees are beyond the reach of the gazelles and the antelopes, but not of the giraffes. The whole of this animal is a miracle of adaptation. Its neck, its mouth, its long twisting tongue and even its viscous saliva are all designed to make the most of the furthest tips of the branches, rich in their protein, if sometimes uncomfortably thorny. A giraffe makes do with exactly the same number of vertebrae as we have, but it has a special lightweight skull, valves in its arteries to stop it blacking out when it bends to drink and neck muscles of extraordinary strength. I have seen a photograph of a drinking giraffe whose head had been seized by a crocodile: in a second frame the giraffe has managed to straighten up and the crocodile is hanging vertically by its jaws. Only the elephant can compete with the giraffe in getting at the tree canopy. It will stand on its hind legs to extend the range of its trunk and, if it is still frustrated, will use its forehead and tusks to knock the tree over. It will also tear open the baobabs with its tusks to get at their moisture.

Ten per cent of the energy trapped by the plants, at the base of the food chain, has now gone up one level as it has been consumed by this vast and diversified army of herbivores. They, too, use up 90 per cent of this energy in movement, digestion, fighting, fleeing, courtship and breeding: only 10 per cent remains for the flesh-eating hunters at the top of the chain. Because the reservoir of energy shrinks each time it goes up a step, the structure of life has been seen by some scientists as a pyramid. The carnivores prowl at the top.

At Kora we see quite a few of the smaller cats, even though they tend to be nocturnal – servals, civets and genets. The most numerous are the lithe golden caracals, with tufted ears like a lynx. They can leap into the air to knock down a dove that is several feet up, and prey on the nimblest of dik dik. One caracal used to come and drink from the water trough, and was regularly teased by a family of dik dik who had learned to take peanuts out of my hand. As soon as the caracal appeared they gave their sneezing alarm call. But if it was out in the open, they would prance up quite close to it, knowing very well that it was far too intent on its drink, and nervous of us, to be tempted into a chase.

A pack of wild dogs occasionally runs through the reserve. Despite their tattered, savage, even sinister, appearance and their macabre habit of devouring their prey before it is dead, they are also models of social decorum. They hunt in intelligent relays, feed in amicable succession and take back food to their dens for mothers and cubs unable to go out themselves.

I often see cheetahs at Kora. More at home on the plains, where their remarkable speed is at a premium in bringing down prey, they have adapted successfully to the constraints of thick bush. But leopards, so secret and solitary, who should thrive in the conditions that prevail here, have been poached for their skins almost beyond redemption. Here, as elsewhere, the top platform of the pyramid is dominated by lions.

But lions are not immortal; within a few moments of death, a predator becomes prey – to the formidable array of creatures which hover over all three levels of the pyramid, waiting to pounce on whatever energy remains to be salvaged. A succession of specialists move in.

The first to arrive are probably the vultures, of which there are several species at Kora. Soaring up on the thermals the large white-backed vultures rely on their phenomenal sight to spot others descending on a kill, or perhaps to detect death for themselves. By the time they have spiralled down they are likely to find that lions, hyenas or jackals have watched the direction of their flight and beaten them to it. Each takes his turn on the carcase in descending order of strength.

Even when the hissing and shuffling circle of birds can get at the shambles, the big griffon vultures may well shoulder out the white-backs, who first sighted the victim. These larger species tend to have bald heads and necks, adapted to their butchery; the small hooded and Egyptian vultures, which hang about on the fringes collecting the scraps, can afford a more normal covering of feathers. Each vulture carries the appropriate beak to its role as surgeon or scavenger. The ingenious Egyptian vulture, endowed with only a slight one, picks up stones to crack open ostrich eggs which it could not otherwise eat.

When the vultures are done there are plenty of other scavengers and decomposers waiting to satisfy their hunger and utilise the last available energy – marabou storks and monitor lizards; mongooses, rats and siafu ants; invisible microbes will bleach the bones white. Because most of these are ugly, and associated with death, they usually fail to excite admiration, affection or interest. But they are as precious as any other link in the food chain, and thanks to them stench and disease are usually swept and kept from the bush.

Jane Goodall, while she was studying a family of jackals, felt her blood freeze when a bateleur eagle stooped on a pup, carried it screaming into the air, and finding her weight too much for its strength dropped her from twenty feet up. I felt much the same about a pair of jackals which lived near our camp. One day the male followed his nose through the gate in search of a bone. Too late he noticed two young lions in the shade of a hut.

He was cornered; but bravely, with bristling ruff – and growling defiance – he rushed into the attack. The end was quick, but the air was long filled with his mate's lamentations.

Mervyn Cowie describes in *Fly, Vulture* an equally chilling experience. Unable to disperse a plague of hyenas by shooting, he was forced to destroy them by poisoning meat. As they died they slunk off to hide, but the vultures knew just where to find them. Vultures in trouble will seek safety in height and as they felt the poison at work they flew higher and higher, until Mervyn could no longer see them with his naked eye. Then, one by one, they came plummeting down, to smash on the plain.

The jaws of a hyena are so powerful that they can pulverise even large bones. The goodness is extracted and the rest excreted as chalk on the dust. The processes of nature ensure that the last vestiges of energy remain in circulation. A particle of potassium, once reluctantly eroded from Kora Rock, is washed down into the soil at its foot where it is absorbed by the grass through its roots, eaten by a zebra and metabolised by a lion, before it is finally returned to the earth to begin the cycle again.

This edifice, whose special status we owed to Christian, was incredibly precarious. I knew that at any moment the most destructive animal of all, man, could wreck it for ever. His bullets had thinned out the elephants and eliminated the rhinos. His cows and sheep would finish off the grass; his goats and camels demolish the browse; deprived of their food the game would disappear; dik dik and hippo, leopard and lion, jackals and vultures, all would be gone. Kora, like too much of Kenya, would become little more than a dust bowl. Its red earth would join the silt in the Tana and, down off the coast, a few more miles of lovely and irreplaceable coral would be smothered in a blanket of mud.

In ancient Egypt a pyramid was both a tomb and a monument. But I didn't look on the new reserve at Kora as Christian's graveyard. For one thing he was only four years old, and a lion can live to twelve or fifteen in the wild. For another, he had blazed a trail across the Tana to the great open hunting ground in the north, and I liked to imagine him exploring its opportunities for a new life; he might have even found his way into Meru with Ugas and Girl. It would therefore be premature and pessimistic to think of the cheerful, mischievous and courageous young lion from London as dust "in that rich earth concealed; a dust whom England bore".

On the other hand I did begin to think of Kora as his monument, and it has often put strength into my fight to protect it as a place where life can continue as it has done for millennia, before it was threatened with dissolution by pressures let loose from other continents in the last fifty years.

Chapter 13
Daniel's Pride
1973–1977

"Leave it to Nature," muttered Terence, one evening at supper. "Abhors a vacuum. There'll soon be more."

Tony and I were discussing our latest loss. Lisa had vanished with her three cubs, Oscar, Kora and Lisette. We had used every trick we could think of to find them during the previous month. We listened for their calls; tracked in widening circles round the camp; followed Juma's spoor into the bush after her evening meals; and sat up over carcases at night in some of Lisa's favourite haunts. We had begun to wonder how we could possibly find some new lions to back up Juma now that she had only her two cubs, Daniel and Shyman, for company.

I was surprised that Terence had deigned to join in our deliberations about the lions, but Tony was not.

"Typical of you, Terence," he said, "to suggest something which will lead to the extermination of George's lions altogether. Christian has disappeared, and Scruffy has made himself scarce lately. So what will happen? The Killer will come back and bump off Daniel and Shyman before mating with Juma. But if he is with lionesses who've got minds of their own, they will soon find a way to get rid of Juma. Our score will be zero, and we might as well pack up camp."

Tony was quite right, Daniel and Shyman were six months old and growing up well, but without Lisa and her cubs, and the support of Scruffy, they stood little chance of holding their own. Terence had the last word.

"Tell you one thing, Tony. There's a limit to the number of lions Kora can stand. You can't go on importing for ever. You'll have to settle for crossbreeds with the local ones soon. Switch to something else. What about the leopards George and Joy keep on about?"

In our hearts we knew Terence had a point. And all of us knew that unless we could keep the encroachment of livestock at bay even leopards would be doomed. Our spirits were low at the end of the next day's search, when Tony saw a single young cub cross the sand of a lugga. I was convinced it was too large to be one of Lisa's, but Tony insisted on following it to a thicket, and grew very excited when he saw the prints of other cubs leading there too.

Patiently I waited in the Landrover and watched him as he eagerly thrust his head into the branches. My attention was rewarded, for in the very next second, almost simultaneously, there was one of the most devastating roars I have ever heard, and Tony shot out of the bush at much the same speed as Christian had bolted with the rhino on his tail. By the time he had reached me he was panting and furious at my laughter. What he had not yet seen was that the lion which had given him the shock of his life was Juma. He was little mollified, as he had been so close when she thundered at him that he had caught the full blast of her sweet-smelling breath on his face.

Nevertheless we agreed to leave her the carcase of the meat we had in the back of the truck, as it was beginning to get dark. Then, just as Daniel and Shyman began to tuck in to the goat, there was a movement at the edge of the lugga – and we could not believe our eyes: emerging from the grass were Oscar, Kora and Lisette. Of Lisa there was no sign.

We wondered how on earth the three cubs had survived on their own, for although their ribs stuck out through their skin, they had quite enough energy to tackle the goat with zest. I knew from their spoor that they had not been with Juma, and it was probable that they had been separated from Lisa for most of the month, or we would have come across her. Presumably they had lived by making small kills of their own or on pickings of carrion.

We never saw Lisa again, or discovered what became of her. She may have been frightened away by, or succumbed to, The Killer and his entourage. I doubt if she was killed by a herdsman, as we would have heard a complaint of her raiding his stock. But recently the local game warden had successfully prosecuted a poacher he had caught with 120 lion claws among his trophies. The tough world of Kora, which one of the government officials had described to us as "unfit for human habitation", was rapidly becoming unfit for lions as well.

Juma immediately adopted Lisa's three young, treating them just like her own; she even succeeded in killing a series of large, 500 lb waterbucks to feed them all. But without reinforcements I did not see how the cubs would grow up to produce a third generation at Kora.

Strangely enough it was the National Parks who came to our rescue and helped to fill nature's vacuum. Now that Kora was accorded the status of National Reserve, and the Parks had too many orphans to handle, Perez Olindo said he thought he could help us.

A young American couple, Esmond and Chryssee Bradley Martin, had become deeply concerned about the catastrophic poaching now rampant in

Kenya and much of East Africa. Esmond began to accumulate a massive indictment of international statistics on the trade in ivory and rhino horn, while Chryssee and a friend devoted themselves to individual animals. One of them was a young lion named Leakey at the Orphanage in the Nairobi Game Park. Like so many orphans Leakey had needed both care and affection to calm him after his capture; the Americans gave him both and were promised by Perez Olindo that he should come to Kora for release in the wild.

While we waited for a message to collect Leakey, who was said to be a bouncy and self-confident young lion, we had one more casualty. Tony had noticed that Lisette was missing and after a long search found her limping badly, and detached from the family. He therefore baited a crate and sat up at night till he trapped her with her brother Oscar, who had also fallen for the easy meal. We took them back to camp and kept Lisette enclosed until she seemed better. When Juma came to talk to her through the wire Lisette fretted so much that we had to let her out. Again she kept falling behind and one day she never caught up. I fear she had a hernia, and was taken by a leopard or hyena.

By the time Leakey was ready for collection we found he had been put on display at the Nairobi Agricultural Show, and he was suffering from a reaction to the noisy ridicule of the crowds who had come to stare and jeer at him. Nevertheless, at one year old, his bounce and resilience had not been broken and we looked forward to his company.

He was the first of five new lions we received in the next year. The second was Freddie, who came from near Garissa, where the game warden had shot his mother for raiding cattle. Hearing about this Tony had gone to see the warden and, finding the cub in a bad way, persuaded him to let us have it. Freddie immediately responded to the love and the time Tony gave him: they played endless games together and Freddie adored being given a swing in his basket. He was one of the gentlest lions we had, except with the ravens, whom he fruitlessly stalked round the camp.

The third cub to arrive was a young lioness called Arusha, via Blydorp Zoo in Rotterdam; she was the last captive-bred lion I took on. Blydorp is the zoo to which Elsa's two sisters went in 1956 and from which Christian's father came to England ten years later. It was the idea of a young vet called Aart Visee to bring Arusha to Kora.

Aart had a number of private patients, as well as looking after animals in the zoo. When a woman in Rotterdam had difficulty in giving her pet lion cub enough exercise – she was neither a footballer nor had access to a friendly graveyard – Aart offered to take Arusha for walks. Rotterdam is a large place, but it is still not big enough to accommodate walking lions once they are full grown. Having heard about Elsa and Christian, Aart wrote to me, and K.L.M. agreed to fly Arusha to Africa free.

We took on Arusha as we desperately needed more lionesses to balance the pride. She was friendly, though stubborn, and soon settled to the rhythm of life in an African pride. Aart Visee and Tony got on well too. Aart was as delighted by Tony's bush lore as we were by the odds and ends which Aart kept on pulling out of his black bag of medical facts.

One morning at breakfast Tony complained that the bacon was too salty and started throwing bits to Crikey and Croaky.

"You mustn't do that," called Aart, and rushed to pick up the bacon before the ravens could get it. "Salt is very bad for birds. They can neither use it nor get it out of their systems unless they are seabirds. Have you noticed seagulls have two holes at the top of their beaks? They are there so they can exude the salt water."

Warming to the subject, Aart told us about a lonely old lady whose husband had just died and whose sole consolation was her budgerigar. She summoned Aart because the budgerigar was suddenly languishing, and after careful examination, he diagnosed an excess of salt, although the old lady adamantly denied giving it to the bird in any form. A week later the budgerigar died, and Aart took it away for an autopsy. Sure enough, he found a fatal build-up of salt. The truth came out when Aart went to tell the woman his findings.

"I shall miss it so much," she said. "You see, when I sat in my chair in the evenings, I would think of my husband. Then the budgie would hop down from its perch and drink the tears as they rolled down my cheeks."

Aart watched Arusha with some amusement — Terence with whole-hearted support — as she began to stalk the guinea fowl round the camp. It took her a little time to discover that her best chance of success lay in feigning sleep and then suddenly pouncing. She must have accounted for at least half a dozen.

As it happened the next two arrivals, from the Nairobi Orphanage, were also lionesses, Growlie and Gigi. Like Juma and Leakey, Growlie's experiences after capture had left their mark on her behaviour. She was always nervous and kept her distance, but never aggressive, and the growl which led to her naming was one of suspicion.

I once had a hell of a shock when I was changing a wheel by the track to the river. I thought I was alone when there was suddenly a blood-curdling growl in my ear. She had crept up behind me and let out her questioning rumble. Tony was convinced that she really longed to be friends and to greet us like the rest of the youngsters. As a tease, when they went for a walk, and she was ahead, he would squeeze her tail, and then look away before she could see what had happened.

The last of the five new arrivals was Gigi, a sweet little cub who was later to have a tough life.

By the time I had ten lions on the go at Kora, life was getting expensive. I reckoned that to raise one lion over two years might cost me £500, and that was only the tip of the iceberg. Beneath the surface someone had to meet the fundamental costs of protecting the reserve.

The Somali herds, the Orma cattle and the Wakamba poachers were each a serious menace. The only hope of protecting the Reserve properly against them was to mark its boundaries clearly, to open up tracks to the extremities so that patrolling was possible, to provide trucks and petrol for the patrols, and to pay for the rangers to man them. The game department and the local Council claimed to have no funds for all of this and neither did I. But I did my best to help raise them.

Joy would still not allow her trustees to vote money for Kora, despite its official status. But the East African Wild Life Society made a contribution; Dr Grzimek arranged for the Frankfurt Zoological Society to provide us with a tractor, a road grader and the money to man and run them for two years; I contributed my share of the income from the film *Christian the Lion*; and the film stimulated individual contributions from viewers in America, swelling those from visitors who now came to see the lions at Kora. Esmond Bradley Martin generously promised us a set of radio collars for the lions, and a tracking device; the equipment would save us many hours a day if we could go straight to the lions rather than follow their zig-zagging movements.

Juma and Growlie had always been too wary to handle, and as with Elsa's cubs we had made a point of never touching any of the lions born in the bush. On the other hand Leakey, Freddie, Arusha and Gigi were all ideal candidates for the new collars. However, before we could get the first collars fitted Arusha delayed our experiments.

I had seen Tony go up the rocks with her one morning. Leakey, Freddie, Growlie and Gigi had gone too: the older lions were off on their own. When I could get away from camp I followed Tony and, seeing that Arusha was lagging behind, I thought it would be fun to ambush her. After a bit of hide and seek, she turned the tables and ambushed me – I lost my footing and fell on a pile of stones. Arusha pounced on me with glee and, as she was fifteen months old, her weight was more than my bones would stand. The pain was exquisite.

Tony was in a better position than I to see exactly what happened next, and this account is taken from one of his letters.

I screamed down the rocks, with Freddie trying to trip me up, and with Gigi's teeth in my bum. No one could have overtaken me at the speed I was moving. Breathless, it took all my strength and the judo throws I thought I had forgotten, to get Arusha off George. She had gone a bit berserk, but hadn't hurt him at all with her teeth and claws. I literally had to flip her on her back and then, when she came again, throw her over my shoulder.

I pulled George up and Freddie and Gigi came to sympathise with him, in their own gentle way. Growlie peered from a distance, looking worried. All George could say was: "Oh God, it's my flaming hip." But I had to get him off the rock, so I carried him down piggy back, with a few stops, as the lions caught up with us again.

George was very faint and in great pain, and had to lie down. But this only set Arusha off again, so I really went for her — no holds barred, fists, feet, teeth, the lot. She submitted as to a superior male. But once she is onto something she is very determined, despite all the rough stuff I was handing out, in real anger now. So I chased her off with a branch and she kept her distance.

Then Freddie came up and said he'd keep her off. He understood that George, propped against a tree now, needed help, and unmistakably told me that he'd look after him, which he did as I ran to camp to get the car. I was back in three minutes or so. I didn't let the shock wear off before I gave George a couple of large slugs of whisky, but he was in great pain. Next day I brought the Flying Doctor in.

I had to spend a week in hospital, as they found that my pelvis was fractured. I was beautifully looked after, and the envy of the other patients, as I was visited each day by Lindsay Bell, one of the most delightful and prettiest, and less ephemeral, of Tony's girlfriends. She worked for a firm chartering small planes at Wilson airport, which was the next best thing to our doorstep. I missed her smiling face and red-gold hair when I was discharged and went to convalesce at Naivasha with Joy. After a fortnight by the lake I grew restless, threw away my crutches and went back to Kora.

Tony had kept things going admirably while I was recovering, but there was no longer any sign of Juma. I thought it unlikely she would willingly have left her own territory, and therefore feared she had been killed by one of the tribes. On the other hand she might have gone off to find a new mate. The timing could have been worse, for her sons and foster children were two and a half years old, and could look after themselves. Daniel was friendly, and turning into a magnificent lion; Shyman was still shy and tricky. Daniel had taken over command of the pride and it amused me to see him dish out the occasional cuff to Leakey who remained pretty bumptious. None of the others was prepared to argue with Daniel.

While I was away Tony had been experimenting with the radio collars,

Opposite: "We made a point of never touching any of the lions born in the bush." Unfortunately they did not feel the same obligation towards us.

and had worked out that if we tagged two of the lions, say Leakey and Arusha, we would in fact be able to keep an eye on four of them. Leakey and Freddie had become firmly bonded and went everywhere together, although there was a year between them and they had been born hundreds of miles apart. In the same way Growlie and Arusha, who had been born in different continents, behaved like two sisters. I was struck by how often the lions formed firm friendships, usually but not always with the same sex, becoming as close as brothers or sisters.

The new gadgets saved us hundreds of hours and miles of laborious tracking under the heat of the sun. It needed two of us working together — one to drive and the other to stand with the direction finder, for it was important to give the antennae as much height as possible, up on the back or the roof of the Landrover. Even so we often had to get out and climb to the top of a hill. When Tony was away I tended to revert to my Robinson Crusoe technique.

Soon after I had recovered from by brush with Arusha, Tony went off to Garissa for a few nights, on a bit of a bender. When he came back, I found myself doing for him what he had done for me — although in this case the situation was a great deal nastier. Old men forget, and I shall rely on an account I wrote at the time.

Late in the afternoon of 12th June (1975) Tony returned from a trip to Garissa. Before doing anything else he went to the back of the compound to greet the cubs who were squabbling over the remains of a guinea fowl Arusha had caught. I was in the main hut having tea. Suddenly Haragumsa came rushing to say that Tony was being attacked by lions. Thinking that the cubs had knocked him over, and were giving him a rough time, I took a stick and went out.

Tony was in the grip of a big lion. I ran at them yelling and brandishing my stick. The lion dropped Tony, slunk away, and crouched looking as if he was about to have another go. A further demonstration sent him into the bush.

Tony was in one hell of a mess. Apparently the lion had caught him unaware from behind as he was playing with the cubs. There were deep gashes in his neck, head and arms, and he was bleeding copiously. Because of all the blood it was impossible to tell how badly he was injured. While Terence and Haragumsa started to clean him up, I got on the radio, and after some delay reached the Flying Doctor at about 5.30 p.m. They said it was too late to fly up to Kora, but would come first thing in the morning.

I gave Tony a shot of anti-biotic, and valium to ease the pain. It was a most anxious night. Tony had lost a lot of blood and complained of difficulty in breathing. He could only mumble incoherently. At dawn we set off on the twenty miles to the airstrip, driving very slowly as the least bump hurt him. We reached the strip at 8.30 and had to wait until after 10.00 before the aircraft arrived with no doctor, only a nurse.

It seems Tony was extremely lucky. One deep gash on the right side of his neck exposed the carotid; another fraction of an inch and he would have had it.

The day after Tony had flown to hospital, Shyman arrived in camp alone. His behaviour was odd. There could be little doubt that it was he who had attacked Tony. There was still dried blood on his coat and his muzzle. He sat near the drinking trough in front of the camp, growling in a menacing manner, quite unlike his normal self. The cubs, who would normally have gone up to greet him, seemed frightened. I was afraid he was going to attack them and therefore drove the Landrover in between. For a long time I watched him carefully. Definitely there was something wrong, and he looked sick. After much hesitation I decided that for the sake of the project he must go. I shot poor Shyman through the brain.

From the beginning I found it very difficult to work out exactly what had happened. Tony had come back from Garissa in a pretty carefree mood, and in his amusement at seeing the cubs playing with the guinea fowl had been less alert than usual. Neither he nor I could believe that any of our lions would savage him like this and assumed that a wild one had come into camp.

On reflection I am sure I was wrong. The night before the accident all the other lions had come in: Shyman alone was away. The day after Tony had been flown to Nairobi, Shyman came in, alone. The blood on his face and coat, added to his unaccustomed and ill-tempered behaviour, were to me conclusive evidence that he was the culprit.

Various possible explanations worked through my mind as I sat and studied him for half an hour before I shot him. He might have had rabies or a tumour on the brain. Alternatively he might have been wounded or poisoned by some of the herdsmen. I have always regretted that I did not examine his body more carefully, but I was too upset at the time to think of it.

I wrote and told Tony in hospital that he should not blame himself for the accident – it was simply one of our occupational hazards. Not that self-reproach is a mood I associate with Tony; once he ceased to be delirious he started threatening to pour brandy through the hole Shyman had made in his trachea. I feared there would be further official displeasure at the incident but after a few quiet words with Tony, the authorities made no formal protests or complaints.

Tony was away for about a month. He was excellently nursed in hospital and Lindsay Bell took more than good care of him when he came out. It was she who had helped get the Flying Doctor up to us in the morning, and had come in the plane herself; she returned him in very good shape except for the formidable puncture scars round his neck.

Most men who had been chewed up by a lion would be reluctant to risk it again, but Tony was as fearless as ever. We were in the middle of a parching drought, the Somalis and their herds were making inroads all down the eastern boundary and poachers riddled the bush. It was exhausting work to restrain the lions from going after the cattle, which were usually herded by small children.

I know the lions killed and ate several Somali cows, although they never attacked men, women or children. Apart from the threat of retaliation the lions were also in danger from poachers, a gang of whom were at large, and we came across the carcases of three rhinos within a mile and a half of our camp. Their great bodies lay rotting in the sun with their horns hacked out. This was really the end of the rhinos at Kora: I have seldom since then seen either a beast or its footprints.

Our resources were so slender that it was with some relish that Terence was able to set a bunch of thieves to catch a bunch of thieves. He was finally clearing a track up the river to the westernmost point of the Reserve, opposite the eastern tip of Meru Park. To save time, and no doubt to get away from my lions, he had set up a camp there.

He was startled and irritated one day when his siesta was ruined by a fusillade of shots that fizzed and whined over the top of his tent. He rushed out in a fury to see a party of Somali rustlers making off across the river, with a herd of Wakamba cattle they had just lifted. They thought that a few well-placed shots would deter Terence from chasing them.

They could not have been more wrong. Nothing on earth would have induced him to go after them. Instead he put it round Kora that a serious feud had broken out on the banks of the river. Both tribes kept their herds well away from his camp for the rest of the drought. Down at our end we had to send for the Police and the Game Department. The Anti-Poaching Unit could only get to us a week after the gang had gone off with their booty. The Police were more timely, and with a combination of force and bluff dispersed the Somalis before the Reserve was laid waste.

The radio collars were a blessing when we had to know quickly where the lions had strayed in the night. They still kept in pairs and we would always find Arusha and Growlie together. What came as an enormous surprise was that Growlie suddenly came into season, a year before normal, when she was only eighteen months old. She behaved with all the abandon of a raving nymphomaniac, casting herself alluringly before Leakey and Freddie.

They were both bewildered by her performance and were at a complete loss to know what to do. But then Leakey, who was always a bit of a bounder, began to appreciate what was offered, and soon took advantage.

Even so, when Growlie's season was over, other attractions proved more powerful and Leakey and Freddie gave in to wanderlust. They began to go roving, increasingly often, on the far side of the Tana. As ill luck would have it, Leakey's battery was a year old, and the signals grew fainter and fainter. By the time Tony got across the river to search for him the battery had faded completely – and we had to reconcile ourselves to never seeing Leakey or Freddie again.

Tony had been with me when Christian had finally left, but he loved Freddie so much that he was even sadder now when these two went off, however much he realised that young lions either have to strike out in search of new mates and new territories or die in defence of the old. There is only one happy ending to a true tale of the wild and that is a question mark.

Not long after Leakey's and Freddie's departure the Somalis returned in unprecedented numbers. A rainfall of less than five inches in eight months, which evaporated almost as soon as it fell, brought a drought and tens of thousands of sheep, goats, donkeys, cows and camels. The cows, donkeys and sheep ate what little grass the Reserve contained. The goats and camels virtually finished off whatever browse was within their reach. My instinctive sympathy for the people and their animals in this plight was overshadowed by the extent of their destructiveness. The magnificent acacias and Tana River poplars were chopped down to provide fodder for the goats and camels, and the damage went further.

When I was out in the bush I would feel the sun suddenly grow cooler on my skin, and looking up see a film of vapour drifting across it. Then I would notice little grey specks floating down on the breeze, just as the smell of smoke reached my nose. The Somalis burned the undergrowth to encourage fresh shoots should there be even a sprinkling of rain. Far more wantonly hundreds of fine palm trees, along the dry water courses, were destroyed by fire in case their young thickets concealed lions, leopards or hyenas. What is more, the herdsmen ruthlessly put out carcases soaked in Coopertox, a proprietary cattle-dip against tsetse fly known to be lethal to carnivores. Many died a terrible death from it. There was not a square yard that was not trampled by stock, and the stench of dung hung over the bush for miles. This is the classic way in which mankind creates deserts all over the world.

My lions were not slow to take advantage of this anarchy. We did all we could to control them, by constant patrolling and increasing their rations of meat at the camp. Despite this they helped themselves liberally to the meat on the hoof. I remember driving past a herd of camels and noticing an odd shape moving beside them.

"*That*'s not a camel," I thought to myself. I braked hard, and reversed, to see Growlie, supported by Arusha, stalking a large camel, which was sitting with its backside towards them. I leapt out of the car and booted the camel in the rump. It turned its long neck slowly and curled its lip in distaste, as if I had very bad breath. But seconds later it spotted Growlie: in a flash it was up and off into the bush like a prizewinner. Just then Arusha's eye lit on a camel calf and, ignoring my blasphemous protests, she sprang on it. Before she could do lasting damage the mother came at her with gaping mouth and yellow teeth bared. Arusha checked and turned at the sound of screaming, as a crowd of Somali children, who had heard the commotion, came rushing up with sticks and stones. Their yells were enough to put Growlie and Arusha to flight. Had Arusha been really hungry I dread to think how the scene would have ended.

Urgent appeals to the authorities to enforce the Reserve's regulations were quite unavailing, as they had not yet been formally ratified by law. The Police sent ten men for three days, but it was hopelessly inadequate. We needed a hundred men for three weeks. Without the resolve, without the funds, and without the laws I began to despair of official protection. Only the rains could save the day.

The older lions, Daniel, Oscar and Kora, had sensed that the Somalis spelt danger, however tempting their cattle. They went hunting in the open country to the north of the river, for longer and longer stretches. They would always come back in splendid condition and must have been killing effectively and regularly. Daniel and Oscar now controlled the Kora range, and together they drove away Scruffy, their father, and protected the rest of the pride from attack or eviction by wild interlopers.

In September Growlie and Arusha displayed a characteristic of lionesses who are close to each other – they came into season together. Daniel and Oscar began to mate with them turn and turn about, and I realised it was going to be difficult to tell who would be the father of whose cubs. I therefore spent the whole of a day studying them very carefully and came to the conclusion that although it was impossible to tell who would sire Arusha's litter, Growlie's would definitely be by Daniel. Both should be born at the end of the year.

That evening a fairly ribald conversation about wife swapping was in progress when Tony had to stand by for the radio. He was still in a flippant mood when a call came up for us.

"I hear you. Vot messich do you say der iss von Friederike Adamson?" There was no love lost between him and Joy and he used to make play of her German names and accent. "Pleece will you say again, over." Then I saw his face suddenly go serious, and he beckoned to me.

"I think you should take this yourself, George," and he gave me an encouraging pat on the shoulder. I was told that Joy had just been rushed into hospital with a broken leg, and that I should stand by again for news in the morning.

The latest catastrophe was the result of one of her impulsive and typical quests. She had taken to walking on the mountains round Naivasha, partly to look for a home for a leopard she hoped she could train for release and partly to keep herself fit – she was now sixty-five, and leopards are much more active than lions. When she was told there were shy and beautiful bongos in a mountain forest just across the lake she was determined to go and look for them. She was expecting two great friends to stay, Billy Collins and Juliette Huxley, and hoped to be able to show them her latest discovery.

Joy had grown very fond of Billy and they had become close to each other over the years, except when it came to making her contracts. Joy always wanted more than the best: Billy remained to the end a true Scot. The hatchet was frequently raised and just as often buried; now he was coming to help her with her autobiography on which she was stuck. Juliette was one of the few people in the world for whom Joy still had genuine admiration and respect.

By way of reconnaissance Joy took a friend into the forest, leaving the friend's husband on the road at the foot of the mountain, as he was convalescing from a major operation on his leg. The two women pushed up higher and higher, along narrow paths forged by buffalo and pitted with their fresh tracks. As the afternoon wore on Joy realised they were lost; climbing over a log she slipped and broke her ankle.

For an hour she hobbled along, leaning on her friend's shoulder, but soon the track was too narrow for both of them. The sun was swinging round and Joy knew she had to get down the mountain before it set, as the paths would be death traps at night. The descent was so steep she decided that the fastest way down was on her bottom and elbows. The race against time was a torture. The track was damp, muddy and chilling. Bamboos split under her weight and cut her. When she came to a train of safari ants they scurried all over her, burning her skin with their bites.

At the edge of the forest they finally knew where they were, but were faced by a wide belt of nettles that brushed their bare legs and arms. Even then the last lap to the road was a treacherous swamp. Together the friend and her husband, despite his bad leg, heroically dragged Joy through the quagmire and back to the car. They got her to hospital in Nairobi at midnight, suffering from shock and exposure, for they had been up to 9,000 feet at the top of the mountain.

Joy's pain was much more than physical. As she lay waiting for the anaesthetic she realised her cherished leopard project would vanish once

With Billy Collins, great friend and publisher who cared so much about our books and the problems of our work.

Arusha with the two lions Daniel and Shyman. Shyman and Arusha managed to send Tony and me to hospital within a few months of each other.

again. Then, when she had come round from the operation, they gave her a telegram. She opened it expecting a message of sympathy. Instead she read that Billy had died of a heart attack. He could never help her finish the book that so much needed his skill.

Her recovery was slow. But when Juliette Huxley arrived Joy poured out her sorrows and hopes, and received in return both wisdom and encouragement to plan for the future rather than weep for the past. On a visit to Lake Nakuru Joy talked and talked. They were so carried away by the sight of the flamingoes, turned red by the glow of the settling sun, that Joy never noticed their car had sunk into the soda crust fringing the lake. Afterwards Joy wrote to Juliette:

> I will never forget our talk on Lake Nakuru. I had been so depressed, feeling my life dwindling away and unable to break new ground with the leopard research . . . I had grown desperate waiting six years in vain for a female cub. I talked to the doctor about my depressions and the tablets help a lot.
>
> . . . I am so glad you enjoyed our trip: for me it was a great treat to be with you, apart from what we saw on safari. Thank you for all your help and patience, because it is a strain to have a friend with you who is unhappy all the time.

When a party came out from the park headquarters to rescue Juliette and Joy they brought a message that was the best cure of all for her sadness. The Warden had a leopard cub which he would send down to Elsamere as soon as she was ready for it.

Joy told me the exciting news about the leopard on the radio and I tried to persuade her to bring it to Kora at once. We had always agreed that it was a perfect home for them, and we already had permission to release any leopard which came from the wild and had not been imported into Kenya. What I did not add was that I should be able to give Joy a helping hand and take some of the heavier work off her shoulders: she could not afford another accident.

I knew our camp looked a bit primitive; but it was really no more uncomfortable than our first house at Isiolo – and a piano was no use to Joy now. I knew also that she and Tony would not get on; but as at Meru with Pippa, she would need a separate camp for the little leopard. Thanks to Terence and Tony the practical arrangements improved all the time. Messages, food, parcels and people could be got in and out with reasonable ease. Terence was not only making the forty-mile boundary on the south-west side of the reserve but was also levelling a new airstrip only three miles from camp.

But Joy maintained that the climate was too hot and that she had to be closer to a post office to handle all her publishing business and the affairs of her Appeal. I was very upset at the time and looking back have sometimes felt that the decision cost her her life.

Tony and I continued to concentrate on the lions. After six years of tracking and plotting I was beginning to understand just how flexible their territorial response had to be to the push and the pull of the bush. Only by riding the pressures – from their own pride, from outsiders, from the Somalis or Orma – and by responding to the attractions – of new mates, richer hunting grounds or havens from herdsmen and poachers – could they hope to survive and succeed in raising their young.

After Boy's death the role of dominant male had been held briefly by Christian, before it had passed to Scruffy and had finally been seized by Daniel. This, with the breaking away of successive lions like Christian, Leakey and Freddie, was the pattern I expected of males. So tough was life in the bush at Kora that no lioness had yet lived long enough to maintain possession of the rocks, though it is usual for lionesses to stick to one territory while the males move on.

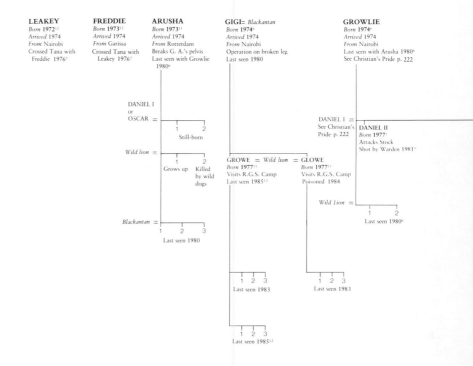

DANIEL'S PRIDE

AT KORA 1974–1985

Now, in December 1976, just as Growlie was about to bear Daniel's cubs, and Arusha his or Oscar's, we suffered yet another defection. Perhaps sensing that a new challenge from outsiders was imminent, Daniel, Oscar and Kora left for the vast open spaces across the river to the north. When I was certain that they would not be back I liked to think that they might be mingling over there with the descendants of Boy, Girl, Ugas and the four Bisletti lions. But I was very sorry Daniel had not waited to see the arrival of his offspring. I was also a little anxious he would not be there to protect them.

Early in January 1977 Growlie and Arusha gave birth to the third generation of the Kora line. We never found Arusha's cubs; her milk dried up in the first few days and they must have died very quickly. Growlie's were born in a secluded lugga half a mile from my camp. Nine years later, as I finish this chapter, one of those cubs, Koretta, has just brought her fifth litter of young to see Tony and me.

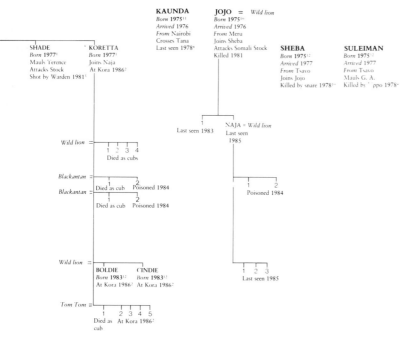

Chapter 14

The Last Walk
1977–1980

The day after Joy and Juliette Huxley had been rescued from the soda crust on Lake Nakuru, Joy went back to claim the little leopard cub.

She was only about two months old and was being looked after by a game ranger called Charles. He and his family had fallen in love with her and she was inseparable from his children. But Joy felt that her own passionate longing to compare a leopard with a lion and a cheetah, and all she would learn about its territorial habits, breeding control and thought communication, justified her in taking over the cub herself. She named her Penny.

Penny was taken to Naivasha by Charles who settled her into a cage near the house. The colobus monkeys hopped down on to the wire and teased her, always keeping just out of reach of her claws. But Joy, who had to win Penny's trust as she had with Elsa and Pippa, was frequently nipped and scratched. She had to learn the language of leopards the hard way and she continued to wear canvas guards on her arms and legs whenever she was out with Penny even though Penny remained genuinely affectionate. She grew rapidly on a diet of chicken, rabbits and mole rats – whose teeth she spat out – and enjoyed walking with Joy in the hills round Hell's Gate.

It is strange that in a country like Kenya it was difficult to find a home for Penny, but the population was rocketing and all land-use was carefully scrutinised; also the National Parks had been merged with the Game Department, which delayed a number of decisions. In the end two of Joy's searches paid off: on one she visited a suitable reserve for Penny's release at Shaba, near Isiolo; on another she discovered that Makedde, the old Turkana scout who had been out with Ken and me on the day we found Elsa, had just retired to Isiolo, and would join her to look after Penny. A little later she also prevailed on Kifosha, our cook in the Elsa days, to work for her again. I made one last attempt to persuade Joy to bring Penny to Kora, but she was adamant, and in August set out for Shaba as soon as permission came through. As she put it to Juliette, "we are off into the real life again".

During the next two years she occasionally wrote to Elspeth Huxley, describing her life.

Shaba is attached to the Samburu and Isiolo Reserves and run by the same warden. It is 100 square miles of beautiful country, with the Uaso Nyiro river as its Northern Boundary.

It took ten heart-breaking months before I was allowed to bring Penny here, and then on condition that the Elsa Appeal helps develop Shaba. We have donated a Toyota pick-up, built an airstrip, financed an anti-poaching camel unit – and there are many more projects to come. The Isiolo Councillors want to restock the reserve with endangered animals as well as eland, grevy's zebra, hartebeest, cheetah, and rhino, over the next two years, before it is filled with tourists.

I have a comfortable camp near a swamp with plenty of water, which attracts lion, buffalo, and all the smaller animals that live in this arid but lovely landscape. We meet them often on our walks with Penny, who roams free within six kilometres round camp. She is utterly different from a lion or a cheetah.

I am indelibly imprinted on her, though I can never relax with her as she is quite unpredictable. But she is most affectionate, intelligent, humorous, fast in her reactions and very independent.

I am now 68 and wish I could have fifty years ahead to do all I would like to do. Apart from a steel hip, a broken hand, elbow, knee and ankle – all on the right side, but mended during the last two years so that I would never know that I have had the breaks – I am very fit (touch wood). I can stumble for hours across wobbling lava in the heat and drench myself, fully dressed, several times a day under the shower to keep mentally active. I have the same game ranger and cook who were with us when we had Elsa, and altogether feel that I have at last come "home" again to the Northern Frontier . . .

George is 72 and as fit as if he were 50. He now looks after fifteen lions at Kora. These are his children and give him the excuse to live in the bush which he loves. Even if I do not agree with the way he shows off his lions to his visitors he is happy there.

＊　　　＊　　　＊

I certainly was happy, because although Joy was now embarking on the most difficult task of her life, one which some experts on leopards thought impossible, I felt that perhaps our worst days at Kora were over. By the time that Joy and Penny were settled into Shaba the number of lions had grown startlingly. For one thing several more of the lionesses had given birth to cubs, and for another we had been given four more youngsters, including Suleiman, who had got the better of me, but had been finally worsted by the hippo.

I never thought Joy's reproaches about showing the lions to visitors were quite fair. Kora was, after all, a National Reserve, from which no one could be kept out. Secondly the lions were not my property, but the state's. Thirdly most people came to see the pride for very good reasons – from the sheer pleasure of looking at them, to the most solemn, if unlikely, research. Our visitors always seemed to include not only conservationists but a fair share of beautiful women: sometimes we scored a left and right. Peter Beard, whose book *The End of the Game* was an early *cri de coeur* on behalf of the animals of Africa, brought Cheryl Tiegs, the loveliest model in America. Happy as we had been to rescue the cosmopolitan boating party spotted by Christian, we were even happier to welcome Candice Bergen, who was filming on a river safari down the Tana; she asked searching questions about our plans for leopards and gave us a big cheque towards them. Later, Ali McGraw came for a night with the lions, after she and I had been filmed over the Mara, in one of Alan Root's balloons, discussing the wildebeest migration.

Prince Bernhardt of the Netherlands, like Prince Philip, has played a really significant part in bringing home to people just how many different kinds of animal are being exterminated all over the world, to the irretrievable loss of future generations. The prince is inquisitive, enthusiastic and fun. When he flew up to Kora we were able to show him the Dutch lioness Arusha, who had not only broken my pelvis but recently bitten me in the leg as I stopped her from bullying Suleiman. After lunch the prince discovered our elephant skull facilities and, seeing the two seats, insisted that we were photographed on them, side by side. On a more serious note he saw for himself a party of Somalis watering several hundred camels, cattle, goats and sheep on the wrong side of the river, and understood their threat to the reserve.

Bernhardt Grzimek has been to see us several times at Kora and but for his generous provision of our tractor, water trailer, road grader and Landrover – with funds towards their running – I don't think Terence would have ever completed the two or three hundred miles of roads which make possible the protection of motor and camel patrols. We have received more help from his organisation than any other. He is an excellent photographer and always curious about the behaviour of animals, even experimenting in the Serengeti with lion-shaped balloons held in place by Alan Root – to see how the real lions reacted.

I discussed with him the varying intelligence and speed of reaction in the lions I had known, and he said a lion can respond to pain instantaneously. When he was director of Frankfurt Zoo, just after the war, a soldier stepped through a safety barrier and stubbed out his cigarette on the tail of a lion, which was lying close to the bars. As he did so the lion whipped out its paw and the soldier's scalp fell, like a flap, over his face.

Among the more abstruse experiments at Kora have been those of Professor Bramacherri of Calcutta and Dr Adriaan Kortlandt of Amsterdam. The professor brought out a large phial of tiger's urine and took away a representative sampling of elephant turds. I have not yet heard how the analysis of the latter compared with the rest of his African collection; and I was as disappointed as he that my lions totally ignored the urine from India, when he sprinkled it on some of their favourite marking bushes.

Dr Kortlandt's activities were a little more technical. Much concerned with the evolution of man and his ancestors, he wondered how on earth they survived on the African plains with only a brain to protect them. He asked to come to Kora to test out a possible answer with the help of our lions. It had occurred to him that early man may have used thorn branches to fend off the attentions of lions and sabre-toothed tigers. As he had not found anyone ready to try out this notion he brought with him a specially constructed battery-driven propeller – to which he attached whispering thorn branches. He brought these, too, in his small saloon car: it must have been an uncomfortable journey.

At the approach of the lioness Koretta, and two of her brothers, he put some camel meat under the blades of the propeller and waited. The lions very soon got the scent of the meat, and just as Koretta put out her leg to get at it Dr Kortlandt pressed the button. With a loud whirring noise the branches began to rotate. The lions looked absolutely astonished, jumped back, and sat down twenty feet away. As they pondered what to do next Dr Kortlandt began to take notes and talk into his recorder. He became so engrossed in this that he didn't notice Koretta suddenly slip forward and flick out the meat with her paw. I saw no mention of this in the article he subsequently wrote, and wondered if he would have modified his theory if he had seen as many lions break through thorn bomas as I had.

Not exactly conformists ourselves, Terence, Tony and I have come to terms with the quirks of most of our guests. In fact I wonder what they make of our meals which have become a bedlam since the guinea fowl, doves, hornbills and squirrels have invited themselves to the table. I also wonder if Hamisi, who was with Terence long before he came to Kora fifteen years ago, thinks all white men live like us. He was, alas, away in hospital when Adriaan Kortlandt demonstrated his propeller.

Hamisi keeps himself sane by going on leave, every few weeks, to a village about thirty miles down the Tana, where his wife and children look after his goats. One evening he went down to wash his goats in the river when a crocodile, about eight feet long, attacked him in the water and tried to drag him by the ankle into the stream. Bending forward, Hamisi called for help and started to gouge the croc's eyes out; it immediately dropped him. But as he struggled to get back to the bank the crocodile seized him again. This time some Somali children, who had rushed to the shouts and the splashing, heaved stones at the croc and drove it away from Hamisi. To this day he carries the ivory scars on his ebony skin.

He remains imperturbable, however many scorpions or cobras invade his kitchen in a corner of the camp: there is only one intrusion he refuses to put up with, and that is being bossed by any of Tony's young ladies who fancy themselves as cooks. At Christmas, exceptionally, when Joy came up to Kora with guests, or Bill and Ginny came out with four children, one turkey, a pudding and two dozen mince pies, he was grateful for some assistance.

*   *   *

I promised to join Joy for her first Christmas at Shaba and looked forward to seeing her. Her camp was, as she had said, very attractive. Its huts and tents stood under a group of tall fever trees. Nearby, the so-called swamp was an emerald oasis of water, grass and tall rushes, on the edge of a burnt-up plain, littered with lava boulders where it was cut by the river. Apart from our two old friends Makedde and Kifosha the cook, Joy had the help of the charming and intrepid Jock Rutherford to look after her camp. He had recently been capturing giraffe from a horse, not with a dart-gun but a lasso. On my first night his truck broke down and he walked across the plain, unarmed, in the dark, so as not to give Joy cause for alarm. She very much needed a man of his calibre in an outpost as lonely as this.

Joy was also being helped by a young man called Patrick Hamilton, who had done two years' research for the Game Department on the translocation of leopards. She treated his statistics as a challenge, for the first ninety leopards that had been trapped for cattle raiding and released in the Meru Reserve for everyone's safety had all disappeared. Joy and Patrick had given Penny, who was a really beautiful animal, a radio collar so they would not lose track of her. Ken Smith, now in charge of developing the reserves, said he would find her a mate. Joy obviously enjoyed our Christmas as much as I did, and wrote of it in her book about Shaba.

> Fishing along the river was idyllic. Its banks were shaded by doum palms, fig trees and poplars. It is true that we had to keep a look-out for crocodiles, and in the thick bush for buffaloes, but listening to the water bubbling over the shoals, the wind rustling through the palms, the rhythm of their swinging fronds and the haunting cry of a pair of crested cranes, I felt that we had gone

back in time, back to the days when George and I spent months on safari in the Northern Frontier District where man was quite unimportant. Today George's hair was white but as we picnicked by the river and I watched him patiently throwing his line again and again until he got a bite, it was as though time had been telescoped.

A little further down the stream Kifosha was fishing, and still further away Makedde was trying his luck.

During the early part of 1978 Joy not only watched Penny like a hawk, sometimes following her movements from the sky, but also put the finishing touches to her autobiography *The Searching Spirit*, which she had completed with the help of Marjorie Villiers. Elspeth Huxley had agreed to write the introduction, and in June Joy sent her the latest news of Penny.

She is now 21 months old and ready to mate. We brought in a male for her last month because the local leopards are too far away for her to meet them.

Since then she first disappeared for two weeks and only by chartering planes to get a better reading for her radio device did we find her 10 km outside Shaba. We assumed the leopard had taken her there and that she was on a safe honeymoon with him, as far away as possible from us, so that we would not interfere.

When I prepared myself to tranquillise her, and drive her back, she walked on her own, apparently without the male. Since then she thrashes herself about in a submissive manner when we locate her in the early morning, growling non-stop, which she never did before, and runs away only to return to more rolling and rubbing herself against our legs. But as soon as she is a few yards away from us she is perfectly normal, and follows us on long walks for more than an hour. She is going through a very important phase, which is different from any behaviour of lion and cheetah, and I have no explanation for it yet.

I intend to camp here for the next three years and to watch Penny's first two or three litters whom I will leave utterly wild. From them I will learn about the behaviour of wild leopards, as Penny is a victim of imprinting and will always be attached to me.

I am very worried about how George can cope with his lions who have landed him in hospital with a broken pelvis and injured neck. But he finds Naivasha too suburban to live there, and wants to remain at Kora however much I plead with him to join me here. It is country which he loves and he could help translocate animals here without the risk of ending up in hospital thanks to a lion kiss.

Later in the year Elspeth told Joy that the producer John Hawkesworth had bought the television rights in *The Flame Trees of Thika* and was coming out to Kenya with his wife to look at the country and decide on possible locations. Joy wrote to her:

Congratulations on *The Flame Trees*. Would it be a good idea for you to join the Hawkesworths? Of course they are welcome. Please warn her that my botanical knowledge is waning and that I am no expert. Now, during the rains, Shaba is unbelievably beautiful and the variety of plants incredible – many new to me.

Penny lost her first litter a week ago. She was away for 17 days during which we expected her to give birth, but she returned without a heavy undercarriage and without cubs. At the same time I broke my knee and am now, for four weeks, to be in plaster from groin to heel.

I am so sorry for Penny, though George consoles me with the fact that one of his lionesses also had a miscarriage of her first litter but later always had healthy cubs. In my own case I had three miscarriages and no children afterwards.

* * *

The lioness who had produced cubs at the second attempt was Arusha and by the end of 1978 we had almost too many lions round the camp. It meant we were kept on our toes, and there was further activity when Alan Root decided to make a film about hornbills.

On any short drive through the bush here you are certain to see, fluttering up into the trees, several hornbills, like small toucans, grey feathered, and with large curving beaks, either yellow or red. The yellow-billed are the commoner and greedier; at meals they push in first, while the red-billed drop in at the end.

Alan particularly wanted to film their elaborate nesting arrangements and knowing that they return, year after year, to the same hollow tree, selected a dead one near camp. He cut through a section, opposite the hole to be used by the birds, inserted a sheet of plate glass, and replaced the section of wood – which could be removed whenever he was filming.

As soon as the female is ready to lay, she enters the hole. She and her husband then wall up the opening, almost to the top, with mud, droppings and fibres. As soon as her eggs have been laid, at intervals, the female moults and is entirely dependent on her mate for her food, which he posts through the slit at the top of the wall. It has been noticed that occasionally when the male has been killed and his mate has called for food, other hornbills have come to her rescue.

The mother is a scrupulous house-keeper and until she has to leave, to help her mate feed the most advanced of the young, she keeps the nest clean by throwing out her droppings. The moment she is out the wall is rebuilt and the young grow up and emerge one by one so that the burden of feeding them is never too heavy. They, too, are immaculately house-trained: they put their tails to the opening and exercise their capacity for high-velocity shitting. I've always admired Alan's insatiable drive to film the enclosed private lives of termites or hornbills at one moment and the expanses of the Serengeti plains or the snow-clad summit of Kilimanjaro, from the swaying basket of a balloon, at another.

After his experiences with the snake, the leopard and the hippo there is no one who could have acted with greater presence of mind than Alan when the next crisis struck. Terence had been re-thatching a roof and early the next morning went to set fire to the debris just outside the gates. Without looking round to see if the coast was clear, he stooped down to put a match to the rubbish, which was damp and slow to get going.

The next thing he knew he was flat on his back with a lion's claws on his neck and his face in its jaws. His labour gang leapt from their truck just beside him and, yelling at the tops of their voices, hurled stones at the lion which retreated, dropping Terence to the ground. Alan and I ran out at the sound of the pandemonium to find Shade slinking off into the bush and Terence with blood streaming down his face.

We wrapped him in blankets and disinfected his wounds which were a terrible sight. There were holes in his neck and we could see his teeth through the tear in his cheek. Alan and Joan dressed his head with cotton wool, bundled him into their plane and headed for Nairobi. Joan held him tight, which he found very romantic. He told her he had never believed Livingstone when he wrote that he felt no pain after he had been mauled by a lion: now he knew it was true, but he felt bloody cold and couldn't stop shivering.

When Alan got him to the hospital, the doctor on duty told Terence he had stitched up both Alan and me, but Terence was only concerned to have a hot bath — his first for more than twenty-five years. The condition of his face was, however, very serious. One of Shade's teeth had just missed his eye and a canine had gone between his carotid and jugular. Despite the skill of the surgeon he found that at first he was unable to blink the lid of one eye. Only a tricky piece of plastic surgery could later restore this.

It was always the young males, between two and three years old, who made these attacks, and it was difficult to see them in perspective just after they had happened. I reckoned that in the last fifteen years, when we had been closely involved with more than forty lions, there had been six serious accidents. Over the same period there had been literally hundreds of maulings and deaths caused by wild lions, although they were seldom reported. On this occasion I did not shoot Shade for he was not sick, as Shyman had obviously been, nor was I asked to. But the Director of Wildlife told me I must cease to rehabilitate lions — and I have not taken one since. On the other hand he did tell me that I could begin to work with some leopards at Kora. Whatever Terence's underlying emotions may have been, he kept them to himself and I did not press him to disclose them. As we both neared eighty we felt it better to live and let live.

*   *   *

Joy's third year at Shaba — 1979 — was more exciting than ever. Apart from the time she devoted to Penny, she had to find a new assistant, carry on her massive correspondence and keep on with the book she was writing about Penny, which she hoped to end with the birth of her cubs.

The camp at Shaba was comfortable, shady and picturesque — but extremely remote. Her nearest neighbour, Roy Wallace, ran a tented safari camp fifteen miles away. Joy demanded much of her assistant, and when Jock Rutherford left she found it impossible to replace him with anyone of his experience and quality. After several misfits she appointed Pieter Mawson, the twenty-two-year-old son of a Zambian game warden, whose ambition was to become a game warden himself.

Joy continued to write to Elspeth Huxley and, hearing that she was working on the history of Whipsnade, expressed her own views on zoos:

> I made a point of visiting every zoo I could during my world travels, so that I could judge from experience what is going on. Of course there are the registered and the unregistered zoos, and what I saw of the latter was unbelievably cruel. But even registered zoos are often far below the required standards and cause unnecessary deaths.
>
> My personal ideal would be that zoos should only acquire animals born in captivity, and thus leave the wild animals, born in freedom, where they belong. Forgive me if I trespass with my ideas, but I am at a loss to see how the often inadequate conditions in zoos can be changed, unless the public is more aware of what goes on behind the curtain.

On 23 May Joy wrote again to Elspeth.

> Today is a big day. I saw for the first time Penny's three-day-old cubs. The day they were born she came off the very rocky mountains to lead Pieter and me to them. She was still bleeding and her teats sticky from being suckled. But as cubs are very vulnerable for a few days — cat mothers sit like incubators to keep their temperature steady — we did not want to disturb them.
>
> But Penny repeated her efforts, so we followed her to her babies — two, under an overhang of large rock, and overshadowed by a tree, which conceals them from birds of prey. She was very beautiful in her new role of mother, so dignified and looking so proud. We sat next to Penny, within one metre. She licked our hands while the cubs cuddled between her front legs, all so sublimely happy.

"Today is a big day. I saw for the first time Penny's three-day-old cubs…cuddled between her front legs."

The general belief is that leopards are the most dangerous of all African animals, and leopardesses with young especially fierce. Either I am exceptionally lucky in having such a good-natured, highly intelligent and affectionate leopard to work with, or Penny proves that most of the accepted beliefs are a fallacy.

She is now two years and ten months old; lives utterly wild for 22 hours a day; walked 25 km in one night; and ranges over 120 square miles – often together with two males – on safaris lasting one or two weeks when she hunts and kills for herself. She has already contradicted many misconceptions, like leopards being treacherous, cunning and even fiendish.

Her wish to share her cubs with us a few hours after they were born is staggering. Her den is high up on a rocky outcrop, and very tricky to reach, climbing across boulders and cliffs, over slippery sand and through devilish thorns. But it was worth all that to see the three-day old cubs, the youngest I have ever seen. Can you understand how happy I am?

The birth of the leopard cubs, one female and Pasha, a male, enabled Joy to finish her book. She posted it off to Marjorie Villiers in London, together with the best of her colour slides and black-and-white negatives: she had taken more than four thousand photographs of Penny.

Joy told me with satisfaction on the radio, one evening, that she had sent off the script and she went on to talk about Penny and problems in the camp with her refrigerator; but the next day she had to face an ordeal that taxed even her remarkable courage and energy. From Joy's letters afterwards, Marjorie Villiers pieced together exactly what happened. It was a Sunday, and Pieter had taken Makedde and Kifosha into Isiolo.

The short rains failed north of the equator and Shaba had become a dust-bowl. The animals congregated near the river. The barren plain became even more denuded and sand-devils of alarming height whirled across it.

I was alone in the camp and started to clean up the dining tent, where work on the fridge had taken place. Suddenly there was an explosion, a flame burst from one of the machines and set fire to the tent. I tried to put it out but the heat was so intense I had to rush into the open. I watched the flames shoot up into the trees and ignite the thatched roof of our living hut, which became an inferno. I dashed inside and grabbed a tape recorder but was nearly suffocated. As though paralysed I stood watching the raging hell all around me. My failure to release the rabbits haunted me for weeks.

Blown at great speed, by a strong wind, the flames crossed the camp approaching the bushes and the plain beyond. I seized a hessian bag and beat back the blaze as it neared the bushes. Passing the rabbit run I recognised the charred remains of my favourite: she had died protecting her young with her body.

I continued beating the flames, urged on by the crackling and heat, though I had difficulty breathing and my skin was scorched. My one aim now was to prevent the fire from reaching the bush. Already the shoulder-high reeds by the swamp were smouldering.

It was not until six in the evening that three rangers, who had seen the fire from the Gate Post of the reserve, walked all the way to camp to help Joy. She had lost all her camp furniture, crockery, cutlery, food and lamps; her books and her papers; her radio receiver for Penny and her own long-distance radio telephone set. Gone were her cameras and most of her four thousand photographs and cine footage of Penny. When Pieter returned she asked him to take the rangers back to their post and to alert the Game Warden. Joy went on:

After they had left I sat on a tin trunk that had contained our provisions, now baked solid. I looked into the darkness and saw the skeletons of the dead trees glowing red against the black velvet of the sky. The scene was beautiful, but those glowing trunks were the sentinels surrounding a tragedy in which countless small creatures had died.

At this critical time Joy needed the support of a man like Jock Rutherford, with a lifetime's experience of working with Kenyans. At the best of times Joy was impatient; in moments like this she gave vent to her temper. Pieter Mawson did his best but he was very young and did not know the local people or speak fluent Swahili. Simple misunderstandings would turn into furious rows, and too often, according to Joy, Pieter would recover from tensions in her camp during the day with parties at Roy Wallace's in the evenings. Any drinking was anathema to Joy and relations sank to their lowest when they needed to be at their best. It was impossible to keep their disputes private in the open camp.

Nevertheless the Isiolo councillors rose to the occasion and sent out help of all kinds. A Turkana, from one of the local manyattas, was engaged to clear up the mess and salvage what he could; and although Pieter may not always have been wise in the people he helped Joy to recruit, five workmen arrived to rebuild the camp only two or three days after the fire. Some had never been in the bush before, and Joy had to restrain one from following his nose into a thicket to discover the source of a "whuff" that obviously came from a lion, an old friend of Joy's. The men worked rapidly and successfully to get the camp up before the rains came.

By the end of November Joy's life at Shaba had more or less returned to normal and to Juliette Huxley she wrote of Penny's cubs at six months old.

> The cubs are utterly wild, and we only get glimpses of them now and again, hiding up on the rocks; it is impossible to get photographs. Pasha is a truly wild leopard and will have nothing to do with us. Penny, touchingly, often tries to bring the cubs near us. She calls them, with her rasping cough, or places herself in full view when the cubs join her high on the rocks, as if knowing how concerned we are that all is going well.

Then Joy was afflicted by more troubles. She was going over to make a radio call from Roy's camp, with Pieter, one evening when her car broke down. Walking back through the dark she fell and cracked her knee. She would never have got home without Pieter's physical and moral support. Once more her leg was in plaster.

A few days later 1000/- was stolen from a cabinet in Pieter's tent and suspicion could only fall on her employees. In the first week of December Joy had a row about his work with a young Turkana, Paul Ekai, who was one of the suspects. He was sacked and paid off. Three nights later, when the camp was empty, a tin trunk in her tent was broken open with a crowbar and some contents removed: Pieter also was robbed.

Joy, often mercurial, was never more so than now. A night or two after these dramas she came up on the radio to say she was flying to Paris for a few days. It was so unlike her to leave Penny, just as her cubs seemed about to break away on their own, and also to spend money on flying to Europe for less than a week, that I could scarcely believe her. But French television had asked her to appear as the star in a series which devoted one evening each week to a famous personality. During Joy's evening they were going to show *Born Free* and a film about her life and work with her animals, which the Elsa Appeal had financed and which had been shown by the BBC. The films were to be followed by a discussion in the studio between Joy and a panel – which included a zoologist, a conservationist, a film critic and Brigitte Bardot who had recently joined the crusade for animal rights. The television company were to pay Joy's first class air fare to Europe, and while she was there she planned to go on to London to approve the edited script, the choice of illustrations and the wrapper for her book about Penny.

She made me promise I would join her for Christmas – the 37th anniversary of our first meeting at Willie Hale's roof party. It would take the whole of the day on most terrible roads to get to Shaba by car. As it only took an hour in a plane I planned to fly over on Christmas Eve. A pilot who was working for a programme of Austrian aid in Kenya, and who was always generous in coming to our help, said he would take me to Joy.

When she arrived in London, for a few hours only on 17 December, Marjorie Villiers went down to greet her at an airport hotel. Joy was still elated by Penny's achievement in raising her cubs and Marjorie found her delighted with the success of her evening on television: she was especially impressed by Brigitte Bardot who had said she would like to come out to see Penny. So mellow was she that all her personal resentments had dissolved and in Paris she had bought Christmas presents not only for Terence and me, but for Pieter and Tony Fitzjohn.

She was immediately pleased with everything planned for the book – only the title remained to be settled. When they said goodbye that evening Joy was as happy as Marjorie had ever seen her since she first told her the story of Elsa twenty years before.

*   *   *

Terence, Tony and I never received our presents from Paris. On 4 January, while I was out looking for the lions, I saw a plane circling the camp. It had become such a frequent occurrence that I thought no more of it and after half an hour or so it took off again. But when I came in at lunchtime, and saw Terence's face, I knew that something was fearfully wrong.

Peter Johnson had flown up in the plane from Nairobi. Late the night before he had been woken by a telephone call from a German doctor in Isiolo, Dr Wedel, who told him that Joy had been killed by a lion: her body was being taken to Meru. As Terence didn't know when I would be back, Peter had decided to fly on to Shaba, to arrange with the warden how best to protect Joy's things and to make plans with Pieter Mawson for looking after Penny.

When my thoughts began to disentangle themselves, the first was a deep and painful regret that I had never been able to reach Joy for Christmas – and would never see her again. The pilot had been called off on an emergency flight over Christmas and so I had not been able to go down to Shaba. Secondly, I felt an immediate and growing disbelief that Joy had been killed by a lion: it was perfectly possible – in fact I knew that a lion lived close to her camp – but somehow the story didn't ring true. Thirdly I was frustrated by being stranded at Kora: it would take me a day to get over to Shaba and all I could do was to wait, as Terence had arranged, until Pieter came up on the radio. When he did, though not till the following day, it was clear I must fly immediately to Nairobi where the dreadful story unfolded.

On the evening of 3 January Joy had gone for her usual evening walk at about half-past six. She was normally back by seven in time to listen to the news on the radio, and before the sun set. Old Makedde was in Isiolo – he had just been married for the third time – and only Pieter Mawson and Kifosha were in camp. Kifosha lit the lamps and by 7.15, when it was quite dark, he and Pieter were worried that Joy was not back. Pieter therefore drove out in the Toyota pick-up to look for her along the track she always took. Two hundred yards from the camp he saw Joy's body in the lights of the truck, lying on the road in a pool of blood.

He immediately tried to reverse the pick-up but got stuck in the mud at the side of the track. So he ran to the camp, called to Kifosha and drove back with him to the scene in Joy's station wagon. They looked at Joy's body, to make certain she was dead, and seeing a large wound on her left arm Pieter told Kifosha he thought it must have been caused by a lion. Leaving Kifosha with the body he drove back to camp to fetch a sheet and a blanket, a rifle and ammunition. He noticed that the lights in the camp had gone out, but thought nothing of it.

With Kifosha's help he wrapped up Joy's body, laid it on the back seat of the station wagon and set off for Isiolo. He left Kifosha with the rifle and ammunition, telling him to guard the camp. Kifosha then discovered that not only were all the lights out, but the two gates to the animal enclosure at the back – the outer one gave on to the bush – were open. Joy had bolted them both before she went out. Kifosha now secured the inner one, but was afraid to go further. Next he saw that Joy's tent had been opened: a trunk had been forced, and papers were scattered around.

In the meantime Pieter stopped briefly at Roy Wallace's camp to borrow some petrol. He told him that Joy had been killed by a lion and pointed to her body at the back. He then drove straight to Dr Wedel's house at Isiolo, getting there at about 9 p.m. Dr Wedel got into the car and they went to the police station, where the doctor examined the body. He simply confirmed Joy's death after observing two wounds on her arm and one on the left side of her chest. Half an hour later the senior police officer, Chief Inspector Gichunga, arrived and it was decided to take Joy's body to the hospital mortuary in Meru, where there was refrigeration. Pieter spent the night with Dr Wedel.

The next morning, 4 January, Mr Gichunga, who was not entirely convinced that Joy had been killed by a lion, went back to Shaba with Pieter, where they were joined by Senior Superintendent Ngansira and other policemen. They examined the blood patch where Joy had died and found her walking stick but had to tow the pick-up back to the camp, as a lead had been pulled off and the battery was missing. There was a crowbar lying in Joy's tent and a metal box, like the trunk, had been prised open: the crowbar, taken from the camp tool shed, was the one that had been used on 10 December. When they went to the gates of the animal enclosure they found prints of shoes or boots leading into the bush.

The police were now convinced that murder had been committed and suspicions fastened on all Joy's employees, particularly on those who had quarrelled with her, including Pieter himself and Paul Ekai, the young Turkana she had sacked.

On the following day, 5 January, a post mortem was carried out on Joy's body, which had been moved to Nairobi, by three doctors. One of them, Dr Geoffrey Timms, was the government pathologist who had been present when the murdered body of Lord Erroll had been removed from his car in 1941. The doctors agreed that Joy had been killed by a sharp weapon, such as a *simi* (short sword); there were two cuts on her arms and a third which had penetrated eight inches into her rib cage, severing the abdominal aorta. Later, Peter Jenkins affirmed in evidence that the wounds could not possibly have been made by a lion.

Meanwhile the suspects were undergoing intensive interrogation. Pieter's was especially fierce and intimidating as his frequent disagreements with Joy had been noisy and impossible to conceal.

On the next day, 6 January, Superintendents Giltrap and Rowe arrived from Nairobi to reinforce the police. The area round the camp was searched but revealed nothing significant except a *rungu,* or knobbed stick, found in the bush, off the road where the body had lain. Very soon all the suspects were cleared except Paul Ekai, who could not be found. But when the police went, with his brother Gabriel, to his father's manyatta at Daba Borehole, several witnesses saw Paul run away before the police party arrived.

For the moment the investigation had come to a standstill. But on 2 February, the police had a stroke of luck and acted very efficiently. That night up at Baragoi, nearly two hundred miles away, and towards the Turkana country round Lake Rudolf, three men reported to the police station that they had been set upon by bandits. The sergeant took down the details and then asked them to produce identification. When one of them handed over his card with the name Paul Ekai, the sergeant recognised him as being on the "wanted" list from Isiolo and he was detained.

Next day, 3 February, Ekai was taken down to Mr Ngansira's office where he was interviewed briefly at about half-past five in the afternoon. He denied any knowledge of Joy's murder, and said he was tired and wanted to rest. He was kept for the night in the police station. Next morning, 4 February, he was interviewed again by Mr Ngansira and made a full confession to the murder.

Ekai said he had been incensed that when Joy sacked him he had not been paid the full wages due to him. He had therefore loitered near her camp intending to remonstrate with her on her evening walk, and when she had grown angry he had stabbed her in a fury. He had then flung his *simi* into the swamp and gone to the camp, intending to rob her tin trunk for money and valuables. But before he could go through it Pieter returned for the blanket and rifle. He therefore hid in the bush until Kifosha came back alone. He then took the battery from the pick-up (presumably intending to sell it) and made his way by a game path to Daba Borehole, concealing the battery under a tree on the way.

Ekai was then taken to Shaba and although he and three policemen looked in the swamp for the *simi* they could not find it; but by now it was a month since the murder, and it could well have sunk in the mud. Next, Ekai led the police to the battery hidden in the bush. Finally he took them to a manyatta near Daba, and pointed to a knife, scabbard and belt, which were taken away.

On the morning of 5 February Ekai was formally cautioned and charged with murder. That afternoon he guided Mr Ngansira and Mr Giltrap to a second manyatta, near the reserve, and showed them a house he said belonged to his sister. From it he produced a haversack containing some of Pieter's clothes that had been stolen on 10 December. He then took down from the roof of another house a torch which had been stolen from Joy on the same night. Later, government chemists established that blood stains on the haversack belonged to Joy's blood group and not Ekai's. He must have handled it shortly after the murder.

The young Turkana was then taken back to Isiolo and examined at the District Hospital, where he was found to be healthy and suffering from no injuries, although he carried the traditional scarring and beauty marks of a Turkana on his skin. These scars are sometimes awarded, like badges of honour, for taking human life, but there was no cause for believing this was so in the case of Ekai.

I waited impatiently for the trial, and its result, but it took an unconscionable time to reach a hearing. There was not even a "preliminary enquiry" at Nyeri, where the trial was to take place, until 26 June, nearly six months after the murder. At this stage Ekai withdrew his two statements, and claimed that on his first night at Isiolo police station he was driven by the police into the country. There he was whipped, kicked, burned with an iron rod, heated in a fire, and tortured, with string round his testicles, into making a confession. For this, or some other, reason the case was delayed still further and, incredibly, did not come up for trial until the middle of the following year.

It lasted three months. Once more Ekai reneged on his confessions, this time under oath. He further claimed that at the time of the murder he was staying with his aunt Rebecca, for three nights, at Isiolo and had been suffering from malaria. His aunt corroborated the story, but the judge rejected the alibi and accepted the original confessions. Ekai was convicted of murder on 28 October 1981.

Because there was some doubt about Ekai's age – he was reckoned to be somewhere between seventeen and twenty – he was sentenced to be detained during the President's pleasure. Had he been older the death sentence would have been obligatory.

Ekai's lawyers appealed on his behalf, largely on the grounds that his confessions were inadmissible, since they were neither voluntary nor true; also because there was doubt about the identity and whereabouts of the *simi* used for the murder. But the three Appeal judges found no evidence of torture, accepted that the two confessions were made voluntarily and seemed to fit all the verifiable facts, and felt that the second robbery was irresistible evidence that Paul Ekai had been at the camp on the night of the murder. On the 14 December 1981 they upheld his conviction.

*   *   *

It was difficult to comprehend that Joy had gone, and dreadful to know the way of her death; far better had it been a lion. Whatever our differences, our fondness remained to the end and had, if anything, deepened over the years.

Her funeral was simple and quiet. The crematorium stands just outside the city on the road to the game park and Lone Tree plain, where we had camped on our earliest visits together to Nairobi. None of Joy's family, or oldest and closest friends, was there that day, for they were either dead or in Europe. But old friends of mine, friends of Joy's later years – Austrian, English and Kenyan – and friends of the wild animals and their country, to whom she had given so much, were present at the service.

I was reminded of lines from the poem by Francis Nnaggenda that Joy used to keep beside her, and which were printed at the end of her posthumous book about Penny:

> The dead are not under the earth,
> They are in the tree that rustles,
> They are in the woods that groan,
> They are in the water that runs . . .
> They are not dead.
> When my ancestors talk about the Creator they say:
> He is with us. We sleep with him. We hunt with him.
> We dance with him.

Later, as Joy wished, I took her ashes to Meru. Some I scattered on Pippa's grave under the tree in her camp where, in a life that was often clouded and stormy, she had been acutely aware of a happiness and peace within herself. The rest I buried with Elsa, near the place of which Joy wrote: "Sitting there, with Elsa close to me, I felt as though I were on the doorstep of paradise."

Chapter 15

Seven Commandments
1977–1985

Four days before she died Joy wrote to Marjorie Villiers: "I have just found out that female cats are called queens, and this gives us the title for the book on Penny – *Queen of Shaba*." So intense was the interest in Joy immediately after her death that two London newspapers wanted to serialise it and the bidding rose to well over a hundred thousand pounds. When Joy married she had no money to speak of and few possessions of value: most precious to her were her piano and easel. When she died she left a fortune.

My most urgent concern was for Penny. Pieter was anxious to stay on and look after her – perhaps even see her through a second litter of cubs – although the family grew wild and perfectly able to fend for themselves. There have been subsequent sightings of Penny with two more litters of cubs.

Pieter was so unsettled by the murder, and the investigations which followed, that when he realised he was not needed at Shaba he left the country for South Africa – only returning once very briefly for the trial. He married and then was tragically killed in a car accident.

Shaba joined Meru and Samburu as one of the National Reserves that owed so much, in their first, vulnerable years to the Elsa Appeal. The Isiolo Council planned to preserve Joy's camp and set up a memorial to her. Several years later the government acquired the land round Hell's Gate in the hills behind Elsamere as a National Reserve. This was one of Joy's most cherished projects and her Appeal is contributing more than $100,000 to its development. Elsamere was left to the Appeal and now offers food, beds and a library to people seriously concerned with conservation.

The bulk of Joy's royalties not spent on her modest living or her handsome donations were invested for the benefit of the Appeal. Peter Johnson as Joy's financial adviser had to press her to retain even a limited sum to support her old age, and she now left me a life interest in the income from this. It amounted to about the same as my pension on which I had been living for the past fifteen years, and although not princely it has helped with the housekeeping bills. Everything that I had received since leaving the

Game Department had gone in this way – mostly on cars, petrol, repairs and camel meat.

The instructions Joy left about her ashes reminded me of a note I had made in my diary as long ago as 1971, when I had only been here a year. I asked that if anything happened to me, my body should not be removed from Kora but buried without fuss in the sand beside Boy's.

In the first five years here both the lions and I had to fight to keep a foothold by the Tana. During the second five our lionesses were almost too successful in establishing the pride: by 1980, at the time of Joy's death, there were sixteen lions round the camp. The situation produced a considerable upheaval in both their lives and ours.

To begin with, the three eldest lionesses seemed to realise that the country was too harsh to feed so many mouths, even allowing for the camels I bought them. The two toughest ones tried to drive away Gigi, the gentlest, and also the four latest newcomers – the last of the lions we brought in from outside. One of them, Kaunda, was quickly adopted by Gigi. Like her he was extremely good natured, and as the pride began to split into groups they would grow restless at Kora and go off on safari. They both paid a price for this dangerous habit.

At 5.30 one morning Tony and I heard with some alarm a car approaching and thought it must be a party of Shifta, especially when the men inside it, who were clearly displeased, brandished guns at us. They were in fact a military patrol in search of cattle thieves. They told us a pride of lions had charged them further back up the road and they had shot one. We hurried out and found Gigi bleeding from two holes in her leg: a bullet had passed straight through it. Luckily it had done no serious damage and she seemed to bear us no grudge.

Kaunda was wounded a few months later when he and Gigi went questing in search of some goats. I realised what they were up to and could follow their spoor for a time but after a bit I lost it and could not get radio readings. Fortunately one of Tony's friends flew in at that moment and took him up with the scanner: they spotted the lions making towards a herd of Somali cattle. Tony was anxious that they might run amok among the cows and be killed by the herdsmen; so he hurried back to camp, collected some meat from the fridge to divert their attention from meat on the hoof, and dropped it down to the astonished lions.

When we went out the following day we found Kaunda had been speared in the shoulder. We lured him into the back of the Landrover and drove him home to camp. As there was no room for Gigi the amiable lioness trotted home in our wake.

From now on, as the lions began to disperse over longer and longer

I had to get them away: the temptation to attack livestock was too great.

Crossing over to Chris Matchett's camp in search of the lion Kaunda. I knew I'd look daft sitting in a rubber boat on the Tana holding a radio mast and looking for lions, but to me it made all the sense in the world.

distances, we relied increasingly on aerial tracking, though we discovered that we had one other trick up our sleeve. It was just now that Terence had hit upon the gift of water divining. I have spoken to too many people who have drawn water he has found to doubt his powers, and they seem to go further.

With the aid of a weight on a string, a pencil, a map and an image or sample of what he has to find, he is prepared to search for almost anything. Concentrating on the sample or photograph, he dangles his pendulum over the map from his right hand and, guided by the force of its circling or swing, gradually pinpoints his quarry with the pencil held in his left.

A retired professional geologist, Don Gordon, now living in Malindi, took Terence up in a plane and watched him draw the line of a geological flaw on his map. Gordon had no idea the flaw existed – nor had anyone else – but he later verified it with instruments on the ground and Gordon said he could not believe in Terence's talent, but he had to accept it.

Another friend who came up to Kora told Terence she had lost touch with her son who was somewhere in Australia. She had brought up his photograph and an atlas: would Terence help her to find him? As he worked over the map with his pendulum his pencil was led to a small town which neither he nor the woman had heard of but which he underlined for her. A year or so later her son confirmed that he had indeed been there at the time.

Tony remains sceptical about Terence's gift for locating the lions: I have found him right about 60 per cent of the time. I have been just as successful in following his advice as I have in tracing the spoor or struggling with radio antennae – and it is much less trouble.

Although by this time Kaunda was fast becoming a spirited young lion he was still not mature and a wild interloper we named Blackantan aspired to take the pride over by storm. In August 1977 he began to court Gigi and as she enjoyed the affair Kaunda wisely kept his distance. Three and a half months later Gigi gave birth to two cubs, Glowe and Growe, whom she cleverly used to ingratiate herself for the first time with the other two lionesses who had been so disagreeable.

In the following year I still kept Kaunda and some of the other young lions shut up in the enclosure at night as on several occasions they had been violently attacked by the older lionesses and their families. Further disturbances were frequently provoked by Blackantan.

In April 1978 he came on the rampage and tried to attack Kaunda through the wire. Kaunda, who had all the enterprising instincts and attack of a successful young footballer, responded in kind. Fearing that the fence would give way, I got into my Landrover and drove him off before the whole thing collapsed. The next morning Kaunda and his companion were so edgy and frustrated at being penned up after once tasting freedom that I had to let them out. It was the last of Kaunda. He vanished from the face of the earth and we could pick up no signals – even from the tops of the hills.

About three months later, Patrick Hamilton, who was helping Joy with Penny while continuing his own research, flew along the Tana about thirty miles west of Kora. He was scanning for his leopards but suddenly he picked up a bleep on Kaunda's frequency. He followed it down to the north side of the river and there, on a rock, sat Kaunda, looking up confidently at the plane – waiting no doubt for the camel meat that would fall from the skies.

A few days later a friend of ours, Chris Matchett, who had set up a tented safari camp on the far side of the river and kept a small herd of goats to provide fresh meat and milk, told us a lion with a collar had taken two of his animals. I rowed over immediately to make amends and apologise – and quickly found Kaunda, quite unrepentant and bouncing with energy. He was as friendly as ever and Tony and I contemplated bringing him back to Kora, but the nearest bridges were at least two hundred miles or more up and down stream. There was no guarantee that he would not go adventuring again so we decided to leave him where he was.

Some weeks after this Tony was again being flown over the area. This time he located Kaunda right on the boundary of the Meru National Park. We were thrilled to know that he had been able to survive on his own for so long and was so close to safety: it also gave us grounds for thinking that Christian, Daniel, Leakey, Freddie and the others who had gone off in the past had fared equally well.

There was soon further evidence for such optimism. Shortly after he had seen Kaunda, Tony was driving a Landrover between Chris Matchett's camp and the boundary of Meru Park. He was taking it slowly through a lugga when he saw a lion and stopped. To his utter amazement the lion walked briskly up to the car, cheekily bumped his head against a door and disappeared into the night. Tony only saw him for a moment but his appearance seemed familiar and his breezy manner unlike that of any lion we had known except one: he was convinced it was Leakey. He turned off the engine to peer into the darkness and listen. At that moment a lion called close by, with an uncanny resemblance to Freddie, his favourite and Leakey's constant companion. Was this another case of the lions' telepathic awareness of our whereabouts? Tony was naturally excited when he came back and told me.

"George, I do promise you I was 'dry' at the time," he added disarmingly. I think this was an allusion to my albino hippo. I had once (just after finishing my eleven o'clock gin) seen a pink hippo in the river with about four normal ones. There were hoots from Tony when I reported the circumstances of the sighting to him and Terence at lunchtime. But when I went back that evening, before our first sundowner, the hippo was still pale pink all over.

It was about now, after Shade's gratuitous assault on Terence had led to the embargo on taking more lions, and the discovery that Kaunda and the others were alive after all and thriving on the other side of the river, that I began to look at the overall results of our efforts.

At Meru I had been given seven lions, including Boy, who had come to Kora after his year's convalescence at Naivasha. At Kora we had taken sixteen more lions – making a total of twenty-three.

The Meru pride had given birth to eleven cubs while I was still there, of which two had probably been taken by a leopard and one killed in the night by the wild lion Black Mane. The survival rate, in the first precarious weeks of their lives, was therefore 70 per cent. At Kora the seventeen lions had produced twenty-five cubs of which eighteen had survived the dangerous early weeks – that is again about 70 per cent. I am told that the average survival rate through this early age for lions in the wild is about 25 per cent.

I was unable to follow up what became of the lions at Meru once I had moved here to Kora, although they were occasionally seen together for the first year or two. At Kora the pattern of their lives seemed to run true to form. As soon as the males grew up they tended to move on – though a lion like Daniel (son of the lioness Juma, who used to creep under the wire), or the wild interloper Blackantan, would dominate the scene for a couple of years. The females, on the other hand, liked to stay put. When the young grew too thick on the ground the lionesses became quite vicious in their attempts to drive the weaker vessels away; once or twice my quixotic attempts at providing protection were rewarded with a bite on the hand or the leg.

One of the worst offenders in these family vendettas was the young lioness Koretta, daughter of Daniel. My camp at Kora has often been called a School of Correction for Errant Young Ladies and Koretta was certainly one of them. Not only did she aid and abet her mother in the persecution of Gigi, but she was seduced at an early age by Blackantan into abandoning her first litter of cubs and going on a honeymoon with him. When she gave birth to his cubs a few months later she abandoned them too, and both would have died had not her companion, Naja, adopted them with her own two cubs. I sometimes think that it was Naja, not I, who proved the salvation of Koretta and reformed her into the pride of our pride.

*   *   *

It was about now that I unwisely undertook to write this book and Chryssee

Bradley Martin, whose husband had given us the radio collars, typed up my diaries. I wrestled with names, dates, my reports, the diaries and smudged carbons of the few letters I had kept. Even so it was impossible to make progress. At the best of times it is difficult to write on the equator: dawn comes soon after six and I tried to keep the evenings free for answering letters or doing my accounts — it did not help that my eyesight was going. Apart from the heat the lions took a toll on my energy during the day and absorbed even more when Tony's attention was diverted to cope with a dream that suddenly came true.

One day Michel Jeannot, our friend who was a senior pilot in Air France, arrived on the airstrip at Kora with a broad grin on his face and a heavy basket on his arm — it was the one we had come to know well and which was so often packed with ham and French cheeses, wine, brandy and his cameras, with photographs and films of our lions. It must also have become familiar to the Customs, for when he had brought his jumbo jet into Kenyatta Airport that morning they had not bothered to look into the basket: had they done so they would have found two tiny leopard cubs.

Michel knew of the embargo on our taking any more lions after Terence's accident; he also shared our enthusiasm for bringing leopards to Kora. He had seen Tony starting to put up a boma and huts at Komunyu waterholes, about seven miles away from our camp, against the day when the leopards arrived. Since then there seemed to be a sudden dearth of these cats and the frustation that Tony expressed in his letters to Michel must have sparked off a brainwave. Two friends of Michel owned a nightclub in Paris whose attractions included a pair of fine leopards: when the leopards had cubs Michel decided to bring them to Kora in the best international traditions of Arusha and Christian.

In all innocence Michel had forgotten it was a condition of our rehabilitating leopards that they should be Kenyan born. I was therefore faced with a series of immediate dilemmas: should we accept or refuse the cubs? If we accepted them should I conceal them or make a clean breast to the authorites? If the authorities rejected them what could I do to reprieve them from life-long captivity? I decided at once to tell the full story and formally apply for permission to keep them — and we waited on tenterhooks for a decision.

The response, which came six weeks later, was an order to return the leopards to Paris at once. By this time we had grown very attached to them and Tony had been obliged to move over to Kampi ya Chui — Camp of the Leopards — for the cubs could not be allowed to grow up near the lions. The next day I therefore went down to Nairobi to see the Director of Wildlife — to ask that the decision be reconsidered and that should we not be allowed to keep the cubs they could at least go to another African country where they would have a chance of being set free. I realised it was an extremely difficult decision for the Director, who had always given our problems at Kora the most courteous and careful consideration, as he still does today.

The wheels of justice and administration in Kenya may sometimes grind slowly but they also grind fairly and small. I received no further word for another four months but this time, when it came, we were told that the leopards – we had called them Attila and Komunyu – might stay.

Kampi ya Chui is about three and a half miles beyond the airstrip near which Tony has nailed to a prominent tree a notice which reads: LIONS ON ROAD – BUZZ CAMP AND WAIT AT PLANE UNTIL PICKED UP. His camp is beautifully situated on sand and is shaded by a grove of acacias. One side is protected by a massive ridge of rocks known as Komunyu Hill; the other gives on to a clearing in the bush which soon became the stage for a variety of spectacles. The leopards were given luxury quarters, a series of linked compounds, the smallest of which enclosed an artificial cave and the largest a full-grown terminalia tree.

The reserve is teeming with easy prey for the leopards – lizards, small birds, guinea fowl, hyrax and thousands of dik dik. As they grew up they were more than able to take on larger game, like jackals, warthogs, gerenuk and lesser kudu. On the other hand, since the native leopards had been shot out – I had seen only two in eleven years at Kora – the baboon population had grown quite out of hand and *en masse* were more of a threat to the leopards than the other way about.

When Attila and Komunyu were fifteen months old, Tony felt they were ready for release. They already had a sense of what they might meet in the real world outside. As they watched the clearing from their enclosure an old elephant wandered past only one pace away on the other side of the wire. Occasionally their natural enemies, such as lions and jabbering baboons, appeared from the wings: early one morning a pack of sixteen wild dogs pulled down a kudu twenty yards off.

Tony collared the leopards with small tracking transmitters and when he first let them out they explored the bush round the camp and followed him back to its security at night. They quickly became adept at killing, Komunyu bringing her first dik dik to Tony, as Girl had brought her Thomson's gazelle to Ginny. Like Christian their instincts had survived at least two generations of captivity, but although they were soon self-sufficient they also came in for some nasty surprises.

On one occasion Attila started stalking, then chasing, three hunting dogs who took to their heels. When twenty other dogs suddenly turned up the tables were turned: Attila was no more than a blur as he streaked up a tree.

Komunyu ran into still more serious danger when Tony was up on the big rock with her and Attila. She was in the lead as they reached the crest of a ridge and suddenly found herself confronted by a troop of over a hundred baboons. Three large males sat in positions of advantage: their army was lined up below. As Komunyu went on towards them a frenzy of blood-curdling shrieks erupted from the ranks who seemed to look to their leaders for orders.

It happened that Tony himself had military support that day. Captain Ron Wilkie, who had been Regimental Sergeant Major in the Scots Guards Battalion of which Boy and Girl were the mascots, was staying at Kampi ya Chui and watched the unfolding action with a professional eye. As the noise from the rock rose to a crescendo it looked as if Komunyu was bound to be torn to pieces by the horde of outraged baboons.

So far Tony had held his fire but now he raised his rifle and let off two shots — with instant effect, although they were only blanks. The baboons yelled louder, scattered and turned. But even as Tony looked on with relief and Komunyu stealthily withdrew to join Attila, who was still well in the rear, the baboons were already regrouping.

"My God," said Ron Wilkie with respect. "Those baboons are much better disciplined than some of the soldiers I have been given to train." He agreed with Tony's conclusion that discretion, in these circumstances, was better than aggression. The four of them made a tactical withdrawal.

Tony noticed that the leopards quickly learnt how to make use of the terrain and especially the trees which were their principal refuge in moments of crisis. On a walk near the rock he came across Attila who for once completely ignored him, staring straight over his shoulder. As Tony followed his gaze he saw a lioness drop to a crouch and slowly back off. Attila stood his ground but the narrowed eyes of the lioness worried Tony so he too backed off to collect his rifle from the Landrover. He returned to the scene just as the lioness sprang at Attila, who took to his heels and flashed up the trunk of the nearest acacia.

For a time Attila looked down at the lioness who balefully glared back: then he slowly descended and with some panache began to mark territory on the opposite side of the tree. This stung the lioness into a second attack, just as she was joined by another and four young cubs. Only then did Tony recognise that the lioness was Koretta — a long way from her territory — and that her companions were Naja and the four cubs she was raising. Until they left — they paid no attention to Tony's commands to disperse — Attila stood furious and impotent up in the branches, dribbling with indignation.

Tony needed all his experience and resolution as an Outward Bound training instructor to coax the young leopards through these ordeals. At the same time he worked hard to safeguard their future and that of others we hoped to release here. He had already set up the Kora Wildlife Preservation Trust in England to raise and administer funds for this programme. Now he was starting to fly in the hope that one day we could afford a plane of our own: it would make it so much easier to get ourselves, our stores and visitors in and out – also to cover wider areas in our radio searches. Once Attila took off into the bush, as he now did, we had no hope of finding him from the ground.

Komunyu, on the other hand, staked out her territory round the rock. She still remains within it, a mile or so from the camp, for much of the time though she wanders afar, and one evening I caught her trespassing. Naja had brought the four cubs into camp and I was just tossing her some meat when I saw a spotted shadow slide along the wire towards her. I realised it was a leopard and must be Komunyu so I relaxed, as a leopard usually will not go for a lion, especially if the latter is on its own ground. It was a convention that must have got lost in Komunyu's European breeding, for she caught the meat before it had landed and was up in a tree before Naja realised she had been robbed. Thus I found myself caught between a vengeful lioness and a defiant leopard – for as soon as I tried to compensate Naja Komunyu came down, as swift as an arrow, and stole the second piece of meat. In the end I added insult to injury by driving Naja away, to give Komunyu a chance to escape – even then she circled the camp several times before going back home.

*   *   *

While Kampi ya Chui was beset by a lion, and Kampi ya Simba by a leopard, in 1983 a third camp was put up on the river about twenty miles to the west, by the Royal Geographical Society of London and the National Museums of Kenya. These two august bodies had assembled a team of more than twenty scientists to explore the reserve. They were led by Dr Malcolm Coe of Oxford University and it was difficult to believe that he had not descended directly into Kora from a cloud.

With his loin cloth, unruly white beard and glittering eye – and given to erudite, colourful and lengthy orations – Malcolm would have matched any Old Testament prophet in his powers of hypnotic persuasion. He was well chosen to catalogue Kora's resources, from its minerals and tiniest organisms to all but the largest of mammals, and to expound to the authorities solutions to any problems which he and his colleagues thought a threat to the future of the reserve.

Elephant, buffalo, waterbuck, hippo and so on were excluded from the expedition's studies, as were our lions. I am not sure who were the more discomfited by their daily encounters, the scientists or Glowe and Growe. Gigi's two daughters was now fully grown, had six cubs between them and had adopted the same stretch of river as the R.G.S. for their home. Richard Leakey, director of the National Museums, said the lions were a constant concern to himself – but I was prepared to bank on their decent behaviour.

The expedition included the river in its scrutiny, as a scheme had been mooted to build yet two more dams on the Tana, one below Adamson's Falls (as they came to be called on the map after I found them during the Mau Mau days), just to the west of the reserve, and the other near the mid-point of our northern boundary: they planned to include the anticipated effects of the flooding in their final report.

I used to enjoy fishing for barbels or catfish, with their sinister whiskers; they are the commonest fish in the river. The tilapia are scarcer and notable for their delicate flavour and the method of raising their young. The male excavates a small pit in the river bed and entices the female to lay her eggs there. The property is usually, but not always, respected as private by other tilapia, who have a taste for one another's eggs. By way of protection the female soon gathers the clutch into her mouth, incubates it and keeps the young in her cheeks until they are old enough to be spewed into the river. An even more sophisticated inhabitant of the Tana is the elephant snout fish which hunts its tiny prey in the mud at the bottom. To do this it generates electricity to power a sonar device and the food, when located, is collected by the little fish's trunk.

The encyclopedic discoveries of Malcolm's colleagues included new species of plants, fairy shrimps, jumping spiders, outsize dung beetles – which roll droppings into a ball that is buried as food for their larvae – and two species adapted to live in the cracks of our rocks, the pancake tortoise and flat-headed bat.

We were amused when these dedicated observers occasionally stooped from their scientific detachment. It was Malcolm who had plucked the lizard from the gullet of a protesting coucal. When he caught a python in the act of swallowing a guinea fowl, he decapitated one and casseroled the other. But the hornbill which swooped down and made off with a four-inch specimen scorpion was allowed to keep its trophy. Terence didn't do too badly either in discouraging scorpions – he accounted for no less than ninety-six of various species when building the R.G.S. camp.

Malcolm seemed to think his team found vicarious release from the inevitable chastity that Kora imposed by studying the mating behaviour of mayflies, foam frogs and our burrowing neighbours, the naked mole rats. According to the rains and the phases of the moon the mayflies would swarm to their mess lamps during supper, when the males would seize the long slim abdomens of the elegant females with a frantic fluttering of wings. I had the expedition's word for it that all mole rats have "degenerate" reproductive organs and, the females, fourteen nipples – yet despite these attributes a pregnant mother was never discovered.

The activities of the foam frogs, which only mate after rain, are enough to shock even Tony. In the middle of the night they make their way to the end of a branch protruding over water, where three males join with one female. While one male embraces her, the other two press themselves to her flanks as she extrudes her eggs and a fluid which all four whip with their legs into foam. The frogs then abandon the eggs which hang from the branch in the foam that hardens into a protective case. Inside, the tadpoles evolve until they are washed down into the water below by the next shower of rain.

However lighthearted Malcolm was in discussing his work, he took it exceedingly seriously and his findings were of the greatest importance – not only to Kora Reserve but to the Tana conservancy and all the *nyika* wilderness of Kenya. His expedition went through the place with mist net and tooth comb, deploying all the wonders of science, including satellite images. From these they could plot the advance and retreat of green vegetation as the seasons rotated – and even pick out the areas burned by Somalis.

The two years of the R.G.S. presence in Kora were a spell of unrelieved drought. The expedition were able to see for themselves the devastation wrought by the Somalis – and to understand the critical problem their migrations create for the government. Many of them have driven their livestock over the frontier from Somalia where, like locusts, they have eaten their own country bare. Advances in veterinary science have produced a pastoral explosion. The Kenyan Government must therefore persuade Somalia to contain its own people and stock. It must also act firmly and moderately *now* to keep out the invasions – or it may be driven to desperate measures which are both too harsh and too late.

The Somalis did not help their own cause by the way they behaved – and it was not just a matter of their wholesale devastation of the bush. As early as 1979, not long after Kaunda stole two goats from it, a Somali gang attacked Chris Matchett's camp on the far side of the river. He, his French wife and their little daughter were returning from Nairobi when his car broke down and they were held up for twenty-four hours. When he got back his camp was in cinders. The day before the Somalis had closed in; three of his African staff had been wounded; a fourth African and his young German assistant had been killed.

"Once the rangers arrived we were less likely to need our slit trenches." Here they are with their first prisoners.

Before it gets dark I prime the pressure lamps, surrounded by guinea fowl, which are apt to sound off in the night like burglar alarms.

In answer the authorities mobilised all the forces they could spare — rangers from the Game Department, armed Anti-Poaching Units and Police — to man what used to be known as "The Somali Line". I was told that a platoon of fourteen rangers had been posted to Kora and would put up a compound a few hundred yards along the ridge from our camp. I wondered if they would be any more alert to nocturnal intrusions than the guinea fowl which were apt to sound off like burglar alarms, or any more of a deterrent than the lions which had acquired a degree of local notoriety.

Just before the post was set up I sent my driver Moti into Asako to buy camel meat: the journey usually takes a couple of hours each way. Three days later he had not come back.

As luck would have it, Jonny Baxendale had just flown over from Meru, where he was working in the reserve, and he offered to take me up to trace Moti's route in the hope of spotting the Landrover. It was not until we were actually over Asako that we saw it standing beside one of the huts. We dropped a message for Moti telling him to meet us at the airstrip twenty miles away.

With some curiosity we waited for his explanation. When he finally turned up he described how he was just leaving Asako to buy a camel from some Somalis out in the bush when a friend warned him that a party of thirteen Shifta were planning to ambush him, seize the car and drive into Kampi ya Simba. As the gates are always opened as soon as my Landrover appears they would have made short work of demolishing us and the camp.

Once the rangers arrived we were less likely to need the slit-trenches we had dug and I stood down my own amateur Home Guard. Even so some Shifta crossed the river and raided a village: no life was taken but the shops were emptied and not a hut was left standing. As I did not want any more confrontations with the lions I warned the rangers to keep to their trucks round Kora, but further afield they patrolled freely through the bush and down Terence's roads. There were several exchanges of fire: on one patrol a Shifta was wounded and caught, another was killed. A member of the platoon was brought back with a bullet through his leg: fortunately it was only a flesh wound and we had a fully trained nurse staying that week.

After all this it came as an anti-climax when Abdi my tracker, on a trip to Asako, was told I had been taken off the hit list. A Somali chief had decided I was not to be killed on any account — I spent so much money on buying dud camels that it would be financial disaster to put an end to this income. They were $100 apiece and from time to time I had to buy a camel a week.

Despite all the counter-measures, Somalis were still flooding into Kora at the height of the drought in September 1984. By now my eyesight had deteriorated further and, however reluctantly, I accepted the advice of an Austrian surgeon to fly to Vienna for a cataract operation; the enterprise was generously financed by a group of fellow Austrians known as The Friends of Kenya. My reluctance to go was due to the realisation of just how much I would be leaving to Tony and Terence: once or twice the boot had been on the other foot.

After Tony had been with me six years I thought I had got used to his unpredictable goings and comings, but once he went along to the airstrip to see off a friend and simply did not come back. Not a word. Then four months later he turned up in camp as if he had been away for the weekend: I was amazed but delighted. He was accompanied by a girl twice his own size and weight. Two mornings later I was not altogether surprised to see his large custom-built bed lying outside his hut in smithereens.

Terence had once done much the same thing. He went off to his house in Malindi for three weeks and was still away three months later. Scandalous rumours — at his age! — reached my ears and he returned with a smile on his face.

When I set off for Vienna Tony was expecting more leopards for release but I left a diminishing pride in Terence's care. Their numbers were down and the four lionesses that remained, all born at Kora, had grown increasingly independent: they were Koretta who was seven, Glowe and Growe now six — each with three cubs — and Naja aged five.

Of the others the four oldest lionesses had gone off on their own; three young males had been poisoned by Somalis; Koretta's two brothers had been shot by rangers for persistently raiding stock near Asako; and one of the younger cubs had been killed by wild dogs.

In bush as thick as Kora's and in conditions as harsh, the lions range more widely and invisibly than in the open grasslands of the Mara or Serengeti plains: it is impossible to monitor all their lives, doings and deaths. But I suspect that the fortunes and fates of the lions we knew were much the same as those of the wild ones who were little more than tawny shapes on the rocks or distant roars in the night.

*   *   *

The surgeon in Vienna told me he was confident he could restore my sight by removing the cataract and implanting a plastic lens in my retina: the technique had been pioneered and perfected after doctors had discovered the human eye did not reject fragments of plastic windshields. However, he added that the operation should wait until March when he would be able to bring in from America an improved version of the lens better suited to my eye and the strength of the African sunlight.

Bill Travers was keeping closely in touch as by a strange coincidence he too was due to have a similar operation on one of his eyes. Hearing about the delay he suggested I came on to England and put the time to good use by working on the book. He and Ginny would have me to stay in the country where he could tape-record everything I wanted to say and have it transcribed. He said he had kept every one of my letters and offered me the use of his entire collection of photographs.

At their house on Leith Hill – from which Christian had set out for Africa – they treated me rather like a spy who had come in from the cold, for England was soon under snow and I was kept in the safest and warmest of houses. Each morning I was settled on the sofa and at eleven o'clock found a gin in my hand; in the evenings at six, the White Horse whisky appeared. When I had finished what I intended to say Bill would begin to ask questions to fill in the background and gaps. Now and again he would lead me into some indiscretion with a joke, or press me like a barrister in court. Occasionally Ginny would join in our sessions. Bill was particularly curious about why Joy and I have come in for criticism from scientists, conservationists, game managers and even safari operators – many of them ex-hunters.

Quite often our work is called a waste of time and resources since leopards, cheetahs and lions are not endangered as species. This is true at the moment but as a yardstick for action is dangerously short-sighted: the same might have been said of rhinos ten years ago. Lions and the other big cats are being confined, as are elephants, to a limited number of pockets which grow fewer and smaller each year: some are threatened, others have already disappeared. If you make it possible for lions to live natural lives you will protect everything else in the pyramid beneath them.

I acknowledge that Joy was not always at her most diplomatic in seeking favours or help from the staff in charge of the parks. I also acknowledge that against the rules I occasionally shot game if I felt that without it a lion might starve or wander away before it was ready to look after itself. I once used my rifle to kill a lion that was dying: its jaw was smashed and it was starving to death. I reported the incident and my rifle was confiscated. All this I regret if it caused provocation but we always had the best interests of the parks and their animals in our minds.

Perhaps the most sophisticated criticism of what we have done is that we imposed great stress on the animals we released, during their months of transition from one kind of life to the opposite. I don't think this applied to leopards and cheetahs, which are more or less solitary once they mature. But lions are basically social and I think Elsa definitely suffered from trying to survive on her own and I always regret we did not keep her sisters so that the family would have supported one another. From the time I took on the lions from the film of *Born Free* I always tried to arrange for new ones to arrive in pairs so that they could explore their strange world together.

There are people who were genuinely concerned that we induced young animals to trust us and so lose their fear of human beings; and that by continuing to feed them I perpetuated this absence of fear and increased the chances of their attacking other people. The truth is that there was no way of keeping the young lions round me, yet free, while I introduced them peacefully into the pride unless they first formed some kind of relationship with me.

I have seen or heard nothing to persuade me that feeding meat to lions that have learned to live on their own, or who were born in the wild, makes them more dangerous to man. When the one Somali was killed by a lion at Kora, all ours were in camp at the time. The frequent and sly, but entirely pacific, inspections of the scientists' traps near the R.G.S. camp by the lionesses Glowe and Growe seem to point to a respect for human beings in no way reduced by how we had treated them.

All lions are dangerous; they have evolved specifically as killers and eaters of flesh yet there is no evidence that the lions and leopards which Joy, Tony and I have released became more dangerous than wild ones. With the exception of Mark Jenkins – and no child should have been taken in an open Toyota so close to a lion – their only attacks have been on people involved with our work. There would have been a great many more attacks had we been living as intimately with *wild* lions, of that I am certain.

Several of my lions have been poisoned or shot for suspected or actual stock raiding. These raids were not due to the way they were fed. As long ago as the Trojan war lions were attacking cattle – Homer alludes to it in his account of the fight between Aeneas and Achilles. For that matter I spent twenty years of my life in the protection of livestock from lions who had never once been offered free food.

Ginny gave me a very long look when I had finished telling her how strongly I hold this opinion.

"I really don't understand all this talk about the need to preserve lions' fear of man," she said. "I have just been reading about Mark and Delia Owens' experience in a part of the Kalahari where no one, perhaps not even Bushmen, had lived before them. On a number of nights a pride came and settled in the middle of their camp and a leopard once slept in their tent. Is there really such a thing as a 'natural fear' of man?"

On reflection I think I share Ginny's doubts about this. Lions probably only fear, or are hostile to, man according to experience. They are afraid of the Maasai and Samburu warriors guarding their cattle but not of a tourist shooting away with a camera. They will attack if you bump into them when they are hungry, threatened, frightened or sexually aroused; but even a man-eater will silently pace past your bed in the night if he is relaxed or replete. Professionals seem to detect a diminishing hostility to man among lions and elephants in places where they know they are safe from confrontations and poaching. If this is so, why should my activities make them *more* dangerous rather than less so?

Certainly our work has its dangers. The risks are only to ourselves – and the people working with us, who know the odds as they would if they joined the army, worked on an oil rig or went down the mines. We have continuously warned them of the dangers and done all we can to protect them; they have been under no compulsion to stay. Two people have been killed in a zoo in England during the time we have been at Kora: on both occasions the zoo was prosecuted – and both times acquitted. Do people seriously think it is possible or even wise to eliminate danger from the human condition? Shouldn't it do for man what lions do for populations of zebra and antelopes – test, winnow and strengthen the strain?

The temperature in England continued to fall as I underwent this debriefing and there was little inducement to go out. For the first time in ages I read the morning papers and we watched television news in the evening: I saw nothing to persuade me to give up my home in the bush for life in a city.

We also watched the documentary films that Bill had made at Meru, Kora and Tsavo, where he had shot most of *An Elephant Called Slowly*, a story whose sequel was both tragic and an inspiration. The real name of the little elephant was Pole Pole and she had been caught as a national gift from President Kenyatta to the Regent's Park Zoo in London. David and Daphne Sheldrick had been asked to get her used to confinement and people.

Bill was given permission to film her but there was nothing he or the Sheldricks could do to prevent her from going to Europe. As soon as she got to London Bill went to see her and, with the keeper's consent, gave her some oranges; but she was so upset when he left that he thought it wiser not to go back.

About fifteen years later, in 1982, Daphne Sheldrick heard that Pole Pole was in a terrible condition. Apparently she had been shut up in the elephant house on her own for two years – quite the wrong treatment for a female African elephant which is by nature gregarious. After a companion had undergone an autopsy near her enclosure and the last one was removed, she had become very disturbed, repeatedly banging her head against the walls, snapping one of her tusks and losing the other entirely.

Daphne alerted Bill, me and a few other friends to the crisis and Bill contacted a number of African reserves to see if we could bring her back home. I heard of an island sanctuary on Lake Victoria, sponsored by Bernhardt Grzimek's Society, which had been successfully stocked with chimpanzees, eland and fourteen elephants: I felt sure the sanctuary would help. When Bill and Ginny spoke to the press about the chance of repatriation they were flooded with contributions, some of £1, others larger and one of £1,000.

The zoo would not hear of the scheme, maintaining – contrary to the experience of experts in Africa – that an elephant returning from London would not survive in the bush. Instead they undertook to send Pole Pole to Whipsnade and the company of her kind. Somehow the transfer was bungled. After several tranquillising injections Pole Pole collapsed in her crate, before it was removed from the zoo – and she died.

Bill, Ginny and a great many others were so distressed and angered by the unnecessary death of an elephant still in her prime that a spontaneous movement sprang up to examine conditions in zoos all over the country. They called themselves Zoo Check, registered as a Trust and found, just as Joy had done, that abuses were widespread and appalling. By coincidence a new Act had just come into force which required the licensing of zoos and Zoo Check's surveillance rapidly led to the closure of some of the worst.

As we talked about zoos Bill reminded me of something Desmond Morris had written about Joy. It meant much to me as Morris had studied human behaviour with exceptional knowledge and perception. He had also been Curator of Mammals at the London Zoo and as such had been asked to analyse the differences in the answers to a questionnaire broadcast by Granada TV before *Born Free* was published and repeated two years later after it had appeared. Children were invited to write in and, among other things, list their ten best loved and ten most hated animals. His staff worked through a total of 80,000 cards and this is what Morris wrote about the second set of answers:

> There was only one significant shift, the lion was more loved and less hated. Joy Adamson's promotion campaign on behalf of the lion had worked. She had achieved the difficult goal of not merely providing passing entertainment, but of actually shifting public feelings towards the animal species. Elsa the lioness had become an ambassador for her kind. She had also done something else. She had made people start to query the morality of keeping animals in

captivity, in zoos and even more so in circuses. The essence of Elsa's story was her freedom.

One afternoon Bill and Ginny brought in a tree – and the children, who had all come back home, began to decorate it. On our first Christmas together, during filming at Naro Moru, there had only been three: William, Louise and Justin. By the next one, ten years ago at Kora, Daniel the youngest took a seven-year-old's pride in watching his namesake lording it over the rest of the lions. Now the family were all grown up and starting to make their way in the world. I wished I could stay to enjoy a third Christmas, in their home this time, but I knew I had to get back to Kora.

So when the evening came I put on the old tweed overcoat that I hadn't worn for years, but which had somehow defied both mould and termites, turned up the collar and set off with Bill through the snow to the airport.

Sitting back in the plane, without much prospect of sleep, I wondered if my worst fears had come true and the Somalis had finally ruined the reserve and finished off the last of the lions. If they had we were back to the law of the jungle. Although man is no longer evolving physically he is said to be developing culturally all the time. Yet there wasn't much evidence of progress in the violence I had seen every day in the news – usually performed in the name of religion or reason, both of which are supposed to set man above the animals.

A tooth for a tooth . . . tooth and claw . . . the phrases went round in my head as I started to doze. I have tried to find out when lions became lions as we know them today. No one is prepared to stick out their neck but one thing is certain: a specialised hunter must evolve with its prey. As antelopes adapt very fast when their environment changes – for instance, if they swim from the mainland to an island or if bush is replaced by open savannah – then the big cats which prey on them must adapt fast too, as has happened with lions. In fact they have probably evolved more recently than man and their code of behaviour is worth our respect: indeed some of their genetic commandments look no worse than ours and are more often heeded. Self-reliance and courage, tenacious yet realistic defence of a realm, the willingness to care for the young of another, brotherhood, loyalty and affection are seven commendable precepts.

I did get some sleep in the end and when I woke up over Kenya my spirits rose – not just to be back in Africa but because even my eyes could make out from the colour of the ground that the rains had broken at last.

The transformation at Kora was spectacular. As we banked for the final run in, the bush was a flourishing green as far as the eye could see. There was not a camel, a cow or a goat in sight – every one of the Somalis seemed to have gone. When we touched down tall, bright grass edged the airstrip; bushes were covered in flower; and leaves everywhere were flushed with colour.

Driving to Kampi ya Simba Tony bubbled over with news of his leopards – he had already released two more and had a third at his camp. Terence asked quietly about England and seemed shy of discussing the lions: at last, when Tony and I had drinks in our hands, he confessed that none of them had been into camp since I left. I wondered how far away, and into what kind of danger, they had wandered before the rains had dispersed all the herds and the herdsmen and brought back the game.

Christmas morning was unusually quiet. Tony was looking after Adnan, the new young leopard, at Kampi ya Chui; Terence had gone off to plan a fresh road; and I sat alone turning over the cards that had piled up in my absence from all over the world. I thought of the Christmases Joy had prepared with such trouble and of her last one at Shaba, alone. The next day she wrote to a friend – the letter arrived after her death – and told her how she had waited for my plane to come in. As the light faded she brushed her anxieties aside, put on some music and gave free rein to her memory, returning as always to Elsa.

I puffed at my pipe and as I strained to decipher a scribble on the back of a card there was a grunt from outside the wire. I looked up straight into the gaze of Koretta: just behind her stood two little cubs we had never seen before.

Epilogue
Evening at Kora
1985–1986

It was a miracle: I could pick out as clearly as ever before the coloured sheen of a sunbird's plumage or the ash-grey lines of a jackal lurking on the rocks in the twilight. After I had been back to Vienna in March, where the lens was grafted into my eye, I found I could also drive the Landrover at night and read without glasses or effort.

Koretta continued to bring back her two cubs – Boldie, the inquisitive, and Cindie who always remained in the background if not by the fire. But there was no sign of Growe and Glowe.

October saw the start of a series of disturbing, curious and significant events. It began when Terence was taken to hospital with pneumonia. Very soon I had to rush down to Nairobi as he had gone into intensive care: his breathing and kidneys had started to fail and they thought he was dying. But Terence is as tough as a boot, and although he had previously suffered a stroke he rallied. By the middle of the month he was flown back to camp, desperately frail but determined.

A fortnight later he was as intrigued as any of us when the clouds parted on a night of full moon to reveal not a disc of shimmering silver but a slender pink crescent. Tony radioed to ask if we had noticed it, and said his Muslim cook was now on his knees at the sign of ill-omen and had started to pray. I wondered how many others in Kenya had not been expecting an eclipse.

The next day I told Terence we had still found no trace of Glowe and Growe and he offered to help. There was a glint in his eye as he picked up his pencil, pendulum and a packet of photographs, while I spread out the map on the table. Terence gazed at one photo and then the other as his pencil followed the swing of the pendulum.

"Glowe is dead. No sign from her," he said, looking up at me. "But Growe is all right. I think she is somewhere in the Kiume Hills."

This was some way off and a few miles from where we had last seen her eight months ago. The moon was full, lions are active after dusk and they often give voice in the night, so I decided to take the Landrover out to the hills and keep watch from the roof, occasionally calling her name. The method had worked very well in the past. Georgina, who was sorting the papers for my book, asked if she could come too — a request I could hardly refuse from a girl who is such fun and so pretty.

We took quite a time to pack up the car with our bedding, the food and some drink for our night's vigil — and meat for Growe should we find her. In the end we did not set out till the late afternoon: the hornbills were going to roost, a few dik dik zig-zagged off through the undergrowth and two kudu paused to stare at us before vanishing into the dusk. It took us an hour and a half to drive along Terence's tracks, down a lugga and finally up through the bush to a point in the hills which looked down on the tops of the thorns.

We were close to a rock where colleagues of Jack Block, who had helped fund the R.G.S. expedition in his memory, had put up a plaque with his name. I could think of no happier place to remember a man who had been so kind to me and had been such a good friend to the wildlife of Kenya.

The moon was getting up in the sky by the time we were heaving our bedrolls on to the roof. Just as she had finished I heard Georgina gasp and blurt out my name. I quickly turned round and there, four paces away, crouching in the bush, was a large lioness making ready to spring at her.

It was Growe all right, looking perfectly well-fed, although I couldn't take a chance on her mood. I therefore told Georgina to stay still as I called Growe's name, over and over again, slowly reaching for the cool-box. Finally I tossed her some meat which she caught in the air and started to eat a few yards away.

She stayed near us through the night and in the dawn we all three watched a herd of elephants move past, tearing at branches and trampling the undergrowth as they went. A little later Growe rose, stretched and was lost among the thorns.

The next morning we had to prepare for the first informal meeting in Kenya of the Kora Trustees. Tony had persuaded an imposing array of busy men to serve on the Trust, if the Director of Wildlife approved its formation. Among others we expected to fly up were Nehemiah arap Rottich of the Wildlife Clubs of Kenya, Ken Smith, now officially retired but working still down on the Mara, Alan Root and Ted Goss, who was in charge of Kenya's 450-strong Anti-Poaching Unit.

The little airstrip was a whirlwind of dust as small planes landed and taxied into what shade they could find. We met them in a shuttle of trucks and went back to Kampi ya Chui where Tony had set up the table in his mess-hut with pencils, paper and jugs of cold drinks. The temperature rose to 100° but in two hours the business was done.

"Well, what do you think of all that?" Tony asked, after everyone had gone and he was putting down some notes. "Will it really change things here for the better?"

I believed at that moment, as I believe now, that although the trustees would help see through plans to improve the Reserve, Tony and I would have to raise most of the money ourselves. But there were two bits of good news. First, Ted Goss said he was bringing in more men to combat the poaching and to keep out the brazen intrusion of livestock. Secondly, a new bridge across the Tana was nearly completed: once it was ready we would need to cut only a few extra miles of road to link Kora to Meru. The project was guaranteed to rejuvenate Terence and, for the first time, open up Kora to all the tourists visiting Meru.

I had not raised at the meeting the subject closest to my heart – the future of our lions and leopards – because I had an uncomfortable feeling that although there would probably be no Reserve today were it not for the lions, and no Trust were it not for the leopards, it was the pyramid that mattered most to the others: Tony and I were the only trustees who were fond of the animals themselves. But would they still have a place here in the future? And if they didn't, would it still be a place for us? Terence, Tony and I had all led our lives in the wild – and I was beginning to sense that the only happy ending we could look forward to, as in other true stories of the wild, was a question mark!

While we talked I could hear a miscellany of Tony's friends – Mohamed, Isaiah, Oil Can and Geoff – repairing our always precarious transport. I could see through the open side of the hut Adnan sprawling magnificently on his rock. He was due to be given his freedom in the next few days and I hoped that Bill and Ginny, who were coming out to help me finish off this book, would get here in time to see him.

They did. They were flown up by Andrew Meyerhold, the Austrian doctor who had taken such care of Terence in Nairobi and who was not going to leave his convalescence to chance. Bill and Ginny embraced the grizzled Hamisi who smiled – and then grinned as they gave him the impressive digital watch he had craved for so long. We talked late into the night.

Towards dawn we were woken by a deep, throbbing roar from a lion I felt I knew well although I had never set eyes on him. His first three loud bellows were followed by a series of deep bass grunts that were so regular, resonant and sustained that I christened him Tom Tom. Each night the drumbeats continued for longer until I could think of only one other lion who roared in this way: it was Boy. Could a voice and mannerism like this be inherited?

Not long after I got back from Vienna, before I even had time to seek out Koretta, I was unexpectedly visited by the Tana River Councillors, who asked if they could see the lions. Having heard from Tony that he had seen confused spoor beyond Kora Tit, I thought I would take a chance, so I took my loud-hailer from the wall and called out "KOR-RET-TA, KOR-RET-TA, KOR-RET-TA."

When nothing happened I regretted my theatrical impulse; we returned to our tea and talk of the roads and the rains. Then Abdi ran up – he has the eyes of a lynx – and pointing to the rocks said: "Simba, Bwana, Simba!" Slowly and majestically Koretta emerged from the bushes in the bowl of the hills and made her way towards us. Boldie was at her side; some way back, as always, was Cindie; but trotting and frisking between them were five very young cubs. As Koretta dropped down in the shade of a tree they started to suckle. Presumably Tom Tom was their father.

We had virtually finished our work on the book when Tony came over to tell us that the leopardess Komunyu, who had been living wild for three years and seemed to cherish a passion for Adnan, had returned to camp and was circling his enclosure. He therefore planned to set Adnan free in the morning. Bill was especially fascinated to watch the first meeting, out in the open, of Komunyu and Adnan and to compare it with the explosion of violence between Christian and Boy. No doubt that had been partly the response of one male to another; but the slow, silent, sensitive minuet of the leopards which now followed also expressed the essence of their secretive natures.

That day the contrast between the habits of the social and the solitary cats was further brought home to us. Abdi had discovered that Koretta, Boldie and Cindie had brought down a waterbuck in a lugga about ten miles from camp. In the late afternoon I took Ginny and Bill down to see them. As we drove up, a handsome young lion, with a dark brown mane, rose to his feet and stalked off through the scrub: it was my first glimpse of Tom Tom.

We frequently come on a kill in a lugga. Each of these rivers of sand that wind through the bush is a natural arena. The timid come here to browse, unaware that the same open space of its bed, which seems to offer protection from stealthy attack, provides a fine field of view for a lion concealed on its bank.

Animal and man are continually drawn to the luggas. They may flow with water only once in ten years but under the surface the water or moisture remains. Their grasses are greener, the fruit on their shrubs is sweeter and juicier, the shade of their trees – which are taller and leafier – is cooler than anywhere else in the bush. They are microcosms of Africa. I had buried Boy in one lugga and Growlie had given birth to Koretta in another.

Now we waited and watched Koretta with her two elder daughters, sitting contentedly over their kill; her five younger cubs tussled and tumbled in the grass close beside her. The dry riverbed was remote and enchanted, shaded by acacias and fragrant with henna. All round us a sprinkling of rain had brought out sprays of delicate flowers – orange, pale yellow, blue and the clear, bright violet of the little Resurrection plant.

* * *

This is where I intended to leave my readers at the end of our eighty-year journey. The anxiety over Terence had relaxed; we had reason for looking forward with renewed hope to the future of Kora; in any case I had no way of seeing round the corner ahead. I am glad that I hadn't.

Although some degree of reticence is appropriate in an author, and although I would have preferred to end this story in a spirit of cheerfulness, I set out at the beginning to tell the whole truth, however unpalatable. I therefore add this postscript.

Under the watchful eye of his doctor, and after an Orma holy man had laid hands on him, Terence slowly recovered a little of his strength. He was no longer carried from his bed to the mess hut; once or twice, when no one seemed to be looking, he made his way with a walking frame to supervise the sharpening of tools on our lathe. Later a young friend took him up in an aeroplane to inspect the half-built bridge and plan a road to link it with Kora.

The Director of Wildlife approved the establishment of the Kora Trust in Kenya: our work with the leopards was to be its principal beneficiary. Komunyu continued to circle round Kampiya Chui; Adnan made off to the west and quite soon Tony could only pick up the pulse of his radio collar from the air.

Life speeded up at Kampi ya Simba. Koretta led her family further and further downstream on the Tana, towards the Somali's legitimate grazing. I therefore tried to lure them back with judiciously placed camel carcases. Increasing numbers of visitors dropped in without warning and expected us to put them up for the night. Finally, a Japanese television company asked to make a film of our daily activities. While they were here fate struck the first of several blows which threaten virtually everything we have tried to accomplish at Kora.

One evening in January, I took them downriver in search of Koretta. Tomoko, the star who was doing the interviews, came in my Landrover. She is as petite as a child, and her English and professional skills are as remarkable as her courage soon proved to be. We found Koretta's family still feeding on a camel; they had the lazy look of the comfortably fed. After watching them we withdrew to a rise. I gave Tomoko a drink and she sat beside the car while I radioed to Tony that we were heading for home.

At that moment I heard a cry of alarm, but there was no sign of Tomoko. Throwing down the handset I dashed round the bonnet and saw that a lion had her head in its jaws: it was obviously Boldie. Yelling at the top of my voice, I rushed at Boldie who immediately let go of Tomoko and trotted back to the pride. Apart from the shock, Tomoko's scalp had been punctured, though not her skull, thank heaven. Early next morning the Flying Doctor took her to hospital, where they kept her for a week.

I was filled with admiration when she insisted on coming back at the beginning of February to finish the interviews – this time with Tony at Kampi ya Chui, where he now had Lucifer, a small wild lion who had been abandoned by his mother. Afterwards Tony invited the Japanese to supper before they left Kora.

Towards the end of the meal, after it was dark, Komunyu took it into her head to scramble over the very high wire fence and to investigate the company Tony was keeping. Rather than bundle his guests into their cars and send them away, Tony chose the other alternative, which had successfully defused Komunyu's suspicions on previous occasions. He introduced his guests to the leopard as he might have done to a guard dog. But as they all sat down again, Komunyu launched herself at Tomoko's back and seized her neck with her teeth: it took all Tony's strength to prise her jaw open.

Once more Tomoko spent a night of physical pain, and who knows what mental anguish, in the heart of the African bush, waiting for dawn and the merciful drone of the Flying Doctor's engines. Once more she was kept in hospital for several days. And once more she insisted on coming back to Kora, this time in a neck-brace, to shoot the final take of the film. My admiration was boundless.

Three reflections occur to me as I mournfully analyse these unpleasant incidents. The first is that untrustworthy lions reveal their characters at an early age. Suleiman, at whom I had to fire my revolver over my shoulder to stop him chewing my neck, had been called Solomon when he came to us; but Tony had felt he was shifty rather than wise and therefore changed his name to that of a dubious acquaintance. Shyman had been so called because he seemed to find no satisfaction in human company: he had savaged Tony. Shade must have shown us the dark side of his nature before he was named: it was he who had mauled Terence. Now Boldie, with excessive audacity and certainly not out of hunger, had deliberately left a kill to stalk Tomoko.

Nevertheless, I still feel that I would have been quite unjustified if I had shot any of them simply on the strength of my instincts.

My second reflection emerges from worrying at the riddle of why Tomoko attracted two unprovoked attacks, from two different species. In the end I have come to the conclusion that unless she possesses some unique personal scent, her child-like appearance, at least to Western and perhaps feline eyes, must have triggered the cats' fatal fascination with children.

The third is that it is impossible to eliminate risk when working with lions and leopards; if Tony and I have sometimes miscalculated the odds the blame lies with us, not with them.

We made sure that the Wildlife Department was fully aware of what had happened, and immediately raised the height of the fences round both camps with strands of electrified wire. I expected some form of reaction from the authorities, but not the finality of the pronouncement that was now delivered to us and which I have reason to believe was formulated before Tomoko's accidents.

On 24 February, the Director of Wildlife wrote a long letter about the future of the reserve to the Game Warden at Kora. The nub of it was that all our work with the leopards must cease. Tony was not asked to leave — he was after all a Kora trustee and founder of the Trust — but it was clear he was regarded as *persona non grata*.

While I was trying to come to terms with this bombshell, Terence complained of feeling unwell, a few days after Easter. His breathing was bad and he could not face supper. We radioed his doctor but by the time Andrew Meyerhold reached us, early next morning, Terence was dead. As once before, an embolism or clot had formed in his bloodstream; this one was fatal. We buried him at Kora. He rests in peace among the flowers and trees he loved so well.

I feel I can no longer go on answering questions about Kora. But I have some to ask. Who will now care for the animals in the reserve, for they cannot look after themselves? Are there young men and women in Kenya who are willing to take on this charge? In the meantime, how soon will the often-promised guards be sent to patrol Terence's roads and stand firm on the banks of the Tana when the reserve is ravaged by drought? Who will raise their voices, when mine is carried away on the wind, to plead Kora's case?

The sands of time are running out. Please spare a deed, a thought, or a word, to help save Christian's pyramid before authority allows it to collapse from neglect.

Acknowledgements

I would like to thank here all those who consciously or unconsciously helped me with this book. I acknowledge with gratitude, below, specific sources on which I have drawn for the text, the maps and the illustrations.

My brother Terence, Tony Fitzjohn and Ted Goss helped me whenever I asked them, just as they did in the rest of my work. Wolfgang and Ingrid Koos in Austria, Bill and Virginia Travers in England, Peter and Mary Johnson, Monty and Hilary Ruben and Jock Dawson and Enid Phillips in Kenya provided generous hospitality during the book's preparation. To some – Juliette Huxley and Elspeth Huxley – I am grateful for the loan of Joy's letters. To others I am grateful for memories – William and Morna Hale, Ken Smith, Virginia McKenna, Alan Root, Monty Ruben, Jonny Baxendale, Simon Trevor, Byron Giorgiadis and Doria Block.

When I look along our crowded yet depleted shelves – the fan-tailed ravens are not the only culprits – at Kora and Elsamere, I realise how much I owe to the books Joy and I have read over the years. I cannot mention them all but first I would like to thank the chairman and trustees of the Elsa Wild Animal Appeal for permission to draw freely on everything written, or painted or photographed by my wife, Joy, whether published or unpublished, and our American publishers listed opposite the title page, for permission to use her published work. Secondly I would like to acknowledge with special thanks material I have derived directly or indirectly from the following:

OUR LIONS, CHEETAHS AND LEOPARDS
Adamson, Joy and George, see opposite the title page of this book;   Bourke, Anthony and Rendall, John, *A Lion Called Christian*;   Hart, Susanne (Sue Harthoorn), *Life with Daktari* and *Listen to the Wild*;   Jay, John Mark, *Any Old Lion*;   McKenna, Virginia, and Travers, Bill, *On Playing with Lions*.

LIONS IN GENERAL
Carr, Norman, *Return to the Wild*;   Patterson, R. J., *The Man-Eaters of Tsavo*; Schaller, George, *The Serengeti Lion*.

AFRICAN ANIMALS AND THEIR ECOLOGY
Cott, Hugh, *Looking at Animals*;   Moss, Cynthia, *Portraits of the Wild*; Croze, Harvey, and Reader, John, *Pyramids of Life*;   Douglas-Hamilton, Iain and Oria, *Among the Elephants*;   Goodall, Jane, and van Lawick, Hugo,

Innocent Killers; Grzimek, Bernhardt, *Serengeti Shall Not Die*; Owens, Mark and Delia, *Cry of the Kalahari*; Pooley, Tony, *Diaries of a Crocodile Man*; Spinage, C.A., *The Book of the Giraffe*.

BIOGRAPHICAL
Cole, Sonia, *Leakey's Luck*; Cullen, Anthony, *Downey's Africa*; Douglas Home, Charles, *Evelyn Baring*; Fox, James, *White Mischief*; Thurman, Judith, *Isak Dinesen* (Karen Blixen); Trzebinski, Erroll, *Silence Will Speak* (the life of Denys Finch Hatton).

MEMOIRS
Cowie, Mervyn, *Fly, Vulture*; Huxley, Elspeth, *Out in the Midday Sun*; Innes, Dorothy Hammond, *What Lands are These?*; Kinloch, Bruce, *The Shamba Raiders*; Morris, Desmond, *Animal Days*; Ruben, Hilary, *African Harvest*; Sheldrick, Daphne, *Orphans of Tsavo*; Wood, Michael, *Go an Extra Mile*; Williams, J.H., *Elephant Bill*.

KORA
Finally there is one book which splendidly encapsulates the vast knowledge gathered by the expedition of the Royal Geographical Society of London and the Museums of Kenya, Malcolm Coe's *Islands in the Bush: A Natural History of the Kora National Reserve, Kenya*.

For the sketch map of Kora I am indebted to Andrew Bruce.

I list below those to whom I am indebted for the photographs in this book. Will Travers kindly helped to assemble them and I have tried to identify their owners: I offer apologies for any errors or omissions.

FOR COLOUR
I am grateful to: Mirella Ricciardi, for me and the lions (p. 16), Terence (p. 17) and lions feeding (p. 241); Simon Trevor, for Kora (pp. 16–17), Boy and Christian (p. 241) and lions (pp. 240–241); Gerald Cubitt, for Tony and me (p. 17); Ken Talbot, for Boy and me (p. 176); David Blasband, for Joy (pp. 176–7); Tony Fitzjohn, for Komunyu (p. 296); and John Reader, for the gerenuk (p. 297). The others belong to Bill Travers, me or Joy's estate.

FOR MONOCHROME
I am grateful to: my cousin Jim Hiddleston, for pages 33 and 36; the National Museums of Kenya, for the fishes (p. 74) and tribespeople (p. 82); Columbia pictures for those on pages 115, 118, 124 and 125; Bernhardt Grzimek, for me with Sam (p. 146); Derek Cattani, for pages 186 and 193; James Hill, for page 224. The others belong to Bill Travers, Tony Fitzjohn, me or Joy's estate.

Index

Abdi, 285, 296
Adamson, Harry (father), 25, 26, 28
Adamson, Joy (wife née Gessner): appearance, personality, 23–4, 64, 75, 76, 109, 129–30, 179; early life, 69–70; meets George Adamson, 64; marriage, 13, 63, 64–5, 66–7, 70–1; at Isiolo, 71–83; paintings, 13, 67, 76–7, 80, 81–3, 86, 177, 228; books and articles, 10, 86, 94, 96–7, 98–9, 101, 106, 111, 114, 144, 181, 183, 228, 249, 259, 266, 272, 290; and lions, 10, 13, 85–108, 126, 128–30, 144, 153–4, 161–2, 226, 227–8, 290; and Elsa Wild Animal Appeal, 99, 111, 266, 272; and films, 105, 108, 109, 110, 119, 120, 121, 142, 144, 153, 154, 159, 164, 179, 183; and cheetahs, Pippa, 13, 123, 136–7, 144, 147, 157, 160, 165, 175–6, 181, 183; at Meru, 133–69, 175–6, 177–9; and leopards, 13, 153, 161, 222, 251, 254–5, 258–60, 262–6; at Lake Naivasha, 63, 156, 157, 172–4, 181–3, 225; injuries, hospital treatment, 161, 162, 163, 165, 248–51, 255; and Kora, 14, 23, 185, 197, 210–11, 215, 222, 227–8, 229, 232, 242, 251–2, 255–6; visit to Russia, 231–2; at Shaba, 13, 254–5, 258–60, 262–5; death, 267–71
Adamson, K. (mother), 25
Adamson, Terence (brother), 10; birth, 25; in Africa, 26, 28–9, 31, 32, 71–2, 147, 185; and elephants, 10, 47; and botany, 10, 16, 73, 233; and Joy, 73; at Kora, 10, 14, 16, 18, 19, 22, 23, 185, 188–9, 191, 195, 201, 202, 205–9, 232, 233, 237, 246, 251, 257, 261–2, 282, 286, 292, 293, 295, 297, 298, 299; builder and engineer, 10, 185, 191, 195, 205–8, 251; and water divining, 208, 275; mentioned, 40, 72, 213
Adnan (leopard), 292, 295, 296, 297
Adukan (poacher), 44
Arusha (lioness), 209, 239–41, 242–3, 244, 246, 248, 253, 256, 260

Astra (lioness), 110–11, 112–13, 121, 126
Attenborough, David, 101
Attila (leopard), 278–81
Ayodo, Sam, 152, 153

Bally, Peter, 63, 64–5, 66–7, 70
Bardot, Brigitte, 266
Baring, Sir Evelyn, 80, 83
Bath, 6th Marquess of, 112, 128
Baxendale, Jonny, 40, 156, 160–3, 167–9, 285
Baxendale, Nevil, 28, 32–40, 172, 188
Beard, Peter, 256
Bell, Lindsay, 242, 245
Bergen, Candice, 256
Bernhardt, Prince, of the Netherlands, 256
Bisletti, Marchese and Marchesa, lions from: for filming, 112, 123; at Meru, 143, 144, 145, 146, 159, 166, 175; young lions: Sally, 144, 167, 175–6; Shaitani, 144, 167; Suki, 144, 160, 161–2, 175–6; Suswa, 144, 159, 166
Black Mane (lion), 134–5, 139, 145, 147–9, 164–5
Blackantan (lion), 54, 275, 277
Blixen, Baron Bror, 30, 31, 53
Blixen, Cockie, 30–1
Blixen, Karen (Isak Dinesen), 30, 31, 53
Block, Abraham, 29, 60
Block, Jack, 60, 171, 179, 184–5, 294
Boldie (cub of Koretta), 293, 296, 297
Boran (tribe), 43, 80
Bourke, Ace, 180–1, 185, 187–95, 197–8
Boy (lion), 13, 112, 215; filming Born Free, 112, 113–14, 117, 117–19, 121, 126; after filming, 128, 129, 130–1; at Meru, 132, 133–5, 137–9, 143, 144, 145, 146, 147, 150, 152, 154–5, 159, 160, 162–3, 164, 165–9; at Lake Naivasha, 170–2, 174–5, 176–7, 179, 179–80, 183–4; at Kora, 191–200, 201–5, 216; death, 213–14
Bradley Martin, Esmond and Chryssee, 238–9, 241, 278
Bramacherri, Professor, 257
Broughton, Sir Delves, 63
Broughton, Diana (Lady), see Delamere, Diana

Brown, Leslie, 181, 182
Brutus (lion), 43, 86

Caesar (lion), 43, 86
Carr, Norman, 99
Cavendish, Hon. Pat, 142
Chapman, Professor David, 141
Charles (game ranger), 254
Christian (lion), 13; in England, 180–1, 183, 184–5; at Kora, 187–200, 202–5, 213, 216, 219–25, 227, 228, 230–1, 236, 299
Cindie (cub of Koretta), 293, 296, 297
Clarke, Ken, 14, 24
Coe, Dr Malcolm, 233, 281–3
Collins, Sir W. A. R. (Billy), 97, 98, 101, 177, 228, 249, 251
Colvile, Gilbert, 29, 63
Cott, Dr Hugh, 212
Cowie, Mervyn, 54–5, 72, 136, 150, 153, 236
Cullen, Tony, 181

Daniel (lion, cub of Juma), 227–30, 237–8, 243, 248, 252, 253
Darling, Sir Frank Fraser, 12
Delamere, 3rd Lord, 29
Delamere, 4th Lord, 63
Delamere, Lady Diana, (Diana Broughton), 62–3, 171
Denis, Armand, 99
Disney, Walt, 99
Djinn Palace, 63, 171
Djuba (lioness), 110–11, 112–13, 121
Dorobo (tribe), 31
Douglas-Hamilton, Iain and Oria, 47, 49, 171, 228
Downey, Syd, 72, 217

East African Wildlife Society, 242
Edmonds, Georgina, 294
Ekai, Paul, 265, 268–70
Eleanor (elephant), 119, 122
Elizabeth II, H.M. Queen, 80
Elliot, Rodney, 200
Ellis, Steven, 116
Elsa (lioness), 10, 12, 13, 85, 134, 195; her mother, 27, 85; early life, 85–90, 287; in the Mara, 91–2; at Meru, 92, 93–6; Born Free, 10, 96–7, 98–9, 290; cubs, 97–8, 99–101; book about her cubs, Living Free, 101, 114; death, 102–3; her "spirit", 129–30

Elsamere, 170–1, 172–4, 272
Erroll, 22nd Earl of, 62–3

Fitzjohn, Tony, 9–10, 11–12, 14, 22–4, 222–5, 226–32, 237–49, 251–3, 257, 273–81, 286, 292, 294–6, 297, 298
Flying Doctor Service, 19, 85, 185, 242, 244, 245, 298
Foreman, Carl, 109, 120, 121, 131
Freddie (lion), 239, 242, 243, 244, 246–7, 276

Geographical Magazine, 76, 77
Gichunga, Chief Inspector, 268
Gigi (lioness), 241, 242, 243, 273, 275
Girl (lioness), 112; filming *Born Free*, 112, 113–14, 117, 117–19, 121, 122, 123, 126; after filming, 128, 129, 130–1; at Meru, 132, 133–5, 137–9, 143, 144, 145, 146, 149, 150, 152, 154–5, 159, 160, 162, 164, 166, 169, 175
Glowe (lioness, cub of Gigi), 275, 282, 286, 288, 293
Goodall, Jane, 12–13, 228, 235
Gopa (lion, cub of Elsa), 98, 99–107
Gordon, Don, 275
Goss, Ted, 130, 132–3, 136, 139, 141, 150–2, 294–5
Graham, R. S. M. Campbell, 130
Grant, Nellie, 90
Grindley, Mrs, 134
Growe (lioness, cub of Gigi), 275, 282, 286, 288, 293–4
Growlie (lioness), 241–2, 242, 243, 244, 246–7, 248, 253
Grzimek, Dr Bernhardt, 104–5, 143–4, 242, 256
Grzimek, Michael, 105, 107
Guggisberg, Charles, 134

Haile Selassie, Emperor, 112, 121
Hale, Morna, 63
Hale, William, 39, 63, 64, 77, 86, 90, 92, 102
Hamilton, Patrick, 258, 276
Hamisi, 10, 14, 22, 201, 257–8, 295
Harari, Manya, 97
Harthoorn, Toni and Sue, 103, 141–2, 143, 166–9, 170, 175, 176–7, 177
Hatton, Hon. Denys Finch, 30, 31, 42–3, 53
Hawkesworth, John, 259
Henrietta (lioness), 114–16, 122, 128
Hill, James, 126
Hohnel, Lieutenant von, 32
Hook, Raymond, 70–1, 75
Hunter, Jack, 43
Huxley, Elspeth, 30, 31, 90, 106, 255, 259, 262

Huxley, Sir Julian, 12, 99–101, 114
Huxley, Juliette (Lady), 99–101, 179, 249, 251
Huxley, Michael, 77

Innes, Ralph and Dorothy Hammond, 23, 228, 229
Ionides, C. J. P., 23, 141
Isiolo, 13, 43, 71

Jeannot, Michel, 278
Jeans, Susi (Lady) and Sir James, 69, 76
Jenkins, Mark, 162–3
Jenkins, Peter, 133, 160, 162–3 (and Sara), 164, 165–6, 268
Jespah (lion, cub of Elsa), 98, 99–107
Jex-Blake, Dr and Lady Muriel, 65, 66, 67, 76
Johnson, Peter, 156, 267, 272
Joseph (assistant warden), 164
Juma (lioness), 23, 200, 201, 202, 203, 213, 216, 219–20, 227–30, 237–9, 242, 243
Juno (lioness, cub of Girl), 154–5, 157–9, 166, 169

Kakamega, 28
Kase, Mr, 226
Katania (lion cub), 183–4, 191–4, 195, 196–7, 198, 200
Kaunda (lion), 273, 275–6
Kenmare, Lady, 142
Kenya, 9, 80–3; early settlers, 26–7, 28–31; Game Department, 41, 43, 66, 150; National Parks, 55, 150; independence, 108
Kenya, Mt, 67, 129, 190
Kenyatta, Hon. Jomo, 80–1, 108, 121
Kifosha (cook), 254, 267–8
Killer, The (lion), 203, 216, 220
Kimani, 208, 213–14
Kirkpatrick, Sir Alec, 30, 43
Klarvill, Victor von, 69–70
Komunyu (leopardess), 278–81, 296, 297, 298
Kora, 9–11, 14–24, 181, 184–5, 190–1, 196, 205–11, 232–6, 242, 277, 297, 298, 299; Kora Rock, 184, 190; Kora Triangle, 190, 232; a National Game Reserve, 21, 232, 255–6, 294–5; Kora Trust, 281, 297, 299
Kora (cub of Lisa), 227–30, 237–8, 248, 253
Koretta (lioness, cub of Growlie), 253, 257, 277, 280, 286, 292, 293, 296, 297
Kortlandt, Dr Adriaan, 257
Krapf, J. L., 32
Kulal, Mt, 35, 36, 89

Lamu, 65–6
Lawick, Hugo van, 12–13, 99, 228
Leakey (lion), 239, 242, 243, 244, 246–7, 276
Leakey, Gray, 81
Leakey, Louis and Mary, 67, 73, 80–1
Leakey, Richard, 39, 282
Lembirdan (game ranger), 43–4, 52, 75
Limuru, 26, 28
Lisa (lioness), 205, 213, 215–16, 219–20, 227–30, 237–8
Lisette (lioness, cub of Lisa), 227–30, 237–9
Little Elsa (lioness, cub of Elsa), 98, 99–107
Little Elsa (film lioness), 114, 122, 128–9, 134, 155–6
Local (game ranger), 136–7, 140, 161
Low, George, 64, 71, 78
Lucifer (lion), 298

Maasai (tribe), 53, 91
MacDonald, Rt. Hon. Malcolm, 107–8, 121, 152
McGowan, Tom, 110–11, 112, 113, 114, 120, 121, 126, 126–8
McGraw, Ali, 24, 256
McKeand, Julian, 89
McKenna, Virginia (Travers): and *Born Free*, 13, 110–30, 144–5, 155; other references, 24, 137, 155–6, 183, 200, 287, 288, 290, 295, 296
Macmillan, Rt. Hon. Harold, 42, 107
Makedde (assistant), 90, 254, 267
Mara (lioness), 116, 121, 123, 126, 128–9, 134, 139, 155–6
Mara Triangle (Maasai Mara Reserve), 91
Markham, Beryl, 30, 31
Matchett, Chris, 276, 283
Mau Mau, 80–3
Mawson, Pieter, 262, 265, 267–8, 272
Maya (lion, cub of Girl), 154–5, 157–9, 169
Meru, 13, 92–3, 130, 132–3, 136, 150, 175–6, 277
Meyerhold, Dr Andrew, 295, 299
Mona (lioness), 205, 213, 215–16
Monalisa (lioness), 200, 201, 202, 203
Monika (lion trainer), 110–11, 113
Moore, Monty, 104
Morris, Desmond, 23–4, 290
Mosandu (tracker), 31–2
Moti (driver), 285
Mt Kenya Safari Club, 112

Muga (labourer), 201–2
Mugwongo Hill, 130, 133
Mutinda, John, 229

Naivasha, Lake, 63, 156, 170
Naja (lioness), 277, 280, 281, 286
Naro Moru, 109–10, 111–12
National Museums of Kenya, 281–3
Ngansira, Senior Superintendent, 268, 269
Nnaggenda, Francis, 271
Norfolk Hotel, 60, 184
Nuru, 86, 96

Ofenheim, Angela and Ernest, 40, 53
Olindo, Perez, 150, 152, 153, 154, 156, 161, 164, 165, 238–9
Orma (tribe), 211
Oscar (lion, cub of Lisa), 227–30, 237–9, 248, 253
Oulton, Tom, 41
Owen, John, 104, 105
Owens, Mark and Delia, 288

Pasha (leopard, cub of Penny), 264, 265
Pati Pati (hyrax), 77, 85, 87, 119, 122
Patterson, Col. R. J., 27
Pearson, Paul, 167–9, 170
Penny (leopard), 254–5, 258, 259–60, 262–4, 265, 272
Philip, H.R.H. Prince, Duke of Edinburgh, 80, 108
Pippa (cheetah), 13, 123, 136, 143, 144, 161, 165, 176; her cubs, 144, 147, 157, 161, 165, 175, 176
Pippin (cairn terrier), 66, 67, 70, 75, 77
Pitman, Captain Charles, 55
Pole Pole (elephant), 157, 289–90

Rebmann, Herr, 32
Remnant, Giles, 132, 143
Rendall, John, 180–1, 185, 187–95, 197–8
Rendille (tribe), 43
Ricciardi, Mirella, 171, 177, 228
Richmond, Mike, 167, 171
Ritchie, Colonel Archie, 42–3, 50, 52, 53, 66–7, 76–7
Rocco, Colonel Mario, 171
Roosevelt, President Theodore, 40
Root, Alan, 99, 140–1, 171, 256, 260–1, 294
Root, Joan, 261
Rottich, Nehemiah arap, 294

Royal Geographical Society, 32, 86, 281–3
Royal Horticultural Society, 76, 77
Ruben, Eddie, 29, 60, 123, 184–5
Ruben, Monty, 123, 152, 181, 184–5, 191
Rudolf, Lake (Lake Turkana), 32, 35–6, 39
Rutherford, Jock, 258, 262
Ryves, Sergeant Ronald, 112, 113–14, 130

Sally (lioness from Marchesa Bisletti), *see under* Bisletti
Sally (lioness with Lyn Temple-Boreham), 91
Sam (lion, cub of Girl), 146, 147–9
Samburu (tribe), 43
Sandie (lioness, cub of Suki), 161–2, 163–4, 166, 175–6
Sayer, Paul, 175, 176, 203
Schaller, George, 104, 159
Scruffy (lion), 54, 220–2, 227, 237, 248
Seago, John, 163–4
Serengeti, 40, 91, 104–5, 106
Shaba, 13, 254–5, 258, 262, 272
Shade (lion), 261, 298
Shaitani (lioness), *see under* Bisletti
Sharma, Arun, 143, 146–7, 155, 156
Sheba (lioness from Ken Clarke), 14, 18–19, 21–2
Sheba (lioness from Marchesa Bisletti), 123, 128
Sheldrick, David and Daphne, 52, 119, 133, 157, 289
Shifta, 24, 132, 145, 212, 285
Shyman (lion, cub of Juma), 227–30, 237–8, 243, 245, 298
Sigara, Mohamed, 226
Smith, Ken, 27, 90, 102–3, 106, 133, 181, 184, 211, 222, 226, 258, 294
Somalis, 11, 24, 43, 78, 211–12, 246, 247–8, 283–5
Stanley (assistant), 137, 140, 144, 161, 172, 183, 191, 195, 201, 208, 213–15
Suki (lioness), *see under* Bisletti
Suleiman (lion), 14, 18–19, 21–2, 255, 266, 298
Supercub (lion), 205, 213, 215–16
Suswa (lion), *see under* Bisletti

Tana (lioness), 142
Tana River, 16, 184, 190, 297
Tana River Council, 21, 184, 226, 229

Teleki, Count, 32
Temple-Boreham, Lyn, 43, 86, 90–1, 153
Thesiger, Wilfred, 23, 181, 217–18
Thompsett, Dick, 171
Tichy, Herbert, 69, 89
Tiegs, Cheryl, 256
Timms, Dr Geoffrey, 268
Tobosh, 35, 37
Tom Tom (lion), 295, 296
Tomoko, 297–9
Travers, Bill: and *Born Free*, 13, 110–30, 144–5, 226; and lions, 13, 128–30, 137, 145, 177, 179–81, 184–5, 187, 191, 200, 226; injured filming, 142, 177; later documentaries, 145, 152, 153, 154, 156, 157, 167, 201, 203–5, 226, 289; and Kora, 13, 184–5, 187, 191, 216, 226, 295, 296; and George Adamson's book, 24, 287, 295; and George Adamson in England, 287, 290–1; and Zoo Check, 290; mentioned, 183
Travers, Virginia, *see* McKenna
Trevor, Simon, 99, 201, 203–5
Tsavo National Park, 52, 119, 157
Turkana (tribe), 39, 43, 77–8
Turkana, Lake, *see* Rudolf, Lake

Ugas (lion): filming *Born Free*, 116–17, 121, 126; after filming, 128, 129, 139; at Meru, 51, 139, 141–2, 143, 144, 145, 146, 150, 152, 155, 159, 166, 175

Victoria, Lake, 26
Villiers, Marjorie, 96–7, 98, 259, 264, 266
Visee, Aart, 239–41

Wakamba (tribe), 211
Wales, H.R.H. Prince of (later King Edward VIII), 30, 31, 42–3, 53
Wallace, Roy, 262
Wateridge, Larry, 93, 94, 99–101, 130
Wedel, Dr, 267, 268
Wilkie, Captain Ron, 280
Williams, Colonel J. H., 46
Wood, Michael, 85
Woodley, Bill, 133

Yusef (cook), 28, 32–5, 37

Zanzibar, 26
Zoo Check, 290